BELMONT UNIVERSITY LIBRARY
BELMONT UNIVERSITY
1900 BELMONT BLVD.
NASHVILLE, TN 37212

Courts under Constraints

This study offers a new theoretical framework for understanding how institutional instability affects judicial behavior under dictatorship and democracy. In contrast to conventional wisdom, the central findings of the book challenge the longstanding assumption that only independent judges rule against the government of the day. Set in the context of Argentina, the study brings together qualitative case studies and statistical analyses with spatial and game theoretic models to explore the conditions under which courts rule against the government. In addition to shedding new light on the dynamics of court-executive relations in Argentina, the study provides general lessons about institutions, instability, and the rule of law. In the process, the study builds a new set of connections among diverse bodies of scholarship, including U.S. judicial politics, comparative institutional analysis, positive political theory, and Latin American politics.

Gretchen Helmke is an assistant professor in Political Science at the University of Rochester. Her research on comparative institutions and Latin American politics appears in several leading journals, including the *American Political Science Review*, *Comparative Politics*, and *Desarollo Económico*. Her research has received grants from the National Science Foundation and the Social Science Research Council. She has been a visiting research Fellow at the Fundación Carlos Nino in Buenos Aires, Argentina; the Kellogg Institute for International Studies at the University of Notre Dame; and the Weatherhead Center for International Affairs, Harvard University.

Cambridge Studies in Comparative Politics

General Editor
Margaret Levi   *University of Washington, Seattle*

Assistant General Editor
Stephen Hanson   *University of Washington, Seattle*

Associate Editors
Robert H. Bates   *Harvard University*
Peter Hall   *Harvard University*
Peter Lange   *Duke University*
Helen Milner   *Columbia University*
Frances Rosenbluth   *Yale University*
Susan Stokes   *University of Chicago*
Sidney Tarrow   *Cornell University*

Other Books in the Series

Lisa Baldez, *Why Women Protest: Women's Movements in Chile*
Stefano Bartolini, *The Political Mobilization of the European Left, 1860–1980: The Class Cleavage*
Mark Beissinger, *Nationalist Mobilization and the Collapse of the Soviet State*
Nancy Bermeo, ed., *Unemployment in the New Europe*
Carles Boix, *Democracy and Redistribution*
Carles Boix, *Political Parties, Growth and Equality: Conservative and Social Democratic Economic Strategies in the World Economy*
Catherine Boone, *Merchant Capital and the Roots of State Power in Senegal, 1930–1985*
Catherine Boone, *Political Topographies of the African State: Territorial Authority and Institutional Change*
Michael Bratton and Nicolas van de Walle, *Democratic Experiments in Africa: Regime Transitions in Comparative Perspective*
Valerie Bunce, *Leaving Socialism and Leaving the State: The End of Yugoslavia, the Soviet Union, and Czechoslovakia*

Series list continues following the index.

To My Father and in Memory of My Mother and Grandmother

Courts under Constraints

JUDGES, GENERALS, AND PRESIDENTS IN ARGENTINA

GRETCHEN HELMKE

University of Rochester

CAMBRIDGE
UNIVERSITY PRESS

PUBLISHED BY THE PRESS SYNDICATE OF THE UNIVERSITY OF CAMBRIDGE
The Pitt Building, Trumpington Street, Cambridge, United Kingdom

CAMBRIDGE UNIVERSITY PRESS
The Edinburgh Building, Cambridge CB2 2RU, UK
40 West 20th Street, New York, NY 10011-4211, USA
477 Williamstown Road, Port Melbourne, VIC 3207, Australia
Ruiz de Alarcón 13, 28014 Madrid, Spain
Dock House, The Waterfront, Cape Town 8001, South Africa

http://www.cambridge.org

© Gretchen Helmke 2005

This book is in copyright. Subject to statutory exception
and to the provisions of relevant collective licensing agreements,
no reproduction of any part may take place without
the written permission of Cambridge University Press.

First published 2005

Printed in the United States of America

Typeface Janson Text Roman 10/13 pt.   *System* LᴬTEX 2$_\varepsilon$ [TB]

A catalog record for this book is available from the British Library.

Library of Congress Cataloging in Publication Data

Helmke, Gretchen, 1967–
Courts under constraints : judges, generals, and presidents in Argentina / Gretchen Helmke.
    p.   cm. – (Cambridge studies in comparative politics)
Includes bibliographical references and index.
ISBN 0-521-82059-6 (HB)
1. Political questions and judicial power – Argentina – History – 20th century.
2. Civil-military relations – Argentina – History – 20th century.   3. Argentina –
Politics and government – 1983–2002.   I. Title.   II. Series.

KHA2533.H45   2004
347.82′012 – dc22   2004052120

ISBN 0 521 82059 6 hardback

BELMONT UNIVERSITY LIBRARY

KHA
2533
.H45
2005

Contents

Contents

List of Tables

Tables

List of Figures

Preface and Acknowledgments

As concern with the rule of law in Latin America and elsewhere continues to grow, this study provides a new framework for understanding how courts under constraints operate. The assumption that only independent judges rule against the rulers has long been the accepted wisdom among social scientists, policy makers, and citizens alike. Although this study initially shared the same premise, it arrives at a markedly different set of conclusions. Set in the turbulent institutional context of contemporary Argentina, the book demonstrates that sometimes the very lack of independence provokes judges to act as a check on their government, including the very government by whom the judges were earlier appointed. I refer to this important, if heretofore unexamined, phenomenon as strategic defection. In elaborating the specific mechanisms through which this dynamic occurs, the book challenges a range of classic and contemporary understandings about judicial behavior under conditions of institutional instability and uncertainty. In addition to solving several theoretical puzzles about court-executive relations in such environments, the study explores the substantive consequences of this reverse political-legal cycle for elites and citizens in Argentina and beyond.

At every stage of writing this book, I have benefited immeasurably from the advice, guidance, and support of others. As a doctoral student at the University of Chicago, I was extremely fortunate to begin this project under the guidance of my thesis advisers, Susan Stokes, Gerald Rosenberg, Cass Sunstein, and David Laitin. Susan Stokes was a constant source of support and inspiration. Gerry Rosenberg provided a wonderful introduction to the field of judicial politics. Cass Sunstein and David Laitin offered thoughtful comments and advice throughout. Along the way, I have also received extremely helpful suggestions from many other scholars and colleagues, including James Alt, Delia Boylan, Carles Boix, Daniel Brinks, Greg Caldeira, John Carey, Mark Chaves, Lee Epstein, James Fearon, John Ferejohn, Barry Friedman, Hein Goemans, Stacia Haynie, Jonathan Katz, Jack Knight, Steven Levitsky, Scott Mainwaring, Luigi Manzetti, Gerry Munck, Guillermo O'Donnell, Adam Przeworski, Richard Snyder, Matthew Stephenson, Georg Vanberg, and Ashutosh Varshney. In particular, Andy Gould gave encouragement and advice throughout my dissertation and the early stages of the book project. Participants in diverse fora at the University of Chicago, Harvard University, University of Michigan, New York University, University of Notre Dame, and University of Washington at St. Louis have also provided provocative questions and helpful suggestions on most parts of this project. Mark Fey, Daniel Gingerich, Macartan Humphreys, Luis Fernando Medina, Elena Plaxina, and Randy Stone provided invaluable advice and suggestions for the formal model contained in Chapter 3. For the final version of the book I am also deeply indebted to two anonymous reviewers at Cambridge University Press, to Margaret Levi for her incisive comments and encouragement, and to Lew Bateman for his support and patience. Whatever errors or insufficiencies remain in the book are entirely my own responsibility.

During my field research in Argentina several people helped to make this project possible. In particular, I want to thank Carlos Acuña, Pedro Caballero, Andrés D'Alessio, Roberto Gargarella, Hernán Goulco, Jaime Malamud-Goti, Jonathan Miller, Guillermo Molinelli, and Catalina Smulovitz, who generously shared their time and insights about Argentine politics and law. I am grateful to Roberto Frenkel and the Centro de Estudios del Estado y Sociedad (CEDES) for their generosity, especially during my pre-dissertation work in August 1996, and to Martin Böhmer and Roberto Saba at the Fundación Carlos Nino. Most of my time in Argentina was spent in the Palacio de Justicia; I am grateful to the librarians at the Biblioteca de la Corte Suprema, Dra. Silvina Oubel de Novo and the staff at the Secretaría de Jurisprudencia, and the staff at the Oficina de Estadísticas and to the many lawyers, judges, and justices in the Tribunales who taught me about both the formal and informal sides of Argentine law. For his excellent research assistance, I thank Pablo Augustín Lafuente, with whom I spent many months coding cases in the upper reaches of the seventh-floor library of the Supreme Court. Above all, I want to thank Mara Rosa Ferino for her friendship and humor.

Field research in Argentina was made possible by grants from the National Science Foundation Graduate Fellowship (SBR-9617896) and the

Preface and Acknowledgments

Social Science Research Council International Dissertation Research Fellowship. The Mellon Foundation Final Year Dissertation Fellowship at the University of Chicago, the Kellogg Institute at the University of Notre Dame, the Weatherhead Center for International Affairs at Harvard University, and the Lanni Fellowship at the University of Rochester provided generous support for writing and additional research. For their outstanding research assistance in helping to extend the Argentina Supreme Court Decisions data set and for sharing their insights about the Argentine judicial system, I am extremely grateful to Maria Eve Miljiker and Santiago Boccardo. For help preparing the final draft of the manuscript, I would like to thank Deniz Aksoy, Tugba Guvenc, Ann Marshall, and, most especially, Elena Plaxina.

Parts of Chapters 2 and 5 have been published in *American Political Science Review* under the title, "The Logic of Strategic Defection: Court-Executive Relations in Argentina under Dictatorship and Democracy" (also translated and reprinted in *Desarollo Económico*). Parts of Chapters 2 and 6 have been published in *Comparative Politics* under the title, "Checks and Balances by Other Means: The Argentine Judiciary in the 1990s."

Throughout this project, I was extremely fortunate to have had the love and support of my family and friends. Most especially, I am grateful to my stepmother, Linda; my aunts, Karen and Jan; and to friends Stephanie, Liz, and Christina. I also want to thank Mitch for his help, humor, and love while I finished this project. Finally, I want to dedicate this book to my father, Stephen, for his constant encouragement and support, and to the memory of my mother, Linda, and grandmother, Nora, who are always with me.

1

Ruling against the Rulers

1.1 Introduction

Latin America's courts are in crisis. Inadequate material resources and infrastructure, outdated procedures, case backlog, corruption, politicization, and cronyism are among the many problems that judiciaries face. Although such difficulties are hardly new to the region, over the last decade the image of the judiciary has grown decidedly worse. According to a recent survey published in *The Economist*, the percentage of Latin American citizens that has confidence in the judiciary has fallen from approximately 35 percent in 1996 to around 20 percent in 2003. In individual countries, the judiciary's image is often far worse. Despite the ineptitude and abuse of power waged by political elites under dictatorship and democracy alike, judges today are less popular than presidents, the military, or the police (ibid.).

Judicial independence has proved particularly elusive. In 1990, Argentina's former President Carlos Menem packed the Supreme Court, proclaiming, "Why should I be the only Argentine President not to have my own Supreme Court?" A few years later, former Peruvian President Alberto Fujimori paralyzed his country's Constitutional Court by impeaching three sitting justices. In Venezuela, President Hugo Chávez dissolved the Supreme Court en masse in 1997, suspended approximately 300 lower level judges, and appointed 101 new judges to the bench. In Ecuador in the same year, the new government carried out a similar purge. In 2003, presidents in Paraguay and Argentina, respectively, launched impeachment proceedings against sitting justices, causing several to tender their resignations.

This was not supposed to have occurred. The wave of democratic transitions that swept the region in the 1980s was initially assumed to be a harbinger of judicial independence and the rule of law. Barring a reversion

1

to authoritarian rule, the early, optimistic view was that young democracies would consolidate and generate a host of auxiliary institutions, including independent judiciaries (O'Donnell and Schmitter 1986; Gunther, Diamandorous, and Puhle 1995). Under stable democratic governance, judges with the "right" kinds of values would be appointed and, once appointed, would serve as stalwart constitutional guardians (Alfonsín 1993). Over time, the growth of judicial power and independence would help to establish a rule of law, simultaneously protecting human and civil rights and encouraging economic investment and growth.

When such a virtuous cycle did not materialize, scholars and policy makers began to conclude that even if democracy was a necessary condition for judicial independence, it was far from sufficient. Hoping to increase judicial legitimacy and strengthen the rule of law, the World Bank launched a series of reform projects throughout the region during the 1990s. Most of these aimed at improving the functioning of the judiciary on the grounds that investors' confidence required an efficient and impartial judiciary (Dakolias 1996). For others, however, the flaws of Latin America's judiciaries defied such a solution. Persistent cultural attitudes, rooted in the civil law legal tradition, meant that, regardless of resources, Latin American judges lacked the values necessary for actively guarding the constitution against popularly elected leaders (Rosenn 1987). Among political scientists, the persistent weakness of the judiciary was viewed as an institutional artifact of hyper-presidentialism, or what Guillermo O'Donnell has termed "delegative democracy" (O'Donnell 1992; Larkins 1998; see also Nino 1992). An inherent feature of this peculiar type of democracy was the inability of other institutional actors to serve as an effective check on presidential power.

Yet even despite such persistent shortcomings, Latin America's courts have become vitally important political institutions. Throughout the region, judges often decide the most important and controversial issues of the day. In the area of human rights, for example, Argentine and Bolivian judges set new standards for transitional justice by trying and convicting top military leaders accused of committing vast human rights abuses (Kritz 1995; but also see Roniger and Sznajder 1999). In social issues, courts have played a key role in adjudicating the rights of indigenous groups, women, and homosexuals. In the economic realm, judges have ruled on policies ranging from privatization to state employment to the scope of emergency powers during economic crises. Judges have also played a

1.1 Introduction

major role in deciding presidents' fates. In Peru and Argentina, judges were called on to rule on the sitting president's eligibility for running for office. In Brazil, Venezuela, Argentina, and Bolivia, judges have been asked to handle corruption cases involving sitting or former presidents. In Brazil and Venezuela, the court played a key role in the impeachment proceedings against incumbent presidents.

Not surprisingly, judges who ruled in favor of the government only fueled further the impression that Latin America's courts lack independence. In Argentina, for example, pundits and scholars alike chronicled a series of almost comically partial decisions handed down by the Supreme Court during former President Menem's first term (Baglini and D'Ambrosio 1993; Verbitsky 1993; Larkins 1998). In the early 1990s, the Argentine Supreme Court allowed the president to freeze private savings accounts, privatize state-owned companies by decree, and trample the independence of other governmental institutions. In one particularly egregious example, known as the Banco Patagónico case (1993), justices appointed by Menem "lost" a decision that was unfavorable to the government. Shortly thereafter, a new opinion emerged that was more in line with what the government wanted (see Baglini and D'Ambrosio 1993; Larkins 1998: 430). Likewise, in Venezuela during the first years of Chávez's presidency, the new Supreme Court regularly caved to the president. In the case of *Elias Santana* (2001), involving a journalist's demand for equal time in Chávez's weekly national radio address, the Court backed the president and denied the claim. Commenting on the Court's rejection of the right of reply, a former justice argued that the Court's decision was "aberrant and erases the word democracy in this country."[1]

Yet even casual observation suggests that judicial behavior within Latin America has been far more varied. From Peru to Guatemala, where judges refused to allow sitting presidents to run for a third term in office, to Venezuela, where Chávez's own judges refused to back his attempts to punish military officers charged with attempting a coup against his government, to Argentina, where judges struck down key provisions of interim president Eduardo Duhalde's economic emergency plans, the fact is that judges do decide cases against the government, and sometimes they decide against the very government by which they were appointed. While it is tempting

---

[1] *Miami Herald,* July 14, 2002.

to dismiss such cases as mere anomalies, the importance and boldness of these decisions demand closer examination.

More generally, the phenomenon of "ruling against the rulers" calls into question several core assumptions about judicial behavior and institutions. First, the fact that Latin American judges are often willing to decide controversial cases casts doubt on the longstanding supposition that judges who lack independence and legitimacy automatically avoid the political fray. Although Latin America's judges have invoked variants of the political questions doctrine, particularly during periods of dictatorship, other evidence suggests that they sometimes go to great lengths to hear politically contentious cases. In Argentina, for example, the use of the writ of *recurso extraordinario*, by which most cases reach the Supreme Court on appeal, has expanded substantially over the last few decades. In 1990 the Court further paved the way for hearing highly political cases by establishing the doctrine of per saltum to hear cases involving the privatization of the state-owned airline. This doctrine, based on U.S. jurisprudence, allows the Supreme Court to seize important cases from the first instance courts, thus "jumping over" second-instance courts all together. Although the Court has used the doctrine only occasionally, even these bursts of boldness rest uneasily with standard notions about how judges under constraints should act.

Second, that even the most compromised judges are willing to rule against the government raises the question of whether political insulation is indeed a necessary condition for checks and balances to emerge. Since Alexander Hamilton's famous defense of judicial independence in *Federalist 78*, scholars have assumed that only politically insulated judges would be willing to "hazard the displeasure of those in power." (1961 [1787]: 471). Variation in judicial behavior in deeply insecure institutional environments, however, invites a reassessment of this fundamental connection.

A brief comparison with one of the world's most independent and powerful courts, the U.S. Supreme Court, helps to underscore further the puzzles raised by Latin American courts. Notwithstanding such well-known disasters as *Dred Scott*, the U.S. Supreme Court has avoided deciding a litany of important issues throughout its history (e.g., see McCloskey [1960] 1994). Even in the area of school desegregation, the Court's famous ruling in the case of *Brown v. Board of Education* (1953) came only after the presidential election had taken place. To paraphrase one of the justices, the Court worried that deciding the matter sooner would have turned the issue into campaign fodder, thereby creating an impossible position for the Court, whose decision would be seen as favoring one political party over the other.[2]

In terms of the U.S. Supreme Court's track record on decisions, a solid body of empirical research shows that the federal government routinely comes out ahead, winning approximately two-thirds of its cases (Epstein et al. 1994). The executive branch, represented by the Solicitor General, does especially well before the highest court. In addition to winning the bulk of its cases (Yates 2002), the Solicitor General exercises an enormous amount of influence on justices' opinions via amicus curiae briefs. Even after controlling for the facts of the case, changes in court membership, and the court's tendency to reverse, scholars have found that the position adopted by the Solicitor General has significant effects on the direction of the Court's opinion (Segal and Spaeth 2002). While such patterns raise red flags about the judiciary's ability to act as a counter-majoritarian institution (e.g., Dahl 1957; Rosenberg 1992), the point of interest here is that if even ostensibly independent judges have a hard time ruling against the current government, why would Latin America's judges ever be willing to do so?

Ruling against the rulers also raises concerns about the proper role of judges in a democratic system. On the one hand, the complaint of scholars in the region has long been that courts too often fail to act as an effective check when leaders violate the rights of minorities. Particularly in light of judges' purported failure to protect human rights under military rule, any willingness to challenge the government, even if only very rarely, should be welcome news. This view would seem to be further shored up by the evidence that, even under democracy, vertical accountability in Latin America is notoriously weak (O'Donnell 1998; Crisp, Moreno, and Shugart 2003; but also see Stokes 2001). In such environments, it would seem that the costs of judges not exercising judicial review are especially high.

Of course, not all proponents of democracy are as enthusiastic about embracing judicial activism. Starting with Thomas Jefferson, skeptics of judicial review have long argued that it is improper in a democracy to allow unelected judges to strike down laws passed by elected legislators. A secondary but related argument is that an activist judiciary poses the potential to generate legal instability. Although such an argument may strike

---

[2] *"The Supreme Court and 'Brown v. Board of Ed': The Deliberations behind the Landmark 1954 Ruling."* National Public Radio, December 2003.

scholars of Latin America as somewhat ironic, North American critics have long charged that because judges are likely to have different ideological views, allowing them to review ordinary legislation on the basis of their own preferences creates problems of inconsistency and instability.[3] Moreover, judicial activism may serve to preclude democratic deliberation by foreclosing important debate between citizens and their representatives (Sunstein 1996b). By these arguments, anti-government decisions handed down by Latin America's courts not only flout our understanding of how dependent judges react, but may also be harmful to new democracies.

In the Latin American context such concerns have been echoed by justices seeking to explain their reluctance to strike down the government.[4] Likewise, regional experts have warned that too much insulation endangers accountability (Fiss 1993; Domingo 1999; Dakolias 1996). Lisa Hilbink (1999) invokes Judith Shklar's critique of legalism to argue against maximizing the independence of Chile's ultraconservative judges. While this book does not aim to settle this controversy, its findings raise new questions about the links between judicial dependence and juridical instability, on the one hand, and the connection between judges' values and their decisions, on the other. Specifically, this study explores the idea that the very absence of institutional security may, under certain circumstances, inadvertently lead judges to shore up respect for basic rights and procedures normally associated with the rule of law. As a result, this analysis highlights an important, if heretofore neglected, tension between rule of law arguments that emphasize stability versus those that emphasize equality and due process.

Taken together, the main point of departure for the book lies in the observation that many of the features normally associated with fragile, dependent courts – insecure tenure, political pressure, and support of the government – may not necessarily co-vary. In established democracies, the incongruence between institutional protections and judicial behavior has generated a long line of research focused around the question of why ostensibly independent judges rarely rule against the government. Turning the focus to Latin America, however, raises a fresh set of puzzles about why, when, and in which types of cases otherwise dependent judges rule against the government. As the following section describes, standard models of judicial behavior derived from the behavioral and institutional literature do not provide sufficient answers. Selection-based theories, which highlight

---

[3] For a formal theoretical approach to this question, see Rogers and Vanberg 2003.

[4] Interview with Justice Moliné O'Connor, Buenos Aires, May 1998.

the government's ability to appoint like-minded judges, lead us to expect unwavering congruence in such settings. Likewise, standard sanctioning-based models, which focus on the ability of the government to punish errant judges, tell us very little about willingness of otherwise dependent judges to rule against the government. Explaining judicial behavior in institutionally insecure contexts thus demands a new analytic framework that can account not only for why judges who lack institutional security support the government, but also why they rule against it.

1.2 Actors, Institutions, and Mechanisms

The vast bulk of the literature on Latin American courts characterizes courts by "adding up" different measures of independence and then evaluating where they fall short (Rosenn 1987; Verner 1989; Dakolias 1996; Larkins 1996; Domingo 1999). This study takes a different tack. Rather than assess Latin America's courts according to an ideal vision of judicial independence, I argue that a more theoretically fruitful approach is to examine the interaction among the various attributes conventionally associated with dependent courts. Such an approach also requires careful description of actors and institutions, but seeks a deeper analytical understanding of the mechanisms by which they are linked. Along these lines, this section considers several models of court-executive relations prominent in the American politics literature. While none of these "off the shelf" theories adequately explains the empirical puzzles at hand, they provide a useful repertoire of ideas and approaches that can be reconfigured to construct a more complete understanding of courts under constraints.

Selection-Based Approaches

When governments control judicial appointments it should hardly come as a surprise that judges rarely rule against them. In established democracies, the selection process has served as a key part of the explanation for the relative harmony among the branches of government. Consider the most well-known example: the United States Supreme Court. Despite a host of institutional guarantees protecting judges against undue pressure, only very rarely is the Court out of line with the government of the day. Starting with Dahl's seminal critique of the counter-majoritarian thesis (1957), such harmony results from the fact that presidents routinely appoint judges to the bench and presidents tend to appoint judges who share their views. The fact that more than 90 percent of all U.S. Supreme Court nominees have come from the president's party provides considerable empirical support for the view that, even among the world's most independent courts, the nomination process is highly partisan (Baum 2001; Carp and Stidham 2001).

Contra Hamilton, the broader implication of Dahl's thesis is that simply granting judges secure life tenure may give them the capacity to rule against the government, but does not ensure that judges will have the inclination to use it. Judges make decisions according to their sincere preferences. But because the elected branches have control over selecting judges, the Court ultimately functions to legitimate, rather than challenge, the power of the government. As long as judges are generally seen as independent, such a situation approximates what Ramseyer and Rasmusen (1996) have argued is the ideal judiciary from the incumbent party's point of view. That is, judges who are viewed as independent will help to make the government's promises credible (Landes and Posner 1975) and help to police the bureaucracy (McCubbins and Schwartz 1984), but will also rule in line with what the politicians in power want.

For governments that respect the basic rule of law principles, there is nothing inherently problematic with this arrangement. Indeed, even the staunchest defender of judicial review would agree with the notion that judges should exercise their power only when governments overstep their limits. Moreover, republican constitutions, such as the U.S. and many Latin American constitutions, are not based on the pure separation of powers, but rather are designed to prevent the concentration and hence abuse of power by a single branch by giving each branch of government a way of exercising influence over the other two (see Manin 1994: 30–31). Giving the other branches a role in selecting judges who share their views may even help to enhance the protections for the judiciary such that politicians do not need or want to violate the independence of individual judges. Along these lines, John Ferejohn (1999) has argued that the structural interdependence among the branches of the U.S. government, which includes the president's and senate's ability to select the justices, contributes to the self-enforcing nature of the constitutional protections afforded to U.S. justices.

Selection, however, is not always foolproof. As Dahl pointed out, sometimes presidents get "unlucky" and fail to have the opportunity to appoint judges to the bench. Such was the fate that befell Franklin Delano Roosevelt, which led to the infamous clash between the Lochner-era Court and the executive branch over Roosevelt's New Deal policies (e.g., see Caldeira 1987). Indeed, although most U.S. presidents get to appoint between two and three justices per term, they do not get to appoint the majority of judges on the bench. Even Ronald Reagan, who had four vacancies on the Supreme Court during his time in office, did not succeed in substantially altering the Court's ideological direction. In Segal and Spaeth's judgment, "the Supreme Court was no more conservative than the one he inherited . . . the twentieth century still ended with organized school prayer unconstitutional and *Roe v. Wade* the law of the land (2002: 217). The larger lesson they draw is that *which* justices' seats become available may be as important as how many.

Senate voting on judicial nominees also can alter the selection process. Research has shown that the success of presidential judicial nominees is highly influenced by the partisan composition of the Senate, the president's popularity, and the timing of the nomination with respect to the president's term (Cameron, Cover, and Segal 1990). Moreover, although most nominees get approved, this may have more to do with presidential strategy, not presidential power. For example, Moraski and Shipan (1992) use a series of simple spatial models to illustrate how the president's ability to select the best new judge depends on the locations of the president's ideal point relative to the current median justice and the median senator. If the president and Senate are located on the same side of the median justice, the president is unconstrained to appoint a new median justice. If the Senate and president are located on opposite sides of the median justice, however, any attempt made by the president to select a new median judge will be rejected by the Senate. By this logic, selection as a mechanism for creating a judiciary that is supportive of the ruling majority requires the additional condition that the preferences of ruling majority are relatively aligned.

Yet even if presidents manage to appoint the judges they want, principle-agent problems may still arise. Presidents may find judges who share their views on some but not all issues. Judges may turn out to behave very differently from what the nominating president anticipates. Or over the passage of time, justices might alter their views. For any combination of these reasons, scholars of the United States have concluded that even judges appointed by the current government are unlikely to support the incumbent president all of the time (Segal and Spaeth 2002).

In Latin America, by contrast, few of the factors mitigating the impact of presidential selection on judicial subservience are in evidence. For example, unlike the United States, Latin American presidents often are able to appoint not merely two or three judges per term but the entire court. Historically, judges have been particularly vulnerable to replacement during periods of regime instability. Incoming authoritarian leaders were able to appoint the majority of justices to the bench in Guatemala (1953), Cuba (1959), Brazil (1964), Nicaragua (1979), and Argentina (1947, 1955, 1956, 1976; Verner 1984). Under democracy, the situation has hardly improved.

The exaggerated capacity of Latin American presidents to select their own judges goes a long way toward explaining the degree of cronyism and corruption that distinguishes Latin American judiciaries from their counterparts in more developed democracies. To see why this is the case, consider the arguments made by Hamilton in *Federalist 76* regarding the importance of the relative balance of power between the executive and legislative branches. According to Hamilton, the dangers of venality that would otherwise come from the executive's ability to nominate judges will be effectively thwarted by the requirement that the president obtain the Senate's confirmation in judicial appointments. In Hamilton's words, "the necessity of the [Senate's] concurrence would have a powerful, though, in general, silent operation. It would be an excellent check upon a spirit of favoritism in the President and would tend greatly to prevent the appointment of unfit characters" (1961 [1787]: 457).

This legislative check, however, is precisely what is often missing in many Latin American countries. Under military dictatorship in which the legislature is disbanded, the selection of judges takes place through a process of negotiations within the military junta. Surprisingly, under democracy the situation may be even worse. As scholars of the region have pointed out, presidents in Latin America are far more powerful than legislatures (e.g., see Morgenstern and Nacif 2002). Under democracy, however, presidents do not even have fellow junta members who must be consulted for their own judges to be appointed.[5] In Argentina, for example, there have been some battles between the Senate and the president over appointing judges

---

[5] In Argentina the most egregious examples of judicial cronyism occurred not under the last dictatorship, but under the democratic government of Carlos Menem (1989-9). For example, Menem's Supreme Court appointees included Justice Eduardo Moliné O'Connor (Menem's tennis partner), Chief Justice Julio Nazareno (a former partner in Menem's family's law firm in Menem's home province of La Rioja), and Justice Vázquez (who on his appointment to the bench publicly proclaimed his personal friendship with Menem on the television show *Hora Clave*; Verbitsky 1993: 52–60; Larkins 1998: 430). In all these cases, the Senate confirmation process functioned only as a mere formality. As under previous democratic governments in Argentine history, the president's nominees were quickly confirmed by the Comision de Acuerdos del Senado (Appointments Committee of the Senate) with virtually no discussion about the nominees' policy preferences, ideology, or even credentials (e.g., see Poder Cuidadano 1997: 21–4).

at the lower level, but no Supreme Court nominees have been rejected since the return to democracy (Molinelli, Palanza, and Sin 1999: 490).[6] Such tendencies are only exacerbated whenever a single party controls both branches of government (e.g., see Iaryczower, Spiller, and Tomassi 2002; Bill Chavez, Ferejohn, and Weingast 2003). Paraphrasing one member of the Argentine Senate's Judicial Commission, Senator Adolfo Gass, once the Peronists gained a majority in the Senate and the Chamber of Deputies, the president of the Judicial Commission was reduced to purely a formal role (Poder Cuidadano 1997: 23).

But precisely in a context such as Argentina's, where executive control over selection appears boundless, the original question of why judges rule against the very government by whom they were appointed becomes all the more intriguing. One possible answer is that, precisely because judges are relatively easy to remove, Latin American presidents may actually face principle-agent problems worse than those of their North American counterparts. Although short tenure removes the possibility of a judge changing his or her ideology over time, selection itself may be less effective. This apparent paradox resonates well with Mark Ramseyer's provocative idea that the easier it is to replace judges, the less time a government will spend on selection.[7] If governments routinely select some portion of judges who do not share their preferences, then judges may hand down decisions against their own appointers. If Ramseyer's view is the right one, then checks and balances emerge because the lack of judicial security undermines the selection mechanism. However, what if judges who do not share the preferences of the government do care about its wrath? If we suspect that judges also care about avoiding sanctions, then we are back to Hamilton's original concern that judicial insecurity leads to judicial subservience, even if selection fails to work perfectly.

Sanctioning-Based Approaches

Within the American politics literature, a growing line of research, known as the separation-of-powers approach, explores the choices judges make by looking at the constraints they face (Marks 1989; Ferejohn and Shipan 1990; Eskridge 1991; Spiller and Gely 1990, 1992; Ferejohn and Weingast

---

[6] The scrutiny with which the Senate approached President Kirchner's nominee to the Supreme Court, Eugenio Zaffaroni, in 2003 suggests, however, that this may be changing.

[7] I thank Matthew Stephenson for suggesting Ramseyer's argument.

1992; Epstein and Knight 1996, 1998; Segal 1997; Rogers 2001). As in the selection-based story, in this account judges are also assumed to have policy preferences. The key difference is that when judges fail to adjust their decisions in light of other institutional actors it has negative consequences: A judge may not get the support of other judges, the executive may refuse to implement the court's decision, or Congress may overrule the court's opinion. To avoid such possible outcomes, a judge will face incentives to forgo his or her most preferred choice and instead choose the next best option that he or she she believes the other relevant institutional actors will support.

Ferejohn and Weingast (1992) capture the basic strategic dilemma imposed on judges by assuming a Court placed in the role of having to interpret statutes passed by an *enacting* or past Congress, in light of the preferences of the *sitting* or current Congress. In their basic model, the Court must choose some outcome K where Q represents the preferences of the enacting legislature and H and S represent the ideal points for the current median member of the House and Senate, respectively.

In Figure 1.1, the space between H and S represents a structurally induced equilibrium such that any judicial decision made within this range is invulnerable to being overturned. Anything outside this range is subject to congressional action, resulting in the compromise equilibrium L. Thus, assuming that the judge's ideal point K matches the enacting legislature's $(K = Q)$, the best strategy for the judge is to enact policy at H, which is the closest point to Q that cannot be overturned. Substantively, what this model shows is the degree to which the judge is constrained by the current House and Senate. In effect, the judge is forced to alter his or her decision to avoid a potentially worse outcome in which both branches move policy further to the right. The more ideologically similar the House and Senate and the more distant both branches are from the enacting legislature, the more constrained the judge is to pursue his or her sincere preferences (ibid.: 267).

Despite its increasing dominance in the judicial politics literature (e.g., see Epstein and Knight 2000), the separation-of-powers approach is not

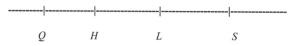

     Q H L S

Figure 1.1 The standard separation-of-powers game. *Source:* Ferejohn and Weingast 1992: 269.

without its critics. Behavioralists, touting the attitudinal model, have been particularly skeptical of its application to the American courts. Although the separation-of-powers approach been used to analyze a handful of case studies (Spiller and Gely 1990; Clinton 1994; Epstein and Knight 1996), critics argue that large-N analyses offer little support (Segal 1997). Scholars have also taken issue with the plausibility of the model's core assumptions. For example, Jeffrey Segal (1997) posits that the costliness of legislation, multiple veto points, and the Court's ability to frame issues substantially reduces the threat faced by U.S. Supreme Court justices. Thus, in Segal and Spaeth's words, "the structure of the American political system virtually always allows judges to engage in rationally sincere behavior" (Segal and Spaeth 2002).

But again, in the Latin American context many of these mitigating factors are far less prominent. Indeed, a growing number of scholars have begun to apply the separation-of-powers framework to account for executive-judicial congruence in institutionally unstable environments (Helmke 2002, 2003b; Iaryczower et al. 2002; Bill Chavez et al. 2003; Scribner 2003). Explaining the full range of variation in judicial behavior in such environments, however, also requires modifying many of the standard assumptions used in the U.S. context.

To bridge the gap between extant theories derived from American politics and Latin American experience, this study begins with the alternative premise that the primary source of the threat that judges face may not necessarily stem from the current government. After all, Ramseyer's point aside, if the current president has been able to handpick his or her own Court, the preferences of the judges and the current administration are already likely to be in accordance. Rapid turnover and presidential control over selection should help to mitigate the need for judges to strategically align themselves with the current executive. Pace Dahl, judges will prefer to support the current government not because they are constrained to do so but because they share its views. As a result, the relevant inter-temporal conflict of interest shifts from the standard scenario of a judge appointed by a *past* government who is primarily constrained by a *current* government to a more uncertain situation in which a judge appointed by the *current* government faces potential constraints at the hands of a *future* opposition government

Starting with this alternative strategic setting, the remainder of this study explores how the interactions among judges' and politicians' goals, preferences, and information shape court-executive relations. Among the several findings is the novel idea that institutional instability does not automatically preclude checks and balances. Rather, institutionally unstable settings generate a reverse legal-political cycle in which judges rule against the current government once it begins to lose power. I refer to this alternative pattern of behavior as "strategic defection." The analysis also helps to shed new light on the puzzle of why judges under attack are willing to handle politically controversial cases. Whereas scholars have long contended that judges without legitimacy should refrain from issuing high-profile decisions, and particularly should avoid making decisions that go against the government of the day, such decisions can potentially serve as valuable signals to incoming governments. The twist here is that judges may be compelled to participate in politically costly decisions precisely because they otherwise lack legitimacy. The study thus offers a new logic for judicial activism that explains when and why judges under attack refuse to duck and cover.

1.3 Design and Overview of the Argument

As one of Latin America's largest and most institutionally unstable countries, Argentina represents the paradigmatic case for exploring the alternative logic of strategic defection that lies at the heart of this book. Precisely because of the chronic institutional instability and the degree of executive control over the Argentine Supreme Court, we should expect to find judges ruling against the government only when they are compelled to do so for strategic reasons. Thus, Argentina offers an ideal, or "most likely," case for evaluating the theory of strategic defection.

Argentina also helps to bring into sharp relief the point that formal institutional provisions may offer dubious criteria for selecting appropriate empirical cases for evaluating strategic accounts. Compared with most Latin American courts, on paper the Argentine judiciary is among the most insulated high courts in the region. The formal institutional design of the Argentine Supreme Court is modeled directly on that of the United States. In addition to provisions that guarantee life tenure, the Argentine Supreme Court is composed of a single chamber, whose number is determined by Congress.[8] Moreover, as in the United States, the Argentine federal

---

[8] During the period under examination, the number of justices has increased from five under the last military dictatorship (1976–83) and under the democratic government of Raúl Alfonsín (1983–9) to nine under both of Carlos Menem's administrations (1989–95 and 1995–9).

judiciary established relatively early in its history the power of judicial review, which has subsequently been codified into law.[9] Although it has generally failed to exercise effective control over its own docket, the constitutional provisions for the Argentine Supreme Court are identical to that of the United States, allowing it to exercise limited original jurisdiction and broader appellate jurisdiction over all federal matters. Its decisions are viewed as binding on all lower courts. The Argentine Supreme Court thus represents the "last word" in the federal judicial system and is the most important judicial body in the country (see Appendix A).

Yet as most scholars of the region have long recognized, in Argentina, as elsewhere in Latin America, the formal provisions regarding the judiciary are often grossly inadequate for understanding the actual constraints that judges face. For most of the twentieth century, chronic regime instability contributed to a pattern of executive incursions against the Court under dictatorship and democracy. As Chapter 4 discusses, formal impeachments were quite rare, but since Juan Perón came to power in the late 1940s, judges were regularly forced to resign with every change in regime.

Following the transition to democracy in 1983, the Court continued to come under severe attack. Although over the past two decades there has been more of an effort to work through the formal institutions to sanction the Court, the justices have still faced considerable threats. For example, since Menem's court-packing plan was passed by Congress in 1990, hundreds of impeachment charges have been filed by the opposition against the justices on the Supreme Court. Most recently, during the 2001–2 economic collapse, the Court became a lightning rod for public criticism, including weekly demonstrations by thousands of angry citizens outside the Court and the justices' private homes. That many of the informal complaints and formal impeachment charges against the judges are based on the very decisions that the judges have handed down suggests a strong empirical link between the choices judges make and the constraints they face.

As a single country study, the research design of the book employs what King, Keohane, and Verba refer to as a methodology of "multiple observations at different levels of analysis" (1994: 208–30). By using individual-level data on judicial decisions under different regimes, different governments,

---

[9] In the case of *Sojo* (1887) the Argentine Supreme Court explicitly invoked *Marbury v. Madison* (1803), arguing that since Argentina's constitutional system was based on that of the United States, it followed that the Argentine Supreme Court should be able to review the acts of the states as well as the other branches of government (Miller, Gelli, and Cayuso 1995).

and at different points within governmental terms, the book expands the number of observations and thus overcomes the problems of causal inference that often plague single-country studies, while at the same time holding constant several competing explanatory factors, such as legal and political culture.

Focusing on a single country also enabled me to conduct the type and quality of research that are necessary for testing explanations that rely on a deep knowledge of actors' preferences, motivations, information, expectations, and beliefs. As in other analytic narrative accounts (e.g., see Bates et al. 1998), this allowed me to trace the sequences of events under various governments and to pinpoint how actors' beliefs and information about the constraints they faced evolved over time.

A key part of establishing the conditions underlying the strategic defection account is information culled from more than thirty interviews conducted with Argentine legal experts and elites.[10] These interviews provide a rich store of information about the internal workings of the Supreme Court as well as a trove of evidence regarding various actors' views about the evolving dynamics between the Court and other institutions, particularly the executive.

In terms of the dependent variable, focusing on a single country made possible the construction of one of the first systematic data sets on judicial decisions in Latin America.[11] The *Argentine Supreme Court Decisions* (*ASCD*) data set includes more than 11,000 individual-level decisions coded on more than fifty variables decided over the last two and a half decades (see Appendix B). In addition to recording the individual justices' votes and

---

[10] Among those I interviewed were several of the current and former Supreme Court justices, including the former Chief Justice under the military and the then-current Chief Justice under President Menem. In addition, I interviewed several clerks for the Supreme Court, three of the five lower level judges from the Federal Court of Appeals that convicted the former military leaders in the human rights trials of the early 1980s, a number of human rights lawyers, law professors from several leading universities, including San Andreas, Buenos Aires, Palermo, and Di Tella, as well as the heads of various legal non-governmental organizations, such as the Centro de Estudios Legales Sociales, Poder Cuidadano, and Fundación Carlos Nino.

[11] Until recently, only a handful of scholars of courts in Latin America gathered systematic data on judicial decisions. González Casanova (1970) and Schwarz (1977) analyze aggregate level data on *amparo* decisions in Mexico. Over the last few years, however, there has been an increasing effort in this direction. For Argentina, see Molinelli 1999; Molinelli et al. 1999; and Iaryczower, Spiller, and Tomassi 2002; for Argentina and Chile, see Scribner 2003; for Argentina and Brazil, see Brinks 2003; for Mexico, see Magaloni and Sánchez 2001; Rios-Figueroa 2003.

the dates on which the decision was handed down, the data set includes detailed information on judges' participation, the issues involved in the case, and lower courts' decisions. This information allows for testing further refinements of the theory and addressing several alternative explanations. To delve further into the dynamics of court-executive relations, the book also draws on a range of qualitative evidence from a variety of secondary and primary sources, including daily newspapers, autobiographies, and Argentine law journals. Such evidence is crucial for examining subtle shifts in the Court's jurisprudence, identifying the most important issues, and exploring more deeply the various strategies of actors that lie at the heart of the theory of strategic defection.

The remainder of the book is organized as follows. Chapter 2, "The Logic of Strategic Defection," provides an informal discussion of the basic ideas and assumptions underlying strategic defection. Building on the standard separation-of-powers approach, the chapter begins by distinguishing strategic defection as an intuitively logical, but heretofore overlooked, pattern of judicial behavior. The chapter then considers how strategic defection emerges in a context where the constraints that judges face stem from *future* as opposed to *current* governments. In addition, the chapter addresses the effects of varying key assumptions regarding judicial motivations, institutional constraints, and information about the incoming government's preferences on judges' willingness and capacity to behave strategically.

Chapter 3, "A Theory of Court-Executive Relations: Insecure Tenure, Incomplete Information, and Strategic Behavior," develops a formal signaling model based on incomplete information. The model provides a unified framework for bringing together the insights of the preceding chapter with the idea that incoming politicians may likewise be uncertain about the types of judges that they face. Specifically, the model endogenizes the constraints that judges face by incorporating politicians' decisions to sanction sitting justices. Under certain conditions, judges strategically defect to maximize their chances of remaining on the bench. In addition to further clarifying the mechanisms driving defection, the model yields several more counterintuitive insights regarding judicial activism and participation. The chapter concludes with a series of testable hypotheses about when and in which types of cases judges will strategically defect.

Chapter 4, "Judges, Generals, and Presidents: Institutional Insecurity on the Argentine Supreme Court, 1976–1999," uses the theory of strategic defection to structure an account of the institutional insecurity that has plagued Argentina under dictatorship and democracy. Drawing on a variety of primary and secondary sources, I explore the type and credibility of threats that judges have faced for the following four governments: the military dictatorship (1976–83), the first democratic government of Raúl Alfonsín (1983–9), and the last two democratically elected governments of Carlos Menem (1989–5 and 1995–9). Within each of the periods examined, I describe the political prospects for the current government and construct a plausible account of the judges' expectations and beliefs. Specifically, the chapter focuses on judges' information about the incoming government's preferences and their expectations about the incoming government's capacity for punishing. It also examines how judges' motivations shape the trade-offs and incentives involved in strategic behavior. While the particular issues, types of sanctions, and the institutional capacities of incoming governments to punish judges vary considerably from government to government, the general conclusion that emerges is that the empirical conditions for strategic defection were present in three of the four contemporary governments on which I focus.

Chapter 5, "The Reverse Legal-Political Cycle: An Analysis of Decision Making on the Argentine Supreme Court," provides a quantitative analysis of several hypotheses that emerge from the theory of strategic defection. Starting with the core timing hypothesis, the evidence overwhelmingly supports the prediction that judges increasingly decide cases against the government once it begins to lose power and that they do so in the most important cases. In addition, the findings of this chapter challenge the conventional wisdom that courts under constraints automatically avoid the political fray. Overall, patterns of abstention, appeals granting, and separate opinion writing suggest little support for the view that judges duck rather than defect. Finally, the chapter concludes with an exploration of several alternative explanations, including the changing composition of the court, changes in issues coming before the court, and changes in the legality of the incumbent government's behavior over time.

Chapter 6, "The Dynamics of Defection: Human Rights, Civil Liberties, and Presidential Power," uses a series of case studies to explore more deeply the causes and consequences of strategic defection. Under the military, I link changes in the Court's jurisprudence on key human rights issues to changes in the political context and test additional implications of the theory by showing how judges deliberately used these changes to ameliorate the threat they faced at the hands of the democratic opposition. Under the Alfonsín government, I reexamine the issue of ducking by surveying the Court's record in handling high-profile decisions. Under Menem, I explore how the rise and decline of Menem's popularity shaped the Court's willingness to support the use and abuse of presidential power. For each of these periods, I then consider the related but separate set of questions about whether strategic defection worked. Finally, I conclude with an epilogue that draws on the theory of strategic defection to make sense of the breakdown of court-executive relations that occurred in the recent political and economic crisis of 2002–3.

Chapter 7, "Conclusion: Broader Lessons and Future Directions," is divided into three sections. Section 7.1 summarizes the main findings of the book with respect to judicial behavior in institutionally unstable environments. Section 7.2 lays the groundwork for future extensions of the theory of strategic defection by examining how well the main propositions work in explaining court-executive relations in three other Latin American countries. Contemporary Venezuela and post-PRI Mexico provide the most likely cases for testing the theory. Chile and PRI-dominated Mexico provide the least likely cases. The chapter concludes with a discussion of the theory's implications for the study of courts and comparative political institutions more generally.

2

The Logic of Strategic Defection

When a judge decides a case in favor of the government, is it because he or she simply agrees with the government's position in the case? Or does his or her decision instead reflect a fear of reprisal were he or she to stand up to the government? Conversely, when a judge decides cases against the government, is it because he or she truly disagrees with the government's position? Or is it for some other reason?

Drawing on the tools of positive political theory, this chapter and the next explore a new set of answers to these questions by recasting fundamentally the connection between the choices judges make and the constraints they face. At the core of the argument is the idea that judges rule against the rulers not because judges enjoy independence in a conventional sense but because they fear being punished by the government's successors. I label this phenomenon strategic defection. Strategic defection constitutes a logical – but heretofore under-theorized – judicial response to a particular institutional setting, namely one in which judges lack institutional security and the main threat to their security stems from incoming political actors rather than incumbents.

To develop this argument, the chapter unfolds as follows. Section 2.1 introduces the standard view of judges as strategic decision makers. Section 2.2 shows how strategic defection differs from several familiar views of judicial behavior. Section 2.3 uses a simple spatial model to offer a first cut at exploring the conditions leading to strategic defection. The next four sections then examine informally the various assumptions on which the logic of strategic defection rests, including judges' motivations, judges' information about the incoming government, and the number of sanctioning players required to punish judges.

2.1 The Standard Strategic Account

In contrast to legalistic accounts that assume apolitical judges and approaches that focus solely on judges' attitudes and ideologies, the standard strategic approach treats judges as rational decision makers who are constrained by other institutional actors. At the heart of this approach is the idea that the "law" depends on the interaction among the various branches of government (Ferejohn and Weingast 1992). The key assumption is that the Court's decisions cannot last for long in institutional settings where other political actors have the power to overturn them. To the extent that judges and politicians share the same preferences over policy outcomes, judges need not worry about trying to make their decisions more palatable to other political actors. Judicial decisions will stand because other actors agree with them. However, because governments change hands, there is always the possibility for an "inter-temporal conflict of interest" that places the Court in the position of interpreting statutes passed by previous legislatures in light of current legislatures (ibid.: 264). Taking this potential conflict as a starting point, the standard strategic setting creates a situation in which judges may prefer the views of the previous government but face constraints to bring their decisions into line with the preferences of the current government.

Perhaps the most well-known example used to illustrate the separation-of-powers approach is *Marbury v. Madison* (1803). Marbury asked the Court to issue a writ of mandamus against Jefferson's newly appointed Secretary of State, James Madison. The writ would command that Madison deliver a federal commission that had been granted to Marbury in the final hours of the outgoing Adams administration. These were the so-called midnight appointments that Adams sought to make before he left office. By all historical accounts, Chief Justice John Marshall would have preferred to give Marbury, a fellow Federalist, his appointment. But doing so would have risked the Court's institutional legitimacy by giving the newly elected Republican president, Thomas Jefferson, the chance to openly defy the Court's ruling. To avoid this outcome, Marshall instead chose the strategy of arguing that the statute giving the Supreme Court jurisdiction to hear the case was in violation of the Constitution. Based on the Court's lack of jurisdiction, Marshall argued, the Court could not grant Marbury the writ. The result was that while Marshall allowed the current government to "win" the case, he also used the decision to introduce the power of judicial review, a power that could be used subsequently to pursue the Court's policy preferences whenever the institutional constraints permitted (Mc-Closkey [1960] 1994; Murphy 1964; Clinton 1994; Epstein and Knight 1996).

Examples of such strategic behavior are hardly limited to exceptional justices or to early U.S. history.[1] Consider the recent Argentine Supreme Court case of *Aerolineas Argentinas*, known formally as *Fontenla* (1990). The facts of *Aerolineas Argentinas* involved a dispute between the ministry of Menem's new government in charge of privatization and members of Congress. Seeking to halt the administration's sale of shares of the state-owned airline, the opposition sought and was granted in a first-instance court an injunction (*recurso de amparo*) against the executive decree 1024/90. Rather than try to get the injunction overturned by the second-instance appeals court (the usual route for appealing decisions), attorneys for the government instead appealed directly to the Supreme Court. The government's argument was that in cases of extreme institutional importance (*gravedad institucional*), the Supreme Court could adopt the doctrine of per saltum. Per saltum, which literally means "to jump," grants to the Supreme Court the power to seize cases directly from a lower first-instance court, thereby skipping over the path of the regular courts of appeals (Carrió and Garay 1991; Carrió 1996).

Aerolineas was the first of the so-called political cases to arrive at the Supreme Court after Menem's increase of the Court's members from five to nine in July 1990 (Verbitsky 1993: 137). Of the previous administration's Supreme Court, only three of its original members remained: Justices Carlos Fayt, Augusto Belluscio, and Enrique Petracchi. The other six justices were all new appointees of Menem and widely viewed as sympathetic to the new government. Thus, even without the support of the held-over justices, the government's attorneys could be relatively assured of getting the majority to vote in their favor. What is of interest here, however, is Justice Petracchi's response. In the case of *Aerolineas* Petracchi not only joined the Menem majority, but actually wrote the Court's opinion permitting the sale of the airline.

Although Petracchi himself was the only Peronist sympathizer among the held-over justices, he can hardly be viewed as a Menem sympathizer. Indeed, in several subsequent cases Petracchi opposed the government's

---

[1] For applications of the separation-of-powers approach beyond the U.S. context, see Vanberg 2000, 2001; Iaryczower, Spiller, and Tomassi 2002; Bill Chavez and Weingast 2003; and Scribner 2003).

policies.[2] Petracchi's opposition to Menem should be viewed as part of the general disaffection between traditional Peronists and the Menemista faction, especially after Menem reneged on his promises to support labor. Nevertheless, in spite of his overall resistance to many of Menem's economic reforms, here Petracchi was also presented with an opportunity finally to adopt for the court the doctrine of per saltum. Since his tenure under President Alfonsín (1983–9), Petracchi had been in favor of allowing the court to seize important cases from the lower courts and had tried to introduce the doctrine in obiter dictum in the case of *Margherita Belen.* According to the account given by Argentine journalist Horacio Verbitsky, when the case first came to the attention of the judges most sympathetic to the Menem government, they contacted Petracchi, saying, "'Enrique, this is your most glorious hour. The time for per saltum has finally arrived" (quoted in Verbitsky 1993: 137, my translation).

Given what we know from other cases about Petracchi's views on the government's economic reforms and Menem's methods for achieving them, it seems likely that Petracchi's first preference would have been to admit per saltum and rule against the government. Yet given the sympathies of the other members of the court with the government, it would have been nearly impossible for Petracchi to achieve his first best option. What is more, ruling against the government would have had virtually no effect on the overall outcome of the case but would have prevented Petracchi from crafting the per saltum doctrine as he wanted. Thus, he settled for making a bargain with the Menemistas, adopting per saltum but ruling in favor of the government.

Occurring in opposite hemispheres and separated by almost two hundred years, what *Marbury* and *Aerolineas Argentinas* have in common is the nature of the strategic setting that each case posed for the judges who were compelled to decide them. In both cases, held-over justices believed themselves to be constrained from implementing their sincere preferences by the government then in power. Marshall calculated that he could not force Jefferson to appoint Marbury. Petracchi realized that he alone could not halt the privatization of his country's airline. But in both instances, Marshall and Petracchi did pursue other goals that they believed would not be challenged by the government. In Marshall's case, the sleight of hand was to enhance the Court's power by articulating its limits. In Petracchi's case,

---

[2] Among the most high-profile of these decisions are *Fiscal Molinas* (1991), *Godoy* (1990, 1991), *Caso Corrientes* (1992), and *Benito* (1994; see Verbitsky 1993; Poder Cuidadano 1997).

deciding a case in favor of the government allowed Petracchi to introduce a doctrine that he believed could, in the future, be used to enact the policies he favored.

Cast in more general terms, the pattern suggested by these stories is one in which judges rule in favor of the sitting government, even though they would prefer not to do so. Standard accounts of strategic judicial decision making thus amount essentially to explaining why judges appointed from a previous government hand down decisions that do not match the justices' first-best option. The answer lies in the constraints hold-over judges face at the hands of the current government. The alternative possibility – that judges may instead act strategically by ruling against the current government – has yet to be explored.

2.2 A New Pattern of Inter-branch Relations

Neither the claim that judges rule against the government nor that judges behave strategically is new. The claim, however, that judges rule against the government for strategic reasons is. Based primarily on examples drawn from the U.S. experience, existing sincere and strategic accounts of inter-branch relations alike tend to reject ipso facto such a connection. On the one hand, sincere-based accounts acknowledging that judges sometimes hand down anti-governmental decisions never address the possibility that this occurs for strategic reasons. On the other hand, strategic-based accounts presuming that judges act strategically tend to focus exclusively on judges adjusting their opinions to rule in favor of the current government. The notion that the constraints judges face may instead lead them to defect strategically against the government has, thus far, been largely neglected.

Generally seen from the perspective of the U.S. institutional context, anti-governmental decisions are assumed to result from the rare combination of the majority of judges held over from the previous administration facing a new government with a different ideology. For example, recall the previous chapter's discussion of Dahl's theory of selection. Given the power of presidents to select their own judges, Dahl argues that the dominant mode of inter-branch relations is that judges rarely are out of step with the ruling majority. Presidents choose judges who share their views, and judges thus tend naturally to rule in the government's favor. Certainly, there may be rare instances where the court ends up in a counter-majoritarian role, but this stems from the fact that while elected representatives may come and go, judges stay on the bench. The Lochner-era Court under Franklin

Delano Roosevelt provides an archetypal example of the view that anti-governmental rulings emerge under only under a new administration that fails to make a sufficient number of appointments to the bench (Caldeira 1987). From this perspective, anti-governmental decisions are thus purely the result of judges behaving sincerely under a new administration, whose views they do not share.

Proponents of the attitudinal model also argue that anti-governmental rulings from the bench have little to do with strategic considerations. Although the attitudinal approach also expects that presidents tend to choose judges who share their views, it assumes that, once justices are appointed, they are virtually unconstrained to behave in accordance with their views, even when the current government strongly disagrees. For example, Segal and Spaeth assert that the U.S. Supreme Court's willingness to defy President Bush and Congress by overturning laws banning flag burning in *Texas v. Johnson* (1989) and *United States v. Eichman* (1990) proves that U.S. Supreme Court justices generally act in accordance with their ideological commitments, not in response to institutional constraints (cited in Segal and Spaeth 1993). Judges' willingness to challenge the government is thus again interpreted solely as evidence against the strategic view.

On the other hand, dating back to Hamilton, the assumption behind the portrayal of the judiciary as the "least dangerous branch" is that, in the absence of institutional protections, the court will be too easily swayed by pressures exerted by the government of the day. From Hamilton's perspective, creating a system where judges constantly cave to the interests of the current ruling majority is problematic because it risks sacrificing the higher law of the Constitution to the fleeting will of the people and their representatives. Constitutions should thus be engineered so as to allow judges to behave sincerely by insulating them from contemporary pressures. In the absence of insulation, however, the danger of strategic behavior is always an excess of pro-governmental rulings.

Similarly, among proponents of the strategic account, the emphasis is entirely on explaining judicial restraint in light of pressures exercised by current governments. Judges' behavior may not comport with the judges' true preferences, scholars assert, but insofar as judicial behavior changes, it tends to be in the direction of bringing the Court's decisions in line with the preferences of contemporary officeholders. Given judges' inherent vulnerability to current majorities, the extent to which judges are able to rule sincerely is a function of whether their preferences converge with those of the current government (Ferejohn and Weingast 1992). This account thus

Table 2.1 *Four Modes of Inter-branch Relations*

	Pro-government	Anti-government
Strategic	Hamilton; conventional separation-of-powers theorists [Examples: *Marbury v. Madison* (1803) Petracchi's opinion in *Aerolineas Argentinas* (1990), *Banco Patagónico* (1993)]	Chapters 5, 6, 7
Sincere	Dahl; attitudinal theorists [Examples: *Ercoli* (1976), *Dufourq* (1984), *Aramayo* (1984), *Videla* (1986), *Peralta* (1990), majority in *Aerolineas Argentinas* (1990)]	Dahl; attitudinal theorists [Examples: Lochner-era cases, *Texas v. Johnson* (1989) and *United States v. Eichman* (1990) *Timerman* (1979), Bacqué's dissent in *Camps* (1987)]

works well to explain why judges rule in favor of governments with different preferences, but the alternative possibility that judges may also sometimes rule against the current government for strategic reasons is not addressed.

Taken together, the competing views of judges can be neatly captured along the two dimensions contained in Table 2.1. The first dimension is whether the outcome is in favor of or against the government. The second dimension is whether the decision is based on a strategic or sincere view of the Court. Both Hamilton's portrait of a non-tenured Supreme Court in *Federalist 78* and the standard separation of powers fit in the upper-left cell in which judges rule in favor of the government for strategic reasons. Justice Marshall's opinion in *Marbury* (1803) is an archetypal example in the United States. In Argentina, the majority opinions in *Aerolineas Argentinas* (1990) and in *Banco Patagónico* (1993), the case in which the Court reissued a pro-governmental opinion after claiming to "misplace" an earlier unfavorable ruling, are illustrative examples.

The lower left-hand cell contains several prominent Argentine cases (discussed more fully in Chapter 6) decided in favor of the government by whom the justices were appointed and thus fits the standard Dahlian critique of counter-majoritarianism. By contrast, the lower right-hand cell fits Dahl's account of the exceptional counter-majoritarian periods in which judges who sincerely disagree with the current government make anti-governmental decisions. In addition to the more familiar U.S. examples, some "exceptional" Argentine cases (discussed more fully in Chapter 6) can also be located here. Note that examples from the attitudinal literature may fit in either of the lower cells, depending on whether judges share the views of the current government. The remaining upper-right cell I have labeled as strategic defection. Conceptually, strategic defection offers a mirror image of strategic support: Whereas strategic supporters share the preferences of sincere defectors, but behave as sincere supporters, strategic defectors share the preferences of the sincere supporters, but behave as sincere defectors. The next task is to explore how this variant of strategic behavior emerges.

2.3 Modifying the Separation-of-Powers Approach

Within the standard separation-of-powers literature, simple spatial models illustrate the strategic interaction between judges and politicians. Although the details of these models vary according to whether presidents, congresses, or agencies are given the last word, all employ three basic elements:

- A fixed sequential structure involving a one- or two-dimensional policy space
- An assumption that actors' preferences are single-peaked
- An assumption that actors have complete and perfect information.

While such an approach obviously dramatically simplifies the real-world complexity of any given situation, it provides a useful way of clarifying at the outset the strategic setting that judges face.

Starting with this basic framework, this section begins with three observations about courts outside the United States. First, in many parts of the developing world, judges face far greater threats than simply having their decisions overturned. In such contexts, sanctions range from impeachment, removal, and court packing to criminal indictment, physical violence, and even death. For example, as Chapter 4 documents, despite clear constitutional provisions granting federal judges life tenure in Argentina, the Supreme Court justices have been removed or threatened with removal with every change in government since the 1940s.

Second, in many developing countries the de facto concentration of power in the executive branch often tends to eclipse the formal institutional judicial sanctioning powers granted to the legislature. This is particularly true throughout Latin America where, despite constitutional guarantees, the functional separation of powers is notoriously weak or absent and power is concentrated heavily in the executive branch (O'Donnell 1999; also see Shugart and Carey 1994). The weakness of these other institutions means that presidential attacks against the judges are unlikely to be successfully blocked by third-party actors such as the legislature.

The third and crucial difference is that in many developing countries the primary threat to judges comes not from incumbent governments but from incoming ones. This follows from the fact that those with the greatest incentives to sanction justices are not those who appoint them, but rather those who succeed the appointing government. Theoretically, this means that the standard inter-temporal conflict of interest shifts from one between *past* and *current* governments to one based on the *current*, incumbent executive and *future*, incoming executive.

Whereas the first two differences suggest that judges' incentives to engage in strategic behavior in developing democracies are potentially far greater than in developed democracies, the third difference opens the possibility for a new repertoire of strategic behavior altogether. Specifically, when judges believe that they are constrained by incoming governments who oppose the incumbent government, their best response may be not to support the current government, but rather to rule against it.

Figure 2.1 provides a simple strategic setting that illustrates the logic of strategic defection. The figure depicts a sequence of decisions with the current government (*G1*) moving first, the Court (*C*) second, Nature (*N*) third, and the future government (*G2*) fourth. In the first stage, the current government acts by selecting justices for the court. In the second stage, these justices rule on policies of this government, either upholding or overruling the policies of the government. In the third stage, Nature selects the next

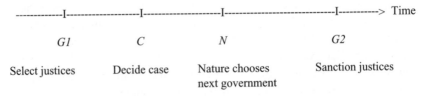

Figure 2.1 The executive selecting and sanctioning game.

2.3 Modifying the Separation-of-Powers Approach

SQ--------------------------G1----------------------G2--------------------------> Policy

Figure 2.2   Policy preferences without inter-temporal conflict.

G1--------------------------SQ----------------------G2--------------------------> Policy

Figure 2.3   Policy preferences with inter-temporal conflict.

government, with a probability p that the incumbents will remain and $1 - p$ that opponents will take office. In the fourth and final stage, the future government decides whether to sanction the court.

For the moment, assume the following basic rule: If the court has decided cases close to the views of the incoming government, the future government will be less likely to sanction the justices, but if the court has decided cases against the views of the new incumbents, the future government will be more likely to sanction the justices. Based on this assumption, the first implication is that under only two scenarios will judges face incentives to continue to support the current government. The first scenario is when the current government itself is strong and able to maintain itself in power; that is, $G1 = G2$. The second scenario if the incumbents lose to the opposition, but the location of the new government's ideal point is such that it prefers $G1$ to SQ, where SQ is the status quo (see Fig. 2.2). Such a circumstance might obtain, for example, if there are relatively few policy differences between the outgoing and incoming governments. Under these circumstances, judges will continue to support the current government, even though it is leaving power.

Under all other circumstances, the rule of selective punishment implies that judges will be better off deserting the current government. If the incoming government opposes the policies of its predecessors such that it prefers that its opponents' policies do not become law, then, in effect, the future government can be said to favor the status quo (i.e., the condition that obtains whenever the policies of the current government are not enacted). Under this scenario, incoming governments punish decisions that fall anywhere between $G1$ and SQ whenever SQ is between $G1$ and $G2$ (see Fig. 2.3). Thus, once the incumbents begin to lose power, judges will face incentives to curry favor with the incoming government by ruling against the policies of their own appointers.

In sum, this illustration represents a stylized version of the strategic situation that occurs whenever incoming governments have full discretion over keeping sitting justices and are able to use that power to reward and punish judges selectively. Its usefulness lies primarily in showing how altering the inter-temporal framework expands the standard repertoire of strategic decision-making to include defection against the current government. Ultimately, of course, whether or not the logic of strategic defection can be sustained demands a deeper analysis of the various assumptions underlying this simple scenario. First, what motivates judges needs to be fleshed out. Second, the consequences of relaxing assumptions regarding the judges' information about the preferences of the incoming government warrant further exploration. Third, more remains to be said about how the incoming government's institutional capacity to punish judges affects the scope of strategic behavior. Fourth, just how and why the selective punishment rule itself emerges begs explanation. In the following sections, I address the first three of these issues. Building on the various observations generated in these each of these sections, the following chapter tackles the fourth issue by developing a game theoretic framework that links endogenously the choices judges make with the constraints that they face.

2.4 Judicial Motivations

An implicit assumption underpinning the logic of strategic defection is that judges place a higher value on avoiding sanctions than on deciding cases in line with their sincere preferences. Yet so far very little has been said about judges' specific underlying goals and how these might affect the trade-offs that judges make between avoiding sanctions and abandoning their preferences. Do judges care only about following precedent, or are they willing to overturn it to make the "right" decision? Or perhaps judges act mainly to further their own careers? Or, to offer another possibility, perhaps they are motivated by enhancing their own reputations or bolstering the legitimacy of the judiciary? Given that it is plausible that judges are motivated by any one of a number of different goals (e.g., career, policy, reputation, legitimacy), it is worth exploring whether and under what conditions assuming different goals clashes with the logic of strategic defection.

Within the U.S. literature the dominant view is that most justices most of the time care about pursuing policy aims. Although other motivational stances have been explored (Ferejohn and Weingast 1992; Baum 1999), the vast majority of strategic-based studies of courts make the assumption that judges seek to bring the law as closely into line with their preferences as they can without being overturned. Along these lines, for example, Epstein and

Knight argue that judicial concern with institutional legitimacy is ultimately best viewed as a means that policy-oriented judges pursue in order to make sure that their rulings are complied with, not an end in and of themselves (1998: 46–9; but also see Munger 2003).

Yet in applying the separation-of-powers model abroad, making a similar assumption about judges as pure policy seekers is undoubtedly premature. For example, in the context of Latin America much is often made of the idea that judges trained in the civil law tradition lack the same values as their common law counterparts. Rarely do civil law judges pursue policy: They act as expert clerks, mechanically matching the facts of the case to the particular statute to deduce their opinions (Merryman 1985: 34–9). Rooted in long-standing notions of judges as merely civil servants, the idea of the judge as an activist pursuing policy aims of his or her own has been – at least until recently – largely unthinkable for observers of Latin American courts (Rosenn 1987).

At the same time, however, it may be that the cultural differences between the ideal-typical civil law judge and the common law judge are overdrawn. The legal systems of late twentieth- and early twenty-first-century Latin America should be viewed as hybrids, sharing features of both the civil law and common law systems. Many Latin American justices enjoy – at least on paper – formal institutional guarantees identical to their U.S. counterparts (Crisp et al. 2003). And most Latin American high courts have long established the power of judicial review and often base their legal reasoning explicitly on important U.S. cases (e.g., see Miller, Gelli, and Cayuso 1995).

Moreover, since the democratic transitions of the 1980s, it is becoming much more acceptable in Latin American legal scholarship to view judges in the role of activists using the law to transform society (Nino 1992; Gargarella 1996). And the judicial profession is in the process of becoming more open. Not all Latin American Supreme Court justices are lifelong judicial employees who worked themselves up through the bureaucratic ladder. They may instead have had experience as legal scholars (traditionally the innovators in the civil law tradition) or even as professional private lawyers. Thus, although certainly many of the norms and institutions of the civil law system remain, it is probably more accurate to describe Latin America as having multiple legal cultures rather than a single legal culture.

Given this pluralism, it is important to examine how and under what conditions the logic of strategic defection holds across judges with different motivational stances. To that end, this section considers three idea typical judges: policy actor, careerist, and professional. The basic point that emerges is that there is nothing inherent in any of these types that necessarily precludes them from behaving strategically. In other words, although it may be tempting to infer that only career-oriented judges are vulnerable to strategic defection, under the right circumstances, judges motivated by more lofty goals may also be led to defect strategically. Incentives to engage in strategic behavior depend on how costly sanctions are for judges given their particular goals, not on the judges' motivational stance per se.

Policy Seekers

To explain my reasoning more fully, I begin by considering the most familiar of the three types, the policy seeker. As in the U.S.-based literature, let us assume that the policy seeker is driven solely by his or her desire to bring the law closest to his or her ideal point. In situations where the main threat involves overturning his or her decision, shifting the inter-temporal context means that he or she will face incentives to ensure that his or her decisions are located in line with the preferences of the future government. Yet it is important to recognize that policy reversal need not be the only threat to which policy-seeking judges will respond strategically.

Consider the situation in which the stakes instead involve the judge's own removal. In this scenario, the cost of losing one's post may override the cost of forfeiting the case for two reasons. First and foremost, for judges who seek to influence policy in the future, removal obviously precludes that. A judge who remains in office may, temporarily, have to alter his or her behavior to accommodate political realities, but he or she also leaves open the possibility that he or she can make an impact on policy if and when the political context shifts. By contrast, a judge who is removed from the bench will not have this opportunity. Thus, as long as this type of judge has a sufficiently high discount rate for the future and some expectation that the power of the future government may eventually wane, judges who care about policy will be adverse to sanctions.

A second and more context-specific reason that policy seekers care about staying on the bench has to do with the particular norms regarding precedent that obtain in a civil law culture. The idea here is that where such norms are relatively weak (i.e., when stare decisis is rarely followed), the lasting effects of judicial decisions are much more uncertain. In such contexts, the ability of a sitting justice to influence policy depends even more crucially on whether the individual judge remains in office. Thus, to the extent that the policy actor believes that he or she stands a chance of remaining in office by modifying his or her actions, he or she will have incentives to defect strategically from his or her appointers in order to retain the ability to affect policy in the future.

Careerists

The second type of judge to be considered is a careerist. The careerist is motivated not by public-regarding goals, but rather by personal career advancement. For the careerist, the costs of removal depend solely on the subsequent career opportunities available to him or her. How careerism plays out is thus ultimately an empirical question that depends on the specific context under examination. For example, in economically volatile settings where state employment ensures judges a steady job and a host of licit (and sometimes illicit) perks, careerists are likely to be averse to making decisions that risk removal.

Or consider the judge who has spent his or her entire professional life working his or her way through the levels of judicial bureaucracy. Having developed few outside professional ties, the judge who is impeached or forced to resign in mid-career may find it considerably more difficult than his or her North American counterpart to enter into a lucrative private law practice.[3] More generally, unless a careerist-oriented judge can count on being better rewarded for his or her loyalty to the outgoing government, switching loyalties to maximize one's chances of remaining in office under a new government is relatively straightforward.

Professionals

The third type of judge is the professional. His or her main motivation is to maintain his or her own personal reputation and to bolster that of his or her institution. Although such goals may ultimately be seen as means to either career advancement or policy making (e.g., see Epstein and Knight 1998), for my purposes here it is worthwhile to consider these as separate motivations. Of the three types, professionally oriented judges would appear to be the least interested in maintaining their posts or ensuring that their

---

[3] Even if a justice were to make the transition to private practice, the reputational effects among the remaining members of the Court may hamper his or her ability to represent clients. Clients are unlikely to choose lawyers against whom they believe sitting judges will be biased.

decisions stand and are thus the least likely to engage in defection. Indeed, to the extent that defection is viewed as politically motivated, judges who care about maintaining their or their institution's reputations should be steadfastly unwilling to engage in it.

Yet taking a slightly different view, the idea that professionally motivated judges might be tempted to defect strategically becomes more plausible. For example, imagine that a judge is primarily concerned with his or her image in the legal community. To the extent that incurring sanctions also risks a judge's reputation within that community, then judges who care about the views of their peers may face incentives that alter their decisions. Likewise, to the extent that the judge cares about the institutional legitimacy of the Court, garnering popular support may be at odds with supporting the outgoing government. An obvious example here is the Roosevelt Court and the so-called switch in time that saved nine (Caldeira 1987). In neither case should we necessarily conclude that the judge who defects is wholly unprincipled (nor really just cares about advancing his or her own career); rather, under certain conditions, the judge is willing to behave strategically in the service of his or her higher principles.

In sum, the overarching point is that the logic of strategic defection does not hinge necessarily on assuming ex ante a single motivational stance. Whether strategic defection makes sense depends on establishing empirically whether a given type of judge values avoiding sanctions relative to deciding a case in line with his or her preferences. While it may be the case that professionally oriented judges generally eschew strategic behavior and careerist judges thrive on it, neither type is automatically precluded from nor automatically prone to behaving strategically. At bottom, whether and under which conditions different types of judges are willing to make this trade-off is an empirical question that needs to be addressed in the application of the theory to real world situations.

2.5 Problems of Information

Standard separation-of-powers approaches begin with the simplifying assumption that actors have complete and perfect information (e.g., see Segal 1997). Similarly, the forgoing discussion assumes that judges know the preferences of the incoming government. Based on this assumption, I derived strategic defection as a logical response used to mitigate sanctions whenever the incoming government has views that are sufficiently different from the outgoing government. While dealing fully with the issue of incomplete information must await until the subsequent chapter, it is worth considering briefly how conventional understandings about certain types of information problems – namely judges' uncertainty over the preferences of the successor government – fit with the core logic of strategic defection.

To assume that judges have full information in any institutional setting is a stretch. In contexts outside the United States, however, such assumptions can appear particularly problematic. Among most Argentine experts, assuming that actors operate in a world dominated by certainty is the exception, not the norm. Military and democratic governments suddenly collapse, economies implode, presidents leave office early, unlikely candidates win office and, once there, often stun their supporters by switching policies (e.g., see Stokes 2001). In such environments, assuming that judges know which government is coming to power, let alone knowing with certainty where the new government's preferences lay, seems naive at best.

Yet on closer examination, asserting that judges may have sufficient information in order to act strategically may not be entirely unwarranted. For example, as we see in Chapter 4, almost daily the Argentine newspapers are filled with politicians weighing in on particular issues and debating the fates of the individual judges. Tribunales Plaza, where the Argentine Supreme Court is located, is regularly filled with mass demonstrations over specific legal issues, ranging from the investigation of terrorist attacks to the privatization of the telephone companies to the government's freeze on private savings. Under President Menem, the political opposition even convened a "shadow court" to hand down rulings on many of the cases being decided by the official Supreme Court.[4] Especially in the most important issues of the day, it seems that judges often do have quite a good sense of the opposition's preferences.

Moreover, the very fact that judges face such high stakes in these contexts may lead them actively to seek out information about where the opposition stands once the incumbent government begins to lose power. For example, in the presidential campaigns of 1989 and 1999, the justices on the Argentine Court met repeatedly with opposition candidates. In the months leading up to the 1999 presidential elections, in which one of the main contenders was the governor of the Province of Buenos Aires, the newspaper *La Nación* quipped that "there are a growing number of federal judges on the highway between Buenos Aires [the seat of many federal judgeships]

---

[4] Interview with Justice Moliné O'Connor, Buenos Aires, May 1998.

and La Plata [where the governorship of the Province of Buenos Aires is located]" (May 15, 1999). The basic message was that judges, worried about their posts, were actively seeking to establish a relationship with the government's successors before the incumbents were out of office.

Still, insofar as judges face some doubt about the preferences of the incoming government, particularly during periods where the incumbent government is just beginning to weaken, the question remains of whether judges might pursue a safer course by avoiding controversy, rather than courting it. Indeed, in the literature on U.S. judicial politics the argument that judges under attack learn to avoid the political fray is hardly new (McCloskey [1960] 1994; Bickel [1962] 1986; Rosenberg 1992; also see Sunstein 1996a, 1996b). The basic lesson of cases such as *Dred Scott* (1857) is that when the Court does not duck, it not only precludes political debate over important issues (e.g., see Sunstein 1996a), but it also puts itself at grave risk.

In situations where judges face additional problems of information over knowing the incoming government's preferences, one plausible option is thus to duck rather than defect. A clear theoretical analogue to this idea appears, for example, in the literature on central banks, which posits that bankers whose appointments depend on the discretion of incoming governments will adopt a strategy of "wait and see" until the new government is already in place (Alt 1991: 65). Applying a similar logic to judges whose fate rests in the hands of the future government, one might reasonably expect judges initially to adopt a prudent strategy of avoiding making high-profile decisions until they are relatively certain about which government is likely to come to power and what its preferences over issues are likely to be.

2.6 Institutions and Sanctioning Players

Institutions shape actors' expectations about the scope and intensity of the constraints that they face. In the forgoing discussion, I have sought to capture the observation that Latin American presidents are all-powerful by modeling the government as a unitary actor capable of removing or keeping judges at will. Clearly, though, this assumption may require modification as circumstances change. As we see below, for example, even in the hyper-presidentialist system of Argentina, Congress has increasingly played a larger role in determining the fate of the Court.

At the most general level, the lesson of separation-of-powers approaches is that adding institutional actors tends to increase the scope of sincere behavior. More specifically, the ability of judges to decide cases in line with their preferences depends on three jointly related variables: the number of political actors who must agree to sanction judges, the location of the sanctioning player's ideal points, and the institutional rules that the relevant actors must follow in order to punish judges.

The first variable, the number of sanctioning players, alternatively referred to as "veto points," "veto players," and "veto gates," emphasizes how institutional arrangements limit or enhance the ability of actors to enact change (Moe and Caldwell 1994; Tsebelis 1997, 2002; Boylan 1999). The central result of this literature is that the greater the number of players required for action, the more difficult it is to change the status quo. With respect to courts, this means that increasing the number of players required to sanction the court potentially increases the judges' discretion to decide cases in line with their sincere preferences (e.g., see Cooter and Ginsburg 1996; Tsebelis 2002).

Building on this point, the second variable refers to the preferences of each of the actors, including those of the Court and the sanctioning players. The preferences of each sanctioning player matter for determining the range of choices that are available to the Court. For example, as Chapter 1 discussed, in the American politics literature the House and the Senate are each assigned an ideal point within a policy space. The ability of the House and the Senate to agree to overturn the Court's decision depends on whether the Court's decision falls between or outside the two ideal points. If the Court's decision is located between the two ideal points, then neither chamber can agree to overturn the decision, since the new legislation would favor one chamber more than the other (Ferejohn and Weingast 1992: 267). Only if the Court's decision falls outside the two ideal points are both chambers able to reach an agreement to sanction the Court. The farther apart the preferences of the two chambers, the more options the Court has. The closer their preferences are, the narrower are the Court's range of choices.

The third variable consists of the rules by which sanctions are imposed. In the models used to depict the United States, the standard sanction that the justices face is to have their decision overturned (Spiller and Gely 1990; Ferejohn and Weingast 1992).[5] In its simplest form, this occurs through the

---

[5] Empirically, the sanctions U.S. judges have faced are far more varied. For example, Gerald Rosenberg distinguishes among at least ten distinct sanctions that have been used to threaten the U.S. Supreme Court (1992: 376). These sanctions include using the Senate's

formal process of passing new legislation, which requires the agreement of both chambers. Yet we have seen in developing democracies that the range of ways in which judges may be punished is often far greater. In Argentina, judges at various times faced threats ranging from informal sanctions such as removal and forced resignations associated with regime transitions to more formal procedures, such as prosecution, court packing, and impeachment.

Each of these sanctions operates according to a specific set of rules and procedures. As Chapter 4 documents, for example, the informal norm of Argentine executives simply removing sitting justices has been mostly associated with regime change as opposed to governmental change. By contrast, sanctions involving court packing and impeachment entail the cooperation of the legislature according to formal procedures that are specified in the Constitution. As in the United States, the Argentine Constitution of 1853 requires that a majority in both legislative chambers approve any law changing the number of judges serving on the bench. Fully two-thirds in both chambers are required to impeach and remove the justices from office. In both cases, the ability of the incoming executives to impose these particular types of sanctions thus depends on achieving support in the legislature. Thus, as scholars have pointed out, whether the president's party controls the legislature potentially makes a big difference for determining whether judges are vulnerable to formal sanctions or not (e.g., see Bill-Chavez et al. 2003).

In sum, although a single-actor model of the government fits well with the conventional understandings of hyper-presidentialism and delegative democracy that mark the scholarship on Latin American politics, the assumptions underlying the logic of strategic defection should be modified to accommodate additional institutional actors depending on the empirical circumstances. Besides increasing the zone of discretion that judges enjoy on any single issue, a further substantive implication of increasing the number of sanctioning players is that it also potentially increases the range of issues across which the Court may continue to behave sincerely. Insofar as different sanctioning players' preferences shift relative to each other across different issues, judges' incentives to defect will be limited primarily

---

confirmation power to select certain types of judges, enacting constitutional amendments to reverse decisions or change Court structure or procedure, impeachment, withdrawing Court jurisdiction over certain subjects, altering the selection and removal process, requiring extraordinary majorities for declarations of unconstitutionality, allowing appeals from the Supreme Court to a more "representative" tribunal, removing the power of judicial review, cutting the budget, and altering the size of the Court.

to issues where a sufficient number of the players prefers the status quo (Helmke 2003). In other words, in contexts where more than a single actor decides the fate of the Court, the issues on which judges will be forced to defect may be limited to only those cases in which all of the relevant actors hold preferences contrary to the position taken by the outgoing government. A discussion of whether increasing the limitations on incoming presidents' ability to remove judges also plays an important role in explaining why judges would ever believe that strategic defection could work must wait until the subsequent chapter.

2.7 Conclusion

Taken together, the forgoing discussion provides the basis for a fresh understanding of court-executive relations in institutionally insecure environments. Building on the simple spatial framework used by separation of powers theorists, I showed that altering basic assumptions about the intertemporal conflict that judges face generates a very different repertoire of strategic behavior. Namely, whenever judges face a threat from future or incoming governments, judges may face incentives to strategically defect against the current government, even though they otherwise share the current government's preferences.

Starting with this basic idea, the chapter then explored how varying assumptions about judges' motives, information, and the sanctions they face affect judges' willingness and capacity to act strategically. Among the most important points to emerge was that strategic defection is not inherently limited to judges with a single motivational stance. This raises the possibility that judges whom we typically tend to think of as stereotypical opposites may, under certain conditions, behave in very much the same way.[6] Potentially more problematic for the logic of strategic defection is the lack of information that judges have over the incoming government's preferences. Although dealing with this issue more fully must wait until the next chapter, here I pointed out that one plausible alternative response open to judges in such situations is to duck, rather than defect. Finally, the chapter considered the effects of varying the institutional constraints

---

[6] Note, however, that at the aggregate level, differences among the different types may be more visible. For example, as Helmke and Sanders argue (2003), given the sequential nature of voting in Argentina, courts composed of different types of judges may exhibit different patterns of unanimity.

that judges face. In line with standard separation-of-powers approaches and veto player theory, I posited an inverse relationship between the number of relevant sanctioning players and the scope of issues along which judges face incentives to defect. Building on these various observations, the task of the next chapter is to deepen our understanding of the mechanisms underlying strategic defection by moving to a formal game theoretic framework that endogenizes politicians' responses to the choices judges make.

3

A Theory of Court-Executive Relations

INSECURE TENURE, INCOMPLETE
INFORMATION, AND STRATEGIC
BEHAVIOR

The previous chapter laid the groundwork for identifying strategic defection as a distinct form of judicial behavior. The main intuition was that whenever judges lack institutional insecurity they will face powerful incentives to rule against the current government, once the government begins to lose power. Yet thus far very little has been said about why exactly judges believe that defection would work. Because defection makes sense only if judges believe that it will improve their fates, the next step is, therefore, to develop a unified theoretical framework that links together systematically judges' and politicians' behavior.

While this chapter retains the core insights of the logic of strategic defection, it thus departs from the previous chapter in two fundamental ways. First, rather than simply treat sanctions as an exogenous constraint that judges face, it offers an endogenous account of why politicians punish loyal judges and reward defectors. Second and relatedly, it develops a formal signaling model of court-executive relations that allows us to capture systematically problems of incomplete and imperfect information. Specifically, the model allows us to bring together the intuitions from the previous chapter regarding judges' uncertainty over the incoming government with the idea that politicians may likewise be uncertain about the type of judges that they face. Although the discussion that follows is somewhat more technically demanding than the previous chapter, the result is a deeper understanding of the conditions that lead to strategic defection as well as a more precise understanding of the various factors that may inhibit it.

The remainder of this chapter is organized as follows. In the next section I introduce informally the main argument of the chapter by addressing politicians' choices over whether or not to retain sitting judges. Next, I present the basic building blocks of a formal theory of court-executive relations. In the following section, I present the model's main results and discuss its implications. Bringing together this discussion with that of the previous chapter, I conclude by proposing a series of original testable hypotheses regarding how, when, and in which types of cases judges will engage in strategic defection.

3.1 Politicians and Uncertainty

Standard separation-of-powers games revolve primarily around exploring the effects of various institutional constraints on judicial decision making under conditions of perfect and complete information (e.g., see Epstein and Knight 1998). Based on modifying core assumptions about inter-temporality, the previous chapter derived strategic defection as a logical pattern of behavior that ensues whenever the current government grows weak, the incoming government's preferences are sufficiently different, and judges wish to retain their posts. I then used this framework to explore informally how relaxing additional assumptions regarding judges' motivations, the amount of information they have about the incoming government's preferences as well as the number of sanctioning players, and the specific type of threat judges face would affect their decision making. The deeper supposition that judges' choices under one government affect their fates under another, however, remained relatively unexamined. The central task of this chapter is thus to begin to fill in this missing piece of the argument by showing how the constraints that judges face are contingent, in part, on the choices they make.

To that end, this chapter expands the substantive focus of the previous chapter by exploring the question of why politicians would decide to retain judges who defect. Although the logic of strategic defection has intuitive appeal, intuition is not a sufficient guide. For example, while the argument thus far has been simply that defection allows judges to appeal to an incoming government by virtue of judges distancing themselves from the outgoing government, one can imagine various objections to such reasoning. From a newly elected president's perspective, for example, why not instead prefer to retain judges who have been loyal? Why assume that judges who ruled against the last government will support your own? To gain a deeper understanding of the logic of strategic defection, then, we need to begin by turning the question around and asking what politicians want and what constraints they might face.

3.1 Politicians and Uncertainty

The model developed below explores the implications of the premise that politicians may care not only about how judges vote, but also about judges' preferences. Although such a supposition may appear odd at first, there are two reasons why it makes sense. First, to the extent that sanctioning judges or overturning their decisions carries some cost to the incumbent government, appointing judges with similar preferences is simply more efficient. Second, following the logic of the standard separation-of-powers game, any change in the current government's ability to constrain the Court poses the risk of allowing judges to shift policy further away from the government's ideal point (cf. Ferejohn and Weingast 1992). Thus, as long as a government believes that there is some chance that its power to constrain judges might wane over the course of its term, it should try to "lock in" judges who share its views whenever it has the chance.[1] For even though appointing judges with similar policy views may not ultimately stem the tide of strategic defection, it may help to prolong a judges' allegiance to the incumbent government until a clear opposition threat emerges.

The problem that politicians face in accomplishing this goal, however, is that they can never observe directly a judges' preferences, only judges' behavior. Such principle-agent problems have long been recognized in the literature on judicial selection. Equally important, but less well understood, is how such uncertainty might affect politicians' decisions about whether or not to retain sitting justices. For although such politicians may have a greater quantity of information about a particular judge's behavior (i.e., the judge's past voting record), the quality of this information is, I propose, inherently ambiguous. In line with the informal model presented in the previous chapter, this problem is likely to be particularly salient for an incoming government who observes how a court interacted with a previous government but is unsure about how its own policies will fare in the hands of the judges. Based on this and depending on the constraints faced by incoming politicians, judges who anticipate a change in government can thus potentially exploit incoming politicians' uncertainty by behaving in ways that are compatible with the incoming government's vision of an ideal judge.

Without changing the core structure of the basic strategic setting for judges, incorporating politicians' uncertainty over the types of judges they

[1] As in most presidentialist systems, this window of opportunity in Argentina has corresponded to the beginning of an executive's term, when he or she tends to be at his or her height of popularity and power vis-à-vis other institutional actors.

face thus creates the opportunity to explore more fully the conditions under which strategic defection is likely to occur. This allows us to both establish more firmly the results of the previous chapter as well as to generate several additional, more counterintuitive insights into how courts under constraints behave. As it happens, judges' uncertainty and politicians' uncertainty will turn out to carry very different implications for judges' behavior. Building on the ideas of the previous chapter, I show here why judges' uncertainty tends to dampen judges' incentives to engage in strategic behavior, whereas politicians' uncertainty enhances it.

In sum, incorporating uncertainty for both sets of actors allows us to move from simply assuming that judges act on the basis of a mutually understood rule (i.e., politicians reward judges who defect and punish ones who do not) toward constructing an explanation of the origins of the rule. In particular, adding politicians' uncertainty about selection and retention allows us to sharpen our understanding of the mechanisms underlying strategic behavior in settings of where the stakes are removal, rather than simply reversal or noncompliance. Although the story that emerges about politicians is still highly stylized, it moves us in a theoretical direction that is arguably closer to reality. Not least of all, this helps to extend rational choice models abroad to contexts where standard assumptions about complete and perfect information are notoriously difficult to defend.

3.2 The Model

This section develops a simple formal model of court-executive relations using a modified version of the familiar Beer-Quiche signaling game designed to capture situations of incomplete information (Kreps 1990; Gibbons 1992). The core components of the model are as follows.

Judges. To capture the incoming government's uncertainty, I assume that there are two types of judges: Liberal Judges (θ) and Conservative Judges ($\sim\theta$). The value of these labels is purely that they allow me to model the compatibility between the judge and the incoming government. The payoffs for both types of judges are determined by two factors: (1) the issue value (α), which is based on whether the judge is able to decide a case in line with his or her preferences, and (2) the post value (β), which is the benefit the judge receives for maintaining his or her post. Although simplistic, this payoff structure is sufficient for developing the discussion regarding judges' motivations raised in the previous chapter. As I show below, for example,

3.2 The Model

Table 3.1 *Judges' and Executives' Payoffs*

		Liberal government		Conservative government	
		Impeach	Not impeach	Impeach	Not impeach
Liberal	L	$\alpha, -c$	$(\alpha + \beta), 0$	$\alpha, -c$	$(\alpha + \beta), -j$
judge	R	$0, -c$	$\beta, 0$	$0, -c$	$\beta, -j$
Conservative	L	$0, -c$	$\beta, -j$	$0, -c$	$\beta, 0$
judge	R	$\alpha, -c$	$(\alpha + \beta), -j$	$\alpha, -c$	$(\alpha + \beta), 0$

α: Judge's issue value.
β: Judge's keeping position value.
c: Government's cost of getting rid of the judge.
j: Government's cost of keeping the judge with different preferences.
Liberal judges $L \geq R$.
Conservative judges $R \geq L$.

it helps to capture the intuition that, depending on the relative value that judges attach to staying on the bench versus deciding cases in line with their preferences, judges with otherwise very different goals may behave quite similarly.

Assuming that $\alpha > 0$ and $\beta > 0$, a liberal judge earns the highest payoff for deciding cases in line with a liberal government and being retained and the lowest payoff for deciding cases in line with a conservative government and being removed (see Table 3.1). Conversely, the conservative judge earns the highest payoff for deciding cases in accordance with a conservative government and being retained and the lowest payoff for deciding cases in line with a liberal government and being removed.

Governments. Analogous to judges, there are two types of governments: Liberal (LG) and Conservative (CG). The payoff for each type of government revolves around two sets of costs. The first cost (j) is the cost that the government bears of keeping a judge with different preferences. In line with the forgoing discussion, I capture the basic idea that a government cares about having judges on the bench who share its views by assuming that $j > 0$. Note that by restricting j to a positive number, the model rules out ex ante the possibility that a government may sometimes prefer to appoint judges on the bench who do not share its views. Solving the model, however, does not depend on this restriction.

The second cost (c) is a generic term that captures broadly the idea that the government's ability to get rid of judges depends on the exogenous constraints that the incoming government faces. Building on the discussion of veto players contained in the previous chapter, this parameter can be used to express the idea that impeaching judges is likely to be more difficult for presidents who face an opposition-controlled Congress than for presidents who enjoy a majority in both houses. Note, however, that the substantive notion of the cost to the government need not be limited purely to the difficulties associated with removing sitting judges. The cost term can also be used to represent the related idea that while removing sitting judges is relatively easy, appointing new judges to replace them is not. The pool of available judges may be limited, the ability of the government to screen judges may be hampered, or the government may be unable to put forward candidates that gain the support of other institutional actors.[2] In short, the government's cost in terms of delay or difficulty can also be cast as a problem of "re-selection," depending on the empirical circumstances.

To illustrate this point briefly, consider Argentina, where the depth of public approbation for the judiciary currently is such that respected jurists are reluctant to serve on the bench. For example, following Justice Bossert's resignation in October 2002, the interim president Eduardo Duhalde's first choice for the post, Carlos Arslanian, declined to be appointed because of concerns over the Court's legitimacy as an institution. Also, in Argentina, despite the Court's unpopularity, the executive has had to bear some cost in terms of its powers of appointment to remove sitting justices. To gain the support of the opposition parties in Congress to move forward with impeachment proceedings against the Chief Justice, Julio Nazareno, the newly elected Argentine president, Nestor Kirchner, was forced to pass a decree limiting his own powers to appoint new justices to the bench. For different reasons, then, both instances suggest that even in contexts where removing justices is relatively easy, the government may still face some cost in changing the Court's composition. Finally, it should be pointed out that in contexts where judges have greater legitimacy, the second cost term could also be used to capture the idea that sanctioning judges is politically costly to presidents in terms of public opinion (cf. Vanberg 2001).

As shown in Table 3.1, the costs borne by both types of incoming governments are symmetrical. Both types of governments pay the same costs for removing either type of judge and for keeping judges with incompatible views. The only difference is that Liberal Governments (LG) pay this second cost (J) for keeping Conservative Judges ($\sim\theta$), while Conservative Governments (CG) pay a cost (J) for retaining Liberal Judges (θ).

[2] I thank Mitch Sanders and Matthew Stephenson for suggesting these other alternatives.

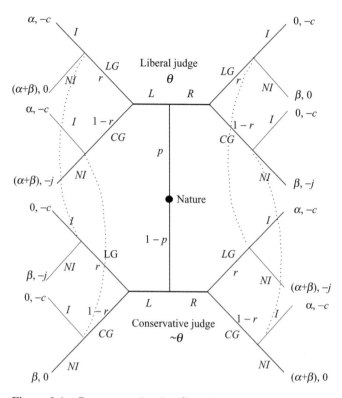

Figure 3.1 Court-executive signaling game.

Structure of the Game. There are three sets of players: judges, governments, and Nature. The game tree shown in Figure 3.1 describes the sequence of moves and the payoffs for both types of judges and governments. To take into account the information asymmetry, Nature makes the first move of the game by choosing a type of judge. The next nodes of the game represent the judges' choices of whether to rule in a liberal direction (*L*) or in a conservative direction (*R*). Because each judge knows his or her own type, each therefore has to make a choice about whether he or she wants to behave sincerely by ruling in line with his or her preferences or against them. In ruling sincerely, each judge either earns the highest payoff or sticks to his or her principles, getting thrown off the bench. In ruling strategically, each judge either remains on the bench in exchange for giving up his or her preferences on an issue, or ends up with the sucker's payoff, deciding the case against his or her preferences and being removed from

47

his or her post. Thus, assuming that a judge places some positive value on (α) and (β), the trade-off lies in whether he or she values remaining on the bench more than deciding issues in line with his or her preferences, or vice versa.

Similar to the depiction of the strategic situation in the previous chapter, the third node is Nature, representing the chance that one type of government will win over another. Here the liberal government wins with a probability of r and a conservative government wins with a probability of $1 - r$. In the fourth and final move of the game, the new government chooses whether to impeach (I) or not impeach (NI) judicial decisions on and off the equilibrium path. Common prior beliefs for each information set involving the government's uncertainty over the type of judge it faces are denoted by (p, $1 - p$). On the equilibrium path, beliefs are denoted by $\mu 1, \ldots \mu 4$ and updated according to Bayes's Rule.[3]

Judges thus have four possible pure strategies: $[(L|\theta; L|\sim\theta); (R|\theta; R|\sim\theta); (L|\theta, R|\sim\theta); (R|\theta; L|\sim\theta)]$. Each of these pairs represents a decision (Left (L) or Right (R)) made by a particular type of judge (Liberal Judge (θ) or Conservative Judge ($\sim\theta$)). The first two of these pairs are pooling strategies. In the first pair, both liberal and conservative judges hand down liberal decisions. In the second pair, both types also act the same way, but instead rule conservatively. The last two pairs represent separating strategies in which different types of judges decide cases differently. In the third pair, liberal judges decide cases in a liberal direction and conservative judges decide cases conservatively. In the fourth pair, liberal judges decide cases in a conservative direction and conservative judges decide cases in a liberal direction.

To solve the game, I use the solution concept of Perfect Bayesian Equilibrium (PBE), which consists of beliefs and strategies that meet the following requirements: (1) at each information set the player with the move has a belief about the previous play of the game; (2) given these beliefs, the player's strategy must be sequentially rational; (3) Bayes' Rule and the players' strategies are used to update beliefs for moves on the equilibrium path; and (4) where possible, the same process of updating takes place off the equilibrium path (Gibbons 1992: 175–80).

---

[3] Bayes's Rule determines the posterior probability of the state of the world by calculating the probability that both the event and the state will occur and dividing it by the probability that the event will occur regardless of the state (Morrow 1994: 164).

3.3 Discussion

Table 3.2 contains the five substantively salient pure strategy equilibria that emerge from the game.[4] The proofs are reserved for the appendix (see Appendix C). In the first equilibrium ("judicial independence") both types of judges act sincerely and neither is punished by the government. This equilibrium is sustained entirely by the costs the government faces in removing sitting judges relative to the costs of keeping an incompatible judge ($c \geq j \geq 0$) and thus comes the closest to capturing the Hamiltonian notion of judicial independence described in the previous chapter. In terms of the recent literature, this result fits nicely with the findings of the veto player literature (Cooter and Ginsburg 1996; Henisz 2000; Tsebelis 2002) and the emerging game theoretic works on public opinion and judicial independence (Vanberg 2001; Staton 2002). Similarly, here the exogenous costs to the government of punishing either type of judge are sufficiently high so as to prohibit either from credibly threatening to remove judges who hand down unfavorable decisions.[5] Thus, judges are free to make decisions in line with their sincere preferences.

In the second equilibrium ("judicial dependence") judges also decide cases sincerely, but here they are punished for doing so. What makes this an equilibrium response is that, regardless of the decision the judge makes, the incoming government always removes sitting judges. Thus, assuming judges place some positive value on issues ($\alpha > 0$), they are always better off ruling sincerely. Note, however, that this equilibrium obtains only in environments where both sets of costs are less than or equal to zero ($0 \geq j \geq c$). In other words, an incoming government must both either face no cost or gain some benefit from removing sitting judges *and* face no cost or gain some benefit from retaining incompatible judges.

Starting with the first condition, in contexts where judges are highly unpopular, it is plausible that removing judges could benefit politicians.

---

[4] In addition to the five pure strategy equilibria identified above, there are three additional equilibria in which both types of judges rule against their type. Substantively, however, these equilibria can be ruled out on the intuitive grounds that they require making the empirically implausible assumption that liberal governments are more likely to punish judges who rule liberally and conservative governments are more likely to punish judges who rule conservatively.

[5] More recently, scholars have also begun to examine how constraints on the government regarding the Court may emerge endogenously from the Court's decisions. For formal game theoretic accounts that examine legitimacy endogenously, see Carruba 2002; Stephenson 2002; and Staton 2003.

Table 3.2 *Equilibria Results*

Pure strategy equilibria	Type of equilibria	Parameters
Equilibrium 1 "Judicial independence"	Separating equilibrium $LG(NI, NI)$ $CG(NI, NI)$ $L\backslash\theta; R\backslash\sim\theta$	$c \geq j \geq 0$ $0 \geq r \geq 1$ $\mu(\theta \mid L, LG) = 1$ $\mu(\theta \mid L, CG) = 1$ $\mu(\theta \mid R, LG) = 0$ $\mu(\theta \mid R, CG) = 0$
Equilibrium 2 "Judicial dependence"	Separating equilibrium $LG(I, I)$ $CG(I, I)$ $L\backslash\theta; R\backslash\sim\theta$	$0 \geq j \geq c$ $0 \geq r \geq 1$ $\mu(\theta \mid L, LG) = 1$ $\mu(\theta \mid L, CG) = 1$ $\mu(\theta \mid R, LG) = 0$ $\mu(\theta \mid R, CG) = 0$
Equilibrium 3 "Judicial principle" if $\alpha \geq \beta$ "Judicial uncertainty" if $\alpha = 0$	Separating equilibrium $LG(NI, I)$ $CG(I, NI)$ $L\backslash\theta; R\backslash\sim\theta$	$j \geq c \geq 0$ $((\beta - \alpha) / 2\beta) \leq r \leq$ $((\alpha + \beta) / 2\beta)$ $\mu(\theta \mid L, LG) = 1$ $\mu(\theta \mid L, CG) = 1$ $\mu(\theta \mid R, LG) = 0$ $\mu(\theta \mid R, CG) = 0$
Equilibrium 4 "Strategic liberalism"	Pooling equilibrium $LG(NI, I)$ $CG(I, NI)$ $L\backslash\theta; L\backslash\sim\theta$	$j \geq c > 0$ $p \geq 1 - c/j$ and $p \geq c/j;$ $r \geq (\beta - \alpha) / 2\beta$ and $r \geq$ $(\beta + \alpha) / 2\beta$ $\mu(\theta \mid L, LG) = p$ $\mu(\theta \mid L, CG) = p$ $\mu(\theta|R, LG) \leq 1 - (c/j)$ $\mu(\theta|R, CG) \leq c/j$
Equilibrium 5 "Strategic conservatism"	Pooling equilibrium $LG(NI, I)$ $CG(I, NI)$ $R\backslash\theta; R\backslash\sim\theta$	$j \geq c > 0$ $p \leq 1 - c/j$ and $p \leq c/j;$ $r \leq (\beta - \alpha) / 2\beta$ and $r \leq$ $(\beta + \alpha) / 2\beta$ $\mu(\theta \mid R, LG) = p$ $\mu(\theta \mid R, CG) = p$ $\mu(\theta|L, LG) \geq 1 - (c/j)$ $\mu(\theta|L, CG) \geq c/j$

Note: See Table 3.1. *LG*: liberal government; *CG*: conservative government; *NI*: not impeach; *I*: impeach; μ: governments' beliefs about type of judge; θ: liberal judge; $\sim\theta$: conservative judge.

Not withstanding problems of re-selection, for example, in the case of contemporary Argentina where more than 90 percent of the population is dissatisfied with the Court, getting rid of judges is likely to improve a politician's image. Indeed, in the midst of the economic and political crisis of 2002, party leaders feared that dropping impeachment proceedings against the Supreme Court would be politically costly.

Moving to the second part of the condition sustaining this equilibrium, however, also requires modifying the earlier assumption that governments either gain some benefit by having incompatible judges serve or that it simply cares nothing about the types of judges they face. Although, as we see below in the case of Argentina, changing either of these assumptions to accommodate this equilibrium is not empirically defensible, it is worthwhile to point out scenarios in which such assumptions could make sense. For example, the notion that a government might derive some positive benefit from appointing an incompatible judge fits roughly with Jean Bodin's classic logic of delegation in which kings create independent judiciaries to deflect criticism away from the Crown (Holmes 1995: 165). Likewise, it could also make sense in an environment where governments use the courts to monitor other branches of government (McCubbins and Schwartz 1984; Rosberg 1995). Note, however, that in both of these examples, the assumption that governments may prefer incompatible judges is used to justify a story of judicial independence, not dependence. Finally, the alternative assumption that governments simply do not care about the type of judges they face would be most plausible in a context where judges' discretion is relatively limited. This, for example, is captured in Toharia's classic study of the Spanish judiciary under Franco (1975). Again, however, in a context such as Argentina, where judges are often routinely called on to decide the most important and controversial cases of the day, this assumption is not defensible.

Putting aside for a moment a substantive discussion of the conditions sustaining separating strategies, these first two equilibria accord well with the intuition that under conditions where removal is either entirely precluded or immanent, judges will behave sincerely. Although clearly judges are better off when governments are constrained (i.e., assuming that $\beta > 0$), as long as removal is certain, judges will also behave sincerely. Empirically, one implication of this for future and current governments alike is that both should have an interest in incoming politicians minimizing judges' uncertainty in either direction. For future governments, reducing uncertainty encourages sincere behavior and allows incoming politicians to learn a judge's true type. Ideally, for incumbents, who are often themselves too weak to threaten their own judges credibly, incoming executives who successfully guarantee either judges' future removal or survival could help to minimize the number of anti-governmental rulings by short-circuiting strategic defection.

The third equilibrium is also a separating equilibrium, but here, along the lines described in the previous chapter, each type of government acts differently ("discriminating"), depending on which type of decision the incoming government observes. Specifically, liberal governments reward judges who choose L and punish judges who choose R, while conservative governments punish judges choosing L and reward judges choosing R. Given each government's willingness to punish different types of decisions, judges' strategies depend on a combination of judges' prior beliefs about the type of incoming government they face (r, $1 - r$), relative to the values that judges attach to deciding issues in accordance with their ideology (α) versus retaining their posts (β). Formally, this parameter is expressed as $(\beta - \alpha)/2\beta \leq r \leq (\alpha + \beta)/2\beta$, and can be rewritten simply as $r^* \leq r \leq r^{**}$ (see Appendix C).

Where governments discriminate, judges separate under two distinct sets of assumptions about the relative payoff values that judges attach to certain outcomes. The first condition under which the equilibrium holds is when judges place a higher value on the issue benefit than on the post benefit. Assuming that $\alpha > \beta$, r takes on any value between 0 and 1 and thus judges act sincerely regardless of their beliefs about which government is likely to come to power. Intuitively, this simply means that because judges care more about issues than their posts, they are willing to be punished if an incompatible government comes to power.

Although such situations of strict dominance may be less interesting from a formal theoretical perspective, such a situation underscores the substantive point that judges with otherwise very different motivations may act similarly with respect to the incumbent government. For example, a professionally oriented judge with divergent preferences from the government who is committed to deciding cases in accordance with his or her vision of the law will continue to rule sincerely under any beliefs he or she may have about the type of incoming government. This fits the classic portrait of a principled judge,[6] but also fits with a more strategic portrait of a judge who

---

[6] An example of sincere defection might be the three judges on Peru's Constitutional Court who, at the height of Fujimori's popularity and power, dared to challenge his bid to run for a third term. These judges were quickly impeached by the C90-dominated Congress.

may be concerned about his or her reputation in the legal community (see Baum 1999: 89–124).

More interesting still, however, is the prospect that such a condition could also depict judges whose career paths are tied exclusively to remaining loyal to the incumbent party. For example, as Magaloni and Sánchez (2001) describe in the case of Mexico, judges are not necessarily always concerned with maintaining their posts. Rather, because of the term limit rule established under single-party hegemony, serving on the bench was a part of the larger process of political elites' circulation under the Mexican single-party state. In such a circumstance, deciding cases in line with one's preferences (which presumably match those of the incumbent party who is in charge of subsequent appointments), takes on a higher value for the judge than does retaining one's post. More generally, this suggests that in any empirical application of the model, ruling out sincere behavior under conditions of a governmental threat requires a clear understanding of how any judge values the benefit of avoiding removal relative to the value of deciding cases in line with his or her preferences (or those of the incumbent government), regardless of his or her underlying motives.

The second condition under which the separating equilibrium is sustained is when $\beta > \alpha$. Under this assumption, separation between judges occurs whenever r lies between a minimum threshold (r^*) and a maximum threshold (r^{**}). Note that when the gap between α and β is relatively small, the distance between the thresholds is relatively wide. In other words, judges have to be fairly certain about the type of incoming government before they are willing to abandon the separation strategy. As the gap between these two values grows, the distance between the two thresholds gets smaller. The intuition captured here is thus that the more value a judge places on the post benefit relative to the issue benefit, the less information he or she requires about the type of incoming government before he or she is willing to forgo separating. A particular case of this equilibrium is when the judge attaches no value to the issues ($\alpha = 0$). Here, the equilibrium becomes knife-edged: Separation occurs only when the chances are evenly split over which type of government will come to power.

With the last two equilibria we come to the conditions for strategic judicial behavior. As in the third equilibrium, both equilibria depend on each

Although since Fujimori's fall, all three have been re-instated as members of the Court, there is no a priori evidence to suggest that their rulings against Fujimori were strategically motivated.

government punishing judges who decide cases against the government's views and rewarding those who side in their favor. But here the crucial difference is that one type of judge acts strategically by pooling with the other type. In the fourth equilibrium, both liberal and conservative judges rule liberally. In the fifth equilibrium, both types instead rule conservatively. As above, both equilibria depend on the judges' prior beliefs about the type of government that he or she is likely to face. As we see below, the judges' priors determine which type of pooling equilibria obtains. But here a more complicated set of restrictions placed on government's prior beliefs also help to drive the equilibria.

Because these are pooling equilibria, no updating takes place on the equilibria path and the governments' posterior beliefs are identical to their prior beliefs ($\mu = p$). Specifically, this means that to sustain these equilibria, both governments' priors about the type of judge that they face must be such that each government is willing to reward and punish according to the strategy profile for each equilibrium. In both cases, solving for p thus leads to two thresholds for liberal and conservative governments, respectively: $p \geq 1 - c/j$, which can be written simply as p^* and $p \geq c/j$, which can be written as p^{**}. Off the equilibrium path, prior beliefs are unrestricted. Posterior beliefs off the equilibrium path, however, must also be such that the governments' threats for punishing deviations from the equilibria are credible.

Translating these thresholds into substantive terms, whether judges have incentives to behave strategically rests on the government's beliefs about the type of judge it faces relative to the costs of removing any judge versus retaining incompatible judges. Given these thresholds, strategic behavior obtains only where $j \geq c > 0$. Note that when these two costs are equal, the equilibria can be sustained under any set of prior beliefs. As the costs of getting rid of judges declines, however, the government's belief thresholds needed to sustain the strategy profile increase. For example, if $c = 2$ and $j = 4$, then a liberal government's priors about the type of judge who hands down a liberal decision must be greater than .50 in order for the government to retain judges who choose L. If, however, the cost c declines to $c = 1$, then the probability that a judge is liberal needed to sustain non-punishment increases to $p > .75$.[7]

---

[7] Conversely, for incoming conservative governments, the threshold $p^{**} = p < c/j$ means that in order to credibly threaten to punish judges who choose L, the government must be sufficiently certain that liberal decisions are more likely to be handed down by liberal judges. As c increases relative to j, a conservative government needs to be more certain that it is facing a liberal judge in order for it to be willing to punish the judge.

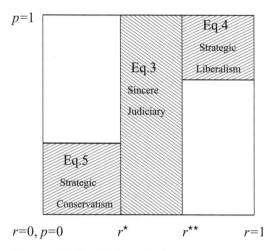

Figure 3.2 Equilibria predictions.

Taken together, distinct relationships among the costs of removal versus the costs of keeping bad judges help to reduce problems of multiple equilibria. As Table 3.2 helps show, the problem of multiple equilibria between the judicial independence equilibria and the third equilibrium is restricted to instances where the costs c and j are exactly equal. In other words, only in this situation is there potential confusion over whether judges rule sincerely because they are constrained, because of their values, or because they are uncertain about which government will come to power. Between the first equilibrium and the last two pooling equilibria, problems of multiple equilibria are further reduced to instances where the costs are exactly equal and where both are greater than zero. Finally, given the initial assumption that $j > 0$ eliminates entirely problems of multiple equilibria that would otherwise appear between the second separating equilibrium ("judicial dependence") and the last two equilibria. Potential overlap between the second and third equilibria occurs only when both costs are equal to zero. In all other scenarios, the model yields unique substantive predictions.

Assuming the basic condition $j \geq c \geq 0$, Figure 3.2 summarizes the last three equilibria along two sets of thresholds described above: the judges' prior beliefs about the type of government, r^* and r^{**}, and the government's prior beliefs about the type of judge that it faces, p^* and p^{**}. As long as both of the government's costs are greater than zero, sincere behavior (captured in the third equilibrium) is driven entirely either by the judges' preferences or

55

by judges' uncertainty. Restating the discussion of the third equilibrium, the boundary of this equilibrium depends fundamentally on the relative value that the judge places on the issue versus the value of the post. Where the value of the issue dominates, the entire area will be subsumed by the third equilibrium. In other words, judges will never pool. When the value of the post dominates instead, the boundaries of the separating equilibrium are contingent on the judge's certainty about the type of government that he or she will face relative to the amount of relative value he or she assigns to keeping his or her post. Again, at the limit ($\alpha = 0$), r^* and r^{**} could reduce to a single point where $r = .50$.

On the y-axis, the overlapping area between the two p values on the equilibrium path determine the boundaries for the fourth and fifth equilibria. Note that whether $p^* > p^{**}$ depends again on the relative value of c and j where $j \geq c$. Building on the point made above, the greater the gap between these two costs, the more extreme the two sets of thresholds will need to be in order to sustain strategic behavior. In other words, both governments will have to have sufficiently high priors that a judge is liberal in order for the fourth equilibrium to hold, while both governments will have to have sufficiently low priors that a judge is liberal in order for the fifth equilibrium to hold.

3.4 Conclusion: Testable Hypotheses

Taken together, this chapter and the previous one have sought to develop a micro-level account of court-executive relations that explains why judges in institutionally insecure environments rule against the government of the day. Beginning with the separation-of-powers approach pioneered by scholars of U.S. judicial politics, each chapter has explored the implications of relaxing a series of assumptions regarding the intensity and source of the constraints judges face and, ultimately, the amount of information that judges and politicians have. Having identified informally a new pattern of court-executive relations in the previous chapter, this chapter has used the tools of formal theory to replicate and deepen our understanding of the logic of strategic judicial behavior. Along the way, I have described both familiar and new patterns of court-executive interactions as unique equilibria that emerge within a unified theoretical framework, depending on the interaction of judges' and governments' beliefs and the relative costs and benefits yielded by different strategies. With these results in hand, it is now time to present the general testable implications regarding when, how, and in which types of cases judges are likely to behave strategically. The first set of hypotheses is about timing. In environments where governments are relatively free to remove judges, we have seen that whether strategic behavior obtains depends on a particular combination of assumptions about judges' preferences and about judges' and governments' beliefs and strategies. Translating these conditions into the judges' perspective, strategic defection thus requires three conditions: (1) the judge must sufficiently care about avoiding punishment, (2) the judge must be sufficiently certain about the type of new government he or she faces, and (3) the judge must be sufficiently uncertain about his or her fate under a new government. Assuming further that the judges' preferences converge with the outgoing government and diverge with the incoming government, the prediction is that once such conditions are met, judges will strategically defect. Stated as a simple testable proposition:

> *Strategic Defection Hypothesis*: Anti-governmental decisions should increase once the incumbent government begins to lose power.

Conversely, if either the incumbent government is likely to remain in office or judges instead believe that the preferences of the incoming and outgoing governments converge, then judges under threat will increase their support for the incumbent government. This leads to a second hypothesis:

> *Strategic Support Hypothesis*: Judges are more likely to hand down pro-governmental decisions if the incumbent government is likely to stay in power or if the incoming government has sufficiently similar preferences to the outgoing government.

The third hypothesis stems from the observation that not all judicial decisions are likely to be politically or legally salient. This is particularly true in a context such as Argentina's, where judges decide thousands of cases every year. From an incoming government's perspective, whether or not the judge rules in favor or against the outgoing government in relatively meaningless cases provides little indication of the judges' type compared with how the judge rules in more important cases. For purely practical reasons, the incoming government is also likely to be focused on how the judge rules mostly in important cases that deal with salient political issues. From the judges' perspective, the incoming government's preferences in such important cases are also likely to be much clearer. Thus, by choosing important cases in which to behave strategically judges help to reduce the risks of the suckers' payoff that comes from defecting and getting punished precisely for such defection. Taken together, these observations suggest that strategic behavior should be concentrated in the most important cases coming before the Court. Stated as a testable hypothesis:

> *Issue Importance Hypothesis*: Strategic defection and strategic support will be concentrated in visible and important cases.

A related set of additional implications surrounds judges' participation. One possibility, raised in Chapter 2, is that in situations of uncertainty and threat judges should automatically duck from controversy. By contrast, although the model developed above does not explicitly include the option of ducking, the logic of signaling suggests that there may be a tension between judges' desire to avoid controversy and their desire potentially to exploit the uncertainty of the incoming government. In other words, although, strictly speaking, no Bayesian updating occurs in pooling equilibria, it could be the case that by not participating judges forgo the opportunity to improve their chances of avoiding punishment at the hands of a successor government. If this is the case, then a more counterintuitive set of implications is that judges under threat should not decrease their willingness to decide cases and, indeed, may increase it. This leads to the following testable hypothesis:

> *Participation Hypothesis*: As judges gain information about which government is likely to be in power in the future, judges under threat will not decrease and may increase their participation in decision making.

Relatedly, for judges facing a threat of removal, separate opinion writing serves as a particularly powerful way to signal one's compatibility (or incompatibility) with the incoming government. In line with the previous observations regarding timing and participation, the first of these two hypotheses predicts that overall judges' willingness to engage in separate opinion increases once a threat to judges emerges. Stated as a testable hypothesis:

> *Separate Opinion Writing Hypothesis*: Judges will increasingly issue separate opinions once the government begins to lose power.

A more refined version of this hypothesis concerns judges' willingness to dissent from majority opinions. Specifically, in situations where the incumbent government is likely to lose power to an opponent with divergent views, the weak version of this hypothesis is that judges should not decrease their dissents with pro-governmental decisions and should not increase their dissents with anti-governmental decisions.

> *Strategic Dissent Hypothesis (1)*: Judges will be no less likely to dissent from pro-governmental decisions and no more likely to dissent from anti-governmental decisions when the incumbent government loses power.

A stronger version of this hypothesis is that judges should increase their dissents with pro-governmental decisions and decrease their dissents with anti-governmental decisions. In a context where the incumbents are likely to stay in power, the expectations for both hypotheses will be reversed. This leads to the following proposition:

> *Strategic Dissent Hypothesis (2)*: Judges will be more likely to dissent from pro-government decisions and less likely to dissent from anti-governmental decisions when the incumbent government loses power.

The last set of hypotheses concerns the scope of strategic behavior on the Court. As the forgoing discussion has made clear, the decision to remove and replace justices may not necessarily reside with a single unitary actor. As the number of sanctioning players increases, the incoming government's capacity to punish the Court decreases. One testable implication of this is that there may be an inverse relationship between the expected number of veto players and the scope of strategic judicial behavior (also see Helmke 2003). For example, judges facing a legislature with divided preferences across issues face fewer incentives to defect against the outgoing government than in the case where Congress is uniformly opposed to the outgoing administration. Thus, the intuition captured by the following hypothesis is that in such contexts judges will face the clearest incentives to behave strategically only in issues in which there is agreement among the relevant veto players. Stated as a testable hypothesis:

> *Issue Convergence Hypothesis*: In contexts with multiple veto players in charge of judges' fates, judges will face incentives to concentrate strategic behavior only in issue areas in which there is agreement among the veto players.

A final hypothesis concerns the target of the threat. In the model, I have assumed that judges face individual threats at the hand of successor governments. This leads to the expectation that only judges who are targeted by the incoming government and who otherwise place a higher value on avoiding sanctions will behave strategically. Stated as a testable hypothesis:

Target Hypothesis: Once the government begins to lose power, defection should be concentrated among judges who face the greatest threat.

To begin the task of evaluating these hypotheses and the assumptions that underlie them, the next chapter returns to the empirical setting of Argentina and to the story of court-executive relations that has developed over the last two and a half decades.

4

Judges, Generals, and Presidents

INSTITUTIONAL INSECURITY ON THE ARGENTINE SUPREME COURT, 1976–1999

The judges, both of the supreme and inferior courts, shall hold their offices during good behavior, and shall, at stated times, receive for their services, a compensation, which shall not be diminished during their continuance in office.

Constitución Federal de la República de Argentina (Art. 96)

Legal guarantees are often not observed, judicial tenure is not respected, and courts are suspended or successively limited in their jurisdiction. The common theme of excessive deviation from the formal rules of the game is valid in Latin American systems as far as the judiciary is concerned.

Von Lazar (1971: 41–2, cited in Verner 1989: 475)

In the last two chapters I have explored the logic of strategic defection, developed a formal theoretical model describing the conditions under which it occurs, and discussed several testable implications that emerge for court-executive relations. The task to which the next several chapters turn is to evaluate how well the model performs empirically by focusing on court-executive relations in Argentina.

To begin to move from a stylized model to an analysis of events in the real world, this chapter focuses specifically on exploring the key assumptions underlying strategic defection. First and foremost, evaluating strategic-based accounts requires establishing ex ante actors' preferences, beliefs, and expectations. In this case, for example, how plausible is it to assume that Argentine judges believed that their fates lay in the hands of incoming governments? Did judges have sufficient information about which government was likely to come to power? And if so, did they have sufficient reason to believe that the direction of their opinions could help to ameliorate the sanctions they faced? To begin to answer these questions, this chapter (along with Chapter 6) draws on a range of qualitative evidence about the

61

threats confronting Supreme Court justices in Argentina. Bringing together information from diverse sources, including newspapers, government documents, interviews, and autobiographies, I develop a plausible, if necessarily incomplete, picture of the underlying beliefs, expectations, and information that judges possessed at various key points under several recent Argentine governments.[1]

In general, the portrait that emerges strongly confirms the notion that, even within Latin America, few institutional actors have faced as much insecurity as the justices who have served on the Argentine Supreme Court. In spite of long-standing constitutional provisions mandating an independent judiciary and life tenure, justices' security has been repeatedly compromised by dictators and democrats alike. In addition to the prospect of removal from their posts, Argentina's judges have faced threats ranging from losing their influence on the Court and their professional reputations to criminal indictment and physical violence. During the cycle of regime instability that plagued Argentina from the 1940s through the 1980s, the members of the Supreme Court were replaced with every change in regime. With the return to democracy in 1983, the insecurity of the Court has continued. Over the last two decades, the fate of justices has been treated as an open political question by each new government. Thus, if the core assumptions underlying strategic accounts apply anywhere, they should apply to the Argentine Supreme Court.

Yet, in contrast to conventional wisdom, the historical narrative developed in this chapter also shows that the level and type of institutional insecurity varies considerably both within and across three of the four most recent Argentine governments. Early in a government's term, once the selection process occurred, justices tended to enjoy a fair amount of independence under both dictatorship and democracy. As soon as the government in power began to lose support, however, judges faced powerful threats at the hands of the opposition. In some of these periods judges had clear information about the preferences of the opposition. In other periods they did not. In some periods judges expected that the incoming government would have a relatively free reign to sanction the justices of the previous government. In other periods the future government's ability to impose sanctions appeared credible but was much more constrained. And in some of these periods, sanctions were targeted at some of the individual justices, while in other

---

[1] For a similar methodological approach to empirically testing rational choice theory, see Stokes 2001: 68.

periods the sanctions were directed at the Court as a whole. What did not vary was the fact that once the incumbents began to lose power, there was very little that the outgoing government could do to counterbalance the incentives leading judges to defect strategically.

The remainder of the chapter proceeds as follows. Section 4.1 describes the origins of insecure tenure in Argentina that emerged out of the regime instability characterizing Argentine politics throughout the mid-twentieth century. Turning to four more recent governments – the military Proceso (1976–83), the Alfonsín government (1983–9), and the two Menem governments (1989–95 and 1995–9), Sections 4.2 to 4.5 examine the changing beliefs that judges had about the ability of the administration to remain in power, the nature of the sanctions posed by the opposition, and the motivations that judges had to behave strategically. The final section concludes with an analytic narrative that summarizes the various elements of contemporary Argentine history according to the core propositions generated by the theory of strategic defection.

4.1 The Gap between Formal and Informal Institutions

A defining feature of contemporary Latin American politics is the gap between formal and informal institutions. Yet it is worth pointing out that in the case of the Argentine Supreme Court such a gap did not always exist. In the late nineteenth and early twentieth centuries the Argentine Supreme Court enjoyed fairly broad authority and legitimacy (Carrió 1996; Miller 1997). As early as 1887 the Court established for itself the power of judicial review in the case of *Sojo*, which based its reasoning explicitly on *Marbury*. From 1903 to 1929 the Court, under the guidance of its most revered Chief Justice, Antonio Bermejo, extended its power of judicial review to cover a number of important areas, such as property rights, equal protection, and labor. Despite its active role in resolving these important and contentious issues, during the institution's first sixty years no justice was impeached or pressured to resign. Perhaps most notably, even under the first of the military governments that ruled Argentina during the 1930s and early 1940s, Supreme Court justices were allowed to retain their posts and continued to assert their authority to assess the constitutionality of the actions of de facto as well as de jure governments (Snow 1975: 606–12).

The watershed in court-executive relations came under Juan Perón's first democratically elected government. Shortly after Perón's victory in the 1946 presidential elections, his supporters in the Chamber of Deputies sought the impeachment of four of the five members of the Supreme Court on fifteen separate charges of misconduct. At the heart of the charges were the Court's earlier decisions on issues important to the new government.

The specific charges leveled against the Court involved two major issues for the Peronist government: the Court's political role and its hostility to labor (Miller 1989). The Court was accused of having exceeded its authority in two separate but identical resolutions passed by the Court in 1930 and 1943 that granted legal recognition to the de facto governments.[2] The specific allegations were that the Court had meddled in political questions and that the Court had decided abstract questions rather than resolve concrete cases (*Acusación de la Cámara de Diputados* 31/10/46, cited in Miller et al. 1995: 875–96).

According to experts, the Court's hostility to Peronist labor initiatives had been spurred by the infamous *Dock Sud* decision handed down by the Court in February 1946 before the election. In this case, the Court struck down as unconstitutional the secretary of labor's initiative to create a national labor relations board. In response, the secretary of labor called for noncompliance and labor organizers debated striking to protest the decision. During his campaign for the presidency, Perón harshly criticized the decision, accusing the Court of being counter-revolutionary and sharing partisan sympathies with the anti-Peronist coalition, Union Democrática (Miller et al. 1995). More generally, this set a precedent in which judges' opinions could be used by politicians as evidence of their misconduct, which, as we see below, has continued to the present day.

Some nine months after the impeachment proceedings began, the Chamber of Deputies impeached three of the five sitting justices and the Senate voted to remove them.[3] Perón's success in ridding himself of his opponents on the Supreme Court had clear and immediate repercussions for his ability to govern as he saw fit. The newly appointed Court did little to challenge Perón's harassment of his political opponents. For example, the new Court refused to overturn the conviction of the leader of the Radical Party, Ricardo Balbín, for allegedly "disrespecting" Perón (Carrió 1996: 52). In the opinion of the Court, the anti-defamation law used to convict Balbín was a legislative act that the judiciary could not question without violating

---

[2] The resolutions were the *Acordada sobre reconocimiento del Gobierno Provisional de la Nacion*, 158 Fallos 290 (1930) and *Acordada sobre reconocimiento del Gobierno Provisional de la Nacion*, 196 Fallos 5 (cited in Miller et al. 1995).

[3] The fourth justice, Roberto Repetto, resigned before he could be impeached.

the separation of powers. The long-term effect of the impeachments was to introduce the informal institution of giving incoming regime leaders the prerogative to retain or remove the sitting justices.

Whereas prior to 1947 the norm had been to respect secure judicial tenure, after Perón incoming governments could expect to remove the justices appointed by their predecessor's regime with very little effort. Over the next three decades, incoming military and democratic regimes alike exercised this prerogative almost without fail.

As Table 4.1 shows, beginning with the military coup overthrowing Perón in 1955, the majority of justices on the Supreme Court were replaced with every change in regime through 1983.[4] Note that in none of these instances were the justices formally impeached. Rather, as Table 4.1 shows, two distinct informal procedures developed. Under the military, sitting justices were removed by decree issued by the executive leadership of the junta. Usually, such decrees included some justification about the new regime's need to appoint justices willing to swear to an oath to uphold the new revolutionary government (Snow 1975: 615). Under the incoming democratic governments the justices simply tendered their resignations once the regime transition occurred.

The effects of these informally institutionalized purges on the length of tenure of justices were profound. In the post-Perón period the average length of tenure fell by more than half. Data compiled from Miller et al. (1995) show that between 1862 and 1946 only thirty-five justices served on the Supreme Court. The average number of years spent on the bench was approximately eleven (see Table 4.2). By contrast, between 1947 and 1999, the number of justices who have served nearly doubled at fifty-seven; the average amount of time spent on the bench fell to less than five years.

In spite of the nearly routine dismissals that occurred at the level of the Supreme Court with each change in regime, the informal institution of insecure tenure was circumscribed in two important respects. First, during the years of regime instability secure tenure remained relatively robust at the lower levels of the judiciary. Although data are notoriously hard to come by, we know that in 1976 at the beginning of the last military government, only the Supreme Court justices, some federal appeals court judges, and the

---

[4] The only exception to this took place in 1962 with the assumption of the presidency by José M. Guido, a civilian, who was chosen by the military to succeed Arturo Frondizi. In 1963 with the subsequent election of another civilian, Arturo Illia, the court was also retained (Smulovitz 1995: 92).

Table 4.1 *Characteristics of Argentine Supreme Court Justices' Tenure, 1955–2003*

Justice	Dates	Justice	Dates
M. Argañarás (DF)	1955–8**	H. Herredia (DF)	1976–8
E. V. Galli (DF)	1955–8**	F. Escalada (DF)	1976
C. Herrera (DF)	1955–8**	A. Gabrielli (DF)	1976–83**
J. Vera Vallejo (DF)	1955–6	A. Caride (DF)	1976–7
A. Orgaz (DF)	1955–60	A. Rossi (DF)	1976–83**
B. Villegas Basav (DF)	1956–64	P. Frías (DF)	1976–81
A. Aráoz de Lam	1958–66*	E. Guastavino (DF)	1978–83**
L. M. Boffi Bogg	1958–66*	E. Daireaux (DF)	1977–80
J. C. Oyananarte	1958–62	C. Black (DF)	1980–2
R. Colombres	1960–6*	C. Renom (DF)	1982–3**
P. Aberastury	1960–6*	J. M. Vivot (DF)	1983**
E. Imaz	1960–6*	E. Gnecco (DF)	1983**
J. F. Bidau (DF)	1962–4	G. Carrió	1983–5
C. Zavala Roch	1964–6*	J. Caballero	1983–90
A. Mercador	1965–6*	A. Belluscio	1983–
E. Ortiz Basuelda (DF)	1966–73**	C. Fayt	1983–
R. Chute (DF)	1966–73**	E. Petracchi	1983–
M. A. Risolía (DF)	1966–73**	J. Bacqué	1985–90
G. A. Borda (DF)	1966–7	J. Oyanarte	1990–1
L. C. Cabral (DF)	1966–73**	R. Levene	1990–5
J. F. Bidau (DF)	1967–70	M. C. Martínez	1990–3
M. Arguas (DF)	1970–3**	R. Barra	1990–3
M. A. Bercaitz	1973–6*	J. Nazareno	1990–2003***
A. Díaz Bialet	1973–6*	E. M. O'Connor	1990–2003***
M. Aráuz Castex	1973–5	A. Boggiano	1991–
E. Corvalán Nancl.	1973–5	G. Bossert	1993–2002
H. Masnatta	1973–6*	G. López	1993–
R. E. G. Levene	1975–6*	A. Vázquez	1975–
P. A. Ramella	1975–6*	J. C. Maqueda	2002–

DF: Justice appointed by a de facto government.
* Justice removed by an incoming de facto government.
** Justice resigned during a democratic transition.
*** Justice formally impeached.
Source: Molinelli et al. 1999.

provincial supreme court justices were removed specifically by decree. All of the other judges had to swear an oath of loyalty to the new government but were allowed to keep their posts (Groisman 1983). In the 1983 democratic transition, over 70 percent of all federal judges kept their posts (Smulovitz 1995: 94).

4.1 The Gap between Formal and Informal Institutions

Table 4.2 *Number of Justices Selected by Each Government, 1862–1995*

Date of government (pre-Perón)	Number of justices selected	Date of govenment (Perón and after)	Number of justices selected
1862	5	1946	5
1868	2	1952	0
1874	3	1955*	5
1880	2	1955*	0
1886	3	1958	7
1890	3	1962	1
1892	1	1963	2
1895	0	1966*	5
1898	3	1970*	1
1904	1	1971*	0
1906	1	1973	5
1910	1	1973	0
1914	1	1973	0
1916	1	1974	2
1922	3	1976*	5
1928	0	1981*	0
1930*	1	1982*	1
1932*	3	1982*	2
1938*	1	1983	5
1942*	0	1989	10
1943*	0	1995	1
1943*	0		
1944*	1		
1862–1944 Average	1.5	1946–95 Average	6.2

* Military government.

Source: Compiled from data in Miller et al. 1995.

Secondly, during this period intra-regime changes did not necessarily result in the dismissal of Supreme Court justices. For example, of the three successive democratic administrations that governed Argentina between 1958 and 1963, five of the seven justices appointed in 1958 served until the coup in 1966 (Miller et al. 1995: 1156–7). Similarly, changes in the military's top leadership did not necessarily amount to changes in the Supreme Court either in the 1955–8 period or in the 1966–73 period.

To sum up, the origins of insecure tenure in Argentina are intimately related to regime instability. Over the past fifty years, the Court has been dismissed en masse six times and the majority on the Court has been replaced fully nine times. Insecure tenure, however, has also been fairly circumscribed. It tended to apply only to Supreme Court justices and then only in particular settings of political change, namely regime change. Having thus established that insecure tenure was part of the informal institutional landscape that dominated postwar Argentina, the following sections turn to consider in much closer detail how judges' expectations have evolved in more recent Argentine history.

4.2 Judges under the Bayonets: The Military "Proceso," 1976–1983

On March 24, 1976, the military staged a coup against the government of Isabel Perón. On seizing power, the new ruling junta, composed of Army General Jorge Videla, Navy Admiral Eduardo Emilio Massera, and Air Force Brigadier General Orlando Ramón Agosti, issued a joint statement from the Casa Rosada. In the "Act Establishing the Purpose and Basic Objectives of the Process of National Reconstruction" the military proclaimed its intentions to "restore the true values of the Argentine nation, eradicate subversion and corruption, and promote the economic development of the state" (Groisman 1983). To exert its control over the state, the "Proceso" government then issued a series of decrees officially removing Isabel Perón from office, dissolving Congress, and removing the elected provincial governors.

In place of the civilian government, the military immediately set about establishing a new institutional order. According to the new rules the supreme power of the state would be shared equally among the three branches of the military, with the commanders of each branch serving a term of three years. An advisory council (Comisión Asesora Legislativa) was created to oversee new legislation. General Videla was appointed as the first executive for a term of four years. In contrast to previous military governments, the junta retained several of the executive's powers, such as the power to declare war and a state of siege and the power to arbitrate between the executive and the advisory council. Finally, the eight ministries were divided equally among the three branches, with the last two posts for the Ministry of Economics and the Ministry of Culture and Education going to the civilians (e.g., see Munck 1998: 57–61).

To accomplish the twin objectives of liberalizing the economy and eradicating subversion, the military also passed a series of decrees severely curtailing civil and political liberties. For example, the military suspended Article 23 of the Constitution, which guaranteed that those arrested under a state of siege had the right to leave the country. Meanwhile, universities were purged and certain departments, such as sociology, were permanently closed. Political party activity was banned and laws were passed that allowed the government to dismiss officials suspected of subversion (Nino 1996: 54). To ensure labor's compliance with the neo-liberal economic policies of the new Minister of the Economy, José Martínez de Hoz, the junta passed blanket decrees, such as 9/76, which suspended "temporarily" all labor activity, including the right to strike (Munck 1998: 67).

In keeping with the informal institution of insecure tenure during regime changes, the military also replaced all justices at the level of the Supreme Court, as well as several federal courts of appeals and state supreme courts. As under the previous military governments that came to power in 1955 and 1966, it was seen as de rigueur that the junta would replace the individual members of the Court with judges who shared the military's basic outlook and ideology. Reflecting this sentiment, the Argentine newspaper *La Nación* commented:

Since the Supreme Court is one of the three powers of the state, the act of swearing in new members formally represents the beginning of a new development in the nation's justice system. . . . The work of selecting the new members is an extremely difficult task for the junta in which the costs of making a mistake are high and the margin of error must be made as low as possible. (cited in Gabrielli 1986: 16)

To find justices who would be able to reorient the judiciary along these lines, the junta asked the Ministry of Justice, which was under the control of the air force, to prepare a list of judges and lawyers who had "distinguished" careers but who had not been previously appointed at the level of the Supreme Court. According to former Chief Justice Adolfo Gabrielli, because the ministry did not know very much about the judiciary, it in turn relied on the civilian institutions, such as the Colegio de Abogados (Bar Association), to help to choose the appropriate justices.[5] In the meantime, the existing members of the Supreme Court, the provincial Supreme Courts, and the attorney general were suspended, officially placed "*en comisión*" (Groisman 1983; Carrió 1996: 93).

It took the junta a total of only eight days to select and swear in its new justices. The five new justices selected to fill the vacancies on the

---

[5] Interview with Justice Gabrielli, Buenos Aires, May 1998.

Supreme Court were Horacio H. Heredia, Adolfo Gabrielli, Frederico Videla Escalada, Alejandro Caride, and Abelardo Rossi. Of these five, four were long-term career judges with conservative leanings.[6] Heredia had been a judge on the federal appeals court for more than eighteen years, Gabrielli and Caride had served in various posts in the federal court system for thirty-four years and forty-five years, respectively, and Rossi had been an appeals court judge since 1958. Only Videla Escalada had not had previous experience as a judge; he was a law professor and author of numerous books on Argentine jurisprudence (Gabrielli 1986: 19–21; Carrió 1996). Videla Escalada resigned at the end of 1976 and was replaced by Pedro Frías, a conservative and respected law professor from Córdoba.

Assessing just how closely aligned were the justices with the military junta is difficult. For example, much has been made of the apparent initial contestation between the junta and the new justices over the wording of the justices' oath of allegiance. Initially, the junta had mandated that the justices swear to respect and uphold the "basic objectives of the junta, the Statute for the National Reorganization, and the National Constitution, insofar as it did not conflict with the other two documents" (Carrió 1996: 94). According to Gabrielli, the ministers were easily able to persuade the junta to remove this final caveat, thereby at least formally putting the Constitution on equal ground with the junta's laws (1986: 23–4). Nevertheless, it is by no means clear that this exchange demonstrates that the justices had ideas substantially different from those of the junta about the Court's proper role. Changing of the oath's wording is also consistent with inferring that the new justices simply did not believe that there were any inherent contradictions between the objectives of the military and the Constitution. Indeed, in an interview I conducted with Gabrielli nearly twenty-five years after the coup, he continued to defend the military's basic objectives of restoring order and ending the turmoil that plagued Argentina in the 1970s. Equally important was that the only threats Gabrielli acknowledged receiving as a Supreme Court justice were from the guerrillas, not the military.

With the various replacements of justices that occurred during the first years of the dictatorship, the military continued to appoint relatively conservative and respected professionals to the bench. In September, Emilio M. R. Daireaux, a judge from Buenos Aires, replaced Caride. Heredia's death in 1978 led to the appointment of Elías Guastavino, who had served as the procurador general (attorney general) under the first years of the Proceso.

[6] Interview with Andrés D'Alessio, Buenos Aires, April 1998.

But in 1980, the quality of the justices began to decline. With Daireaux's death in 1980 César Black was appointed. Black was seen as loyal to the military but not of the same caliber as the other justices.[7] In 1981, Frías was replaced by Carlos Renom, a justice on the provincial Supreme Court of Buenos Aires. In September of 1983, Black and Renom were replaced by Julio J. Martínez Vivot and Emilio P. Gnecco. In the end, only Gabrielli and Rossi served on the Court the entire six-year period. Yet out of the several membership changes that occurred on the Court during the dictatorship, only Frías's resignation appears to have been motivated by political reasons. Although many of the details are unclear, it seems that Frías's nephew was among those "disappeared" by the military and that this was part of the motivation for his resignation.

Beginning in the late 1970s the Court began to come under scrutiny, particularly for its decisions dealing with writs of habeas corpus. During this time the Court was visited on three separate occasions by international organizations, such as the Organization of American States (OAS), and by foreign governments, including the United States, that demanded information on the whereabouts of thousands of political detainees and prisoners. At the same time, the Court received thousands of petitions for habeas corpus and hundreds of letters from concerned individuals and groups worldwide. Although public debate during this period under the dictatorship was severely limited, many of the Court's decisions were also widely discussed in law journals and in the daily media (e.g., see Gabrielli 1986).

Yet for the most part, during the first four years of the military junta the justices on the Court were under very little obligation to respond to this pressure. The military remained firmly in control of the state and was developing plans to institutionalize its rule (Bombal González 1991). For example, as early as 1977 the military began to claim victory in its war against subversion and to develop a political party that would be able to overcome the divisions wrought by Peronism.[8] As far as organized opposition to its economic policies went, the junta managed fairly early on to reshape labor through co-opting some leaders and crushing the rank and file (Munck 1998: 71–102). And through a combination of terror and propaganda, the military succeeded in de-politicizing most sectors of the society. In 1978

---

[7] Ibid.

[8] The war also provided a useful pretext for crushing other perceived "enemies" of the regime, thus the military did not declare the war officially over until much later (Nino 1996: 58). In fact, it was not until 1980 when General Videla officially declared that the war was over (*Clarín*, May 31, 1980, cited in Bombal González 1991: 22).

most of the attention within Argentina focused on winning the World Cup, not on visits from Amnesty International (Malamud-Goti 1996). Throughout the first four years of military rule, there were no indications that the military government would hand over power to the political parties without demanding and receiving institutional guarantees that insulated its power or that the eventual departure of the military from power would not be directed by the military itself. As Videla's minister of the interior, General Albano Eduardo Harguindeguy, put it in September of 1980:

Will 1981–1984 be the last military government? It is a very difficult question to answer. To the extent that the objectives of the military are achieved in three years – something which seems very difficult to do in my view – one could say that this will be the last military government. But if these objectives are not achieved, it will not be the last military government. The basic objectives are the following: the formation of large political parties that help the country [to achieve its goals] and an economic transformation.[9]

Moreover, during these first years the justices not only expected the junta to remain thoroughly in control of any eventual transition, they also expected that if and when a regime change did occur, the junta would be able to break the informal norm of replacing judges. This expectation makes sense when we consider that the military's overarching goal was to reform the Constitution to ensure for itself broad spheres of influence over political and economic policies once democracy was restored (Bombal González 1991). Keeping their own justices on the Court was thus a logical aim of the military. In the late 1970s, the government sponsored a series of meetings on the subject of judicial reform. Although many of the proposals dealt with basic issues such as exterminating rats in the Tribunales, fixing the elevators, and establishing a research library for use of the justices and their clerks, proposals were also made to ensure that judges' tenures would be respected. Indeed, in the proposals that emerged from the series of judicial reform meetings held in Mar del Plata in 1977 and 1978 and attended by the members of the Supreme Court and several other federal courts, one of the top priorities listed was that secure tenure be respected (Gabrielli 1986: 356).

In the early 1980s, however, the scenario for the military government changed considerably. According to Gerardo Munck, in spite of the military's attempts to exert control over the state, the junta had never managed to institutionalize fully its rule (1998: 105). The problems within the military leadership became salient during the process of selecting a replacement

---

[9] *Clarín*, September 12, 1980, cited in Bombal González 1991: 23.

for the military president, General Videla. A split emerged between two factions. One supported General Viola, a soft-liner who favored a gradual political opening and opposed the harsh austerity measures adopted by Minster of the Economy José Martínez de Hoz. The other faction supported General Galtieri, a hard-liner who favored continuing the military's rule indefinitely and de Hoz's economic liberalization program (Munck 1998: 106–8). The military's waning ability to manage the economy helped to tip the balance in favor of Viola.

The more moderate Viola assumed the presidency in March of 1981 and began a dialogue with the political parties.[10] However, as has been argued by scholars of democratic transitions, the Argentine government's attempt to liberalize only succeeded in further destabilizing the dictatorship (O'Donnell and Schmitter 1986; Przeworski 1991). Thus, over the next six months a political crisis escalated between the hard-liners, who opposed the dialogue, and the political parties, who had joined together in a multi-party alliance to demand further concessions. Joining the party alliance were labor organizations and the increasingly powerful human rights groups. The first wave of public protests began in late 1981. Involving unions, human rights groups, and the political parties, it was the largest public demonstration since 1976.

The protests, coupled with severe inflation, provoked Galtieri and the hard-liners to seize power in a putsch against the soft-liners at the end of 1982. Yet as it turned out, the hard-liners would not be any more successful in thwarting the demand for a democratic transition. Galtieri issued thinly veiled threats to wage another war against subversion, but mass protests against the regime only increased (Bombal González 1991: 115). On March 30, 1982, tens of thousands of people marched in the Plaza de Mayo to denounce the political, social, and economic policies of the dictatorship (Nino 1996: 60). Less than a week later the military sent forces to confront the British over the Falkland-Malvinas Islands. Although the populace generally supported the war at the beginning, the total defeat of the Argentine forces in June led to the rapid downfall of Galtieri and to the final transition to democracy. General Bignone assumed power in June 1982 and called for elections to be scheduled for the following fall.

---

[10] It should be noted that an initial political dialogue was opened in 1980 between Videla and the political parties. The main difference between the first and second dialogue is that in 1980 the hope of the military was still to create its own military party, the Movement of National Opinion (MON), to which it could transfer power (Bombal González 1991).

Although we now know the outcome was democracy, the situation from 1981 to 1983 was marked by profound uncertainty for all actors, including the judges. Although it ultimately became apparent that the military could not negotiate the terms of the transition, this was not always entirely clear. As a result, this meant that beginning in 1981 up until Alfonsín's surprising victory in 1983, the future tenure of the Supreme Court justices was an open question. Although past experience suggested that the judges would be automatically removed, there was some movement to keep the court intact. Among the voices in favor of keeping the military justices on the bench was the highly respected constitutional scholar Bidart Campos, who argued that compared with the cycle of juridical instability that had plagued Argentina, keeping the current Court was the lesser of two evils (cited in Gabrielli 1986). Indeed, right up until the very end of the regime, the military government made concerted efforts to keep the judges on the bench under the next government. Following the Malvinas fiasco, for example, the military explicitly included in their list of demands from the democratic opposition the continuity of the judiciary.

In addition to uncertainty over staying on the bench, however, was the looming question of how the judges' reputations would be viewed under the new democracy. As the transition gained momentum and the human rights groups played a more central role, confronting the military's abuses in the Dirty War took center stage. The discovery of mass graves during the electoral campaign further fueled this concern (Nino 1996). Closely tied to these events was a growing debate over the role that the Court had played and whether it had done enough to protect human rights from state abuses.

Although it is doubtful that the judges themselves would have been criminally prosecuted along with the generals,[11] their behavior was thus under increasing scrutiny at the end of the military regime. In particular, the judges' reputations most at risk were those who had served under the military during its most repressive years and who remained on the bench: Chief Justice Adolfo Gabrielli, Abelardo Rossi, and, to a lesser extent, Elías Gaustavino.[12] Indeed, from the perspective of these justices in particular, the strength of the human rights movement and the growing public

[11] I thank an anonymous reviewer for clarifying this point.

[12] Although Justice Guastavino was not one of the original members of the military's Supreme Court, he served as the attorney general under the dictatorship prior to being appointed as a justice in 1978 and thus played a role in many of the early human rights cases coming before the Court in the mid-1970s.

perception that the military's leaders had to be punished trumped the uncertainty over which of the two political parties would win. Most observers during the campaign expected the Peronists to win, but this expectation would hardly have given much comfort to the judges. Although it is true that the Peronists were not as committed to punishing human rights abuses as were the Radicals, who had put human rights at the center of their campaign, it was also far from clear that the Peronists would protect the military's justices. The experience under Perón's 1946–55 government had established that the Peronists could hardly be counted on to refrain from scapegoating the individual justices when it served their political interests to do so. Moreover, unlike the several union leaders connected to the Peronist movement, who formed their own pacts with the outgoing military government (Munck 1998: 149–53), the military-era justices and the Peronists had no special agreement.

From this narrative we can thus summarize who the military regime judges were and how their beliefs about their futures changed over the course of their tenure. The judges who stayed on the bench under the military were politically conservative jurists with strong professional qualifications who cared about retaining their posts and, perhaps even more strongly, about their professional reputations. During the first four years, the judges reasonably expected that the military regime would sustain its hold on power until it had succeeded in reshaping society and in setting Argentine politics on a new trajectory. Moreover, during this initial period, the judges could even expect that if a transition took place they would still be able to retain their posts, to say nothing of their reputations. Beginning in 1981, however, it became plausible that a transition would take place sooner rather than later and, increasingly, that it would not be on the military's terms nor include reserved domains of institutional influence. This emerging threat posed by the likely regime transition and the prospect of judges losing their posts was exacerbated further by the additional threat to the justices' professional images that came from serving under an increasingly reviled regime.

4.3 Judges under the Alfonsín Government: The Return to Democracy, 1983–1989

On October 30, 1983, a Radical Party presidential candidate, Raúl Alfonsín, stunned the country by defeating the Peronists for the first time ever in an open election.[13] Against the Peronist candidate, Italo Luder, Alfonsín won the presidency with 52 percent of the vote (Catterberg 1991: 84–5).[14] In the midst of tremendously high expectations, the Alfonsín government immediately set about seeking to fulfill its campaign promises to punish the former military leaders for abuses committed during the Dirty War and to install a democratic regime that would ensure a new level of respect for human and civil rights. Three days after taking office, Alfonsín announced a broad package of backward-looking and forward-looking human rights proposals. To deal with the crimes committed by the former regime, the government proposed nullifying the military's self-amnesty law, modifying the Military Code to give broad powers of review to the civilian courts and to reduce the scope of impunity for lower-level officers, and issuing decrees necessary for beginning the prosecution of the guerrilla leaders and the military. To prevent future abuses from occurring, Alfonsín further proposed repealing all of the anti-subversive laws passed by the military, ratifying several international human rights treaties,[15] reforming the federal criminal procedural code, and modifying the Military Code to eliminate the jurisdiction of the military court's over civilians (Nino 1996: 69).

In the context of these legal reforms, the question of what the incoming democratic government should do regarding the federal judiciary came to the fore. Once the election had taken place, the main debate was over the degree to which the new government should purge the judiciary. There

---

[13] Since the party's birth in 1945, the Peronist Party had never lost in an open election. The victories that the Radicals had achieved since then – for example, in 1958 with Arturo Frondosa's election – took place under the proscription of the Peronist Party from electoral competition (O'Donnell 1979; Cavarozzi 1986; Collier and Collier 1991).

[14] In retrospect, the Radical's victory is somewhat less surprising. In contrast to polling done in early 1982, six months prior to the election public opinion polls showed the Radicals leading Peronists by 20 percent to 18 percent, with at least 55 percent of the voters undecided (Catterberg 1991: 77). The victory of the Radicals can be seen as a result of structural changes in the economy as well as changes in the attitudes of the electorate. The drastic neo-liberal policies enacted under the military shrank substantially the traditional working-class sectors that had provided the core support base for Peronism in the post-war era (Cavarozzi 1986: Levitsky 2003: 94–8). In the context of growing support for human rights, the Peronist campaign made several blunders that Alfonsín was able to exploit. For example, Alfonsín's clear and immediate rejection of the military's "self-amnesty" law in Alfonsín's statement entitled "This Is Not the Final Word" contrasted sharply with the Italo Luder's far more tepid disapproval of the law (e.g., see Nino 1996: 65; Munck 1998).

[15] The human rights treaties included the American Convention of Human Rights (which entails the jurisdiction of the Inter-American Court of Human Rights, the United Nations Covenant on Civil and Political Rights, and the United Nations Covenant on Economic and Social Rights; Nino 1996: 69).

were basically three proposals that emerged during this period. The first proposal, put forth by the human rights group Asamblea Permanente por los Derechos Humanos, was to remove immediately all of the federal judges who had served under the military. The second proposal, made by the conservative legal group Foro de Estudios Sobre la Administración de Justicia (FORES), proposed instead to keep all the judges appointed by the military, with recourse to the impeachment procedure for those individuals who had violated their mandate. The third proposal, of the Buenos Aires Bar Association, fell somewhere in the middle of these two extremes, calling for approximately half of the existing federal judges to be denied confirmation by the Senate (Smulovitz 1995: 93). Yet all of these debates were mainly about the lower levels of the judiciary. At the level of the Supreme Court there was ultimately relatively little controversy over what steps the new government should take.

The basic view of Alfonsín's transitional team was that it was absolutely necessary to replace the justices on the Supreme Court.[16] According to Carlos Nino, one of Alfonsín's leading legal advisers, the very fact that the justices had been sworn in by a de facto government meant that the tenure of the sitting justices would not be respected by the incoming democratic government (Nino 1996: 67). Thus, after winning the election in October, Alfonsín's legal advisers immediately began to prepare a list of possible candidates to fill the Supreme Court posts.

In contrast to the concerns of the military junta, the Alfonsín administration seemed to place very little priority on building a strictly professional court or one that was even necessarily politically homogeneous. Rather, according to Alfonsín's attorney general and former judge Andrés D'Alessio, the Alfonsín court was best characterized as composed of individual "stars" rather than as a team of players with a common set of objectives.[17] The post of the chief justice was initially offered to Italo Luder, the Peronist candidate whom Alfonsín had defeated (Carrió 1996: 116; Larkins 1998: 439). After Luder refused the post, it was subsequently offered to Genero Carrió, a well-known law professor and human rights attorney who had served as Jacobo Timerman's defense lawyer during the military government. The four other justices selected were Augusto Belluscio, José Severo Caballero, Carlos S. Fayt, and Enrique Petracchi. Belluscio and Caballero were both lower court judges with ties to the Radical Party, Petracchi was a

---

[16] Interview with Jaime Malamud-Goti, Buenos Aires, March 1997.
[17] Interview with Andrés D'Alessio, Buenos Aires, April 1998.

high-profile Peronist labor lawyer from Buenos Aires, and Carlos Fayt was a socialist lawyer (Carrió 1996; Molinelli 1999: 684). Of the five original appointees, only one justice resigned. In 1985 Carrió stepped down for health reasons and was replaced Jorge Bacqué, a private lawyer with a successful law practice in Buenos Aires. All of the nominees were unanimously approved without discussion either before or during the Senate confirmation proceedings (Carrió 1996: 116).

In spite of the high-profile status of the new Supreme Court justices, during the first years of the democratic government most of the attention was on the lower courts of appeals in which most of the human rights trials would take place (Smulovitz 1995). The most important of these was the Cámara Federal de Buenos Aires (the Buenos Aires Federal Appeals Court). According to the legal procedures established for trying the former military leaders, if the military courts did not carry forward the investigations and prosecutions in a timely fashion, the Appeals Court would have the jurisdiction to take over the proceedings. Here the administration was clearly less committed to ensuring "diversity" and more prone to appoint judges with established records on protecting human rights. For example, both Jorge Torlasco and Guillermo Ledesma, who were appointed to the Cámara, had ruled against the military in numerous human rights cases and were among the first lower court judges to declare the military's law of self-amnesty unconstitutional.[18] Two other judges, Andrés D'Alessio and Gil Lavedra, had been members of Alfonsín's transitional team itself and had played a key role in coming up with the legal strategy that was used to prosecute the military leaders. Given the impending military trials, accepting a post on the Cámara entailed both a great deal of prestige as well as sacrifice on the part of the judges. According to D'Alessio, the day he was asked to accept the post the minister of justice called him and said, "Take a seat, Andrés, this afternoon I'm going to screw up your life."[19] By contrast, with most of the spotlight on the Appeals Court, the justices on the Supreme Court enjoyed relative peace and security in the first few years following the democratic transition.

Between 1983 and 1986 the social and economic policies of the Radical government were largely successful. Although the government faced some opposition from the Peronist-controlled Senate, most of the

---

[18] Interview with Jorge Torlasco, Buenos Aires, April 1998; interview with Gil Lavedra, Buenos Aires, April 1998.

[19] Interview with Andrés D'Alessio, Buenos Aires, April 1998.

administration's laws dealing with human rights issues were approved.[20] In September 1984 the Comisión Nacional sobre la Desaparición de Personas (National Commission for Disappeared Persons), otherwise known as CONADEP, published its final report, *Nunca Más* (*Never Again*), which detailed the human rights atrocities committed during the military regime. Drawing on information gathered by human rights groups and the testimonies of thousands of witnesses, the commission's report was widely hailed as an impartial, representative, and politically independent source of information about the fate of the disappeared (Roniger and Sznajder 1999: 63; but see Gabrielli 1986).

In the economic realm the government also initially managed to avoid several major disasters. For example, in spite of its early failures to defy the international banking community by suspending payments to the IMF, the Austral Plan, launched in June 1985, exceeded initial expectations and pulled the country from the brink of hyperinflation (Smith 1991: 9–11). With the Peronist Party still reeling from its defeat in 1983, the Radicals managed to retain their majority in the Chamber of Deputies by winning the 1985 midterm elections with 42 percent of the vote.[21] During this period, opinion polls showed the government enjoying an average of 44 percent positive approval ratings, while Alfonsín's personal ratings stood at an average of 76 percent public approval (Catterberg 1991: 91). But in 1986 things started to fall apart for the Radicals. On the economic front, the government's attempts to cut spending led to a series of strikes in the public sector. By the end of year, the problems with the Austral Plan were becoming apparent as inflation began to grow. Never supporters of the government's heterodox economic strategy, the Peronist unions began a series of massive strikes at the end of 1985, with prominent union leaders, such as the CGT's (General Labor Confederation) Saúl Ubaldini, calling on the government to "get out and stop lying" (cited in Rock 1985: 400).

Alfonsín's human rights policies also began to run into trouble in 1986 and 1987. Following the unprecedented conviction of the military junta's

---

[20] Among the most important can be included Law 23.040, declaring the nullification of the "self-amnesty" law, unanimously approved by both houses of Congress, the so-called Defense of Democracy and Constitutional Order, the ratification of the American Convention on Human Rights, and the modifications of the penal code regarding torture and the Federal Code of Criminal Procedure regarding the duration of trials and procedures of due process (Nino 1996: 74–5).

[21] Election data retrieved May 1, 2000, from http://www.georgetown.edu/pdba/Elecdata/Arg/cong83.html.

leaders by the Federal Appeals Court in 1985, Alfonsín took a number of measures designed to limit the scope of the verdict and the potential for further indictments. In 1986 the government issued the Instrucciones a los Fiscales Militares (Instructions to Military Prosecutors), the Ley de Punto Final (Full-Stop Law), and the Ley de Obedencia Debida (Due Obedience Law). The first law included a detailed set of instructions to prosecutors that limited the categories of military personnel that could be put on trial. The Full-Stop Law sought to limit the trials further still by establishing a fixed period of time in which proceedings for human rights abuses could be filed. In 1987 the government proposed the Due Obedience Law, which made those who had "acted under orders" exempt from prosecution (Garro and Dahl 1987; Nino 1991; Acuña and Smulovitz 1995).

Nevertheless, the military was not appeased. In 1987 during Easter Week, the military staged its first of four uprisings (Norden 1996). Although the rebellion was quickly put down, it showed the inability of the civilian government to impose their command and maintain order (Acuña and Smulovitz 1995: 107). Meanwhile the public registered its outrage with the government's "betrayal" by staging a series of massive protests. In Buenos Aires alone tens of thousands marched in protest against the Full-Stop legislation (Roniger and Sznajder 1999: 70).

During this period, the Renovation faction assumed control over the Justicialist (Peronist) Party (PJ) leadership in November 1987, enabling the Renovation opposition to reposition itself to take advantage of the mounting problems in the Alfonsín administration. As Steven Levitsky argues, the Renovation wing of the Peronist Party abandoned the party's traditional strategy of linking itself exclusively to organized labor and adopted a "catch all" strategy that moved the party in a liberal and socially progressive direction (2003: 119). The Peronists were able to capitalize on their minority position by opposing the Alfonsín government's attempts to limit the trials and joining the labor main organization, the Confederación General del Trabajo (CGT), to protest against Alfonsín's economic plan as "liberal" and favorable to the International Monetary Fund (IMF; Levitsky 2003: 119). This time, to the surprise of almost no one, the Peronists roared back in the electoral arena, increasing the party's vote share in the 1987 midterm elections from 35 to 43 percent and winning seventeen of the twenty-two governorships (Levitsky 2003: 119–20).

During the final two years of the Alfonsín administration the government proved completely incapable of managing the state and the economy. In

4.3 Judges under the Alfonsín Government

1988 Argentina was forced to suspend debt payments to the IMF, consumer purchasing power declined by more than 50 percent, and food riots in several provinces broke out. As one scholar writes, "no one knew what the value of the currency was. Banks and money exchanges simply closed their doors. Argentina was left virtually 'stateless'" (Smith 1991: 28–29). With each new crisis the approval ratings of the government plummeted: From 1987 to 1988 the percentage of people polled who had a positive evaluation of the government fell from 30 to 11 percent. In 1989 positive evaluations of Alfonsín went from 15 percent in May to an all-time low of 9 percent in April (Catterberg 1991: 91). Observers at the time, after the 1987 Peronist victory, would have overwhelmingly assumed that the Peronist opposition would win the presidential election in 1989.

How then did the Radical's collapse post-1987 affect the justices' expectations about their futures? First, even in spite of the military uprisings, very few observers believed that there was a serious possibility of a reversion to military rule. In public opinion surveys conducted in March, June, and November of 1988, only 1 percent of respondents ranked "relationship with the military" as the country's most pressing concern (Catterberg 1991: 95). The possibility that the judges' fates would lie in the hands of a military government was therefore not a major concern for the justices. And given that in the past the norm of insecure tenure had been limited to regime transitions, there was thus no clear expectation on the Court that the justices would be automatically removed in the next two years.

What is more, the transition to democracy had, at least temporarily, transformed the public's perception of the judiciary. Largely through the judiciary's role in the human rights trials, the public ceased to view many of the judges and prosecutors as anonymous bureaucrats and began to perceive them as true "civic heroes" (Smulovitz 1995: 98). In fact, this role became even more pronounced toward the end of the Alfonsín administration, culminating most dramatically in the events that took place during the month of January 1987. Part of the Alfonsín administration's efforts to end the military trials involved limiting the trials to the January holiday that is generally taken by federal and provincial judges. (Acuña and Smulovitz 1995: 21–99). This was the reason for passing in December the Full-Stop Law – which set a limit of seventy days in which lawsuits could be filed. But the plan backfired. To the chagrin of the government and the delight of the public, many federal courts of appeals judges canceled their January holiday that year, processing as many cases as they could before the deadline passed. By the end of February 1987 more than 300 high-level officials had been indicted on charges of violating human rights (Acuña and Smulovitz 1995: 61).

Still, justices at the time could hardly have regarded the stability of the Court guaranteed. In the wake of the disastrous aftermath (from the government's perspective) of the Full-Stop Law, a series of negotiations began between the Radicals and Peronists to increase the number of justices on the Court. At first, the issue of increasing the number of justices emerged as part of the Alfonsín's own proposals for judicial reform that emerged in the wake of the human rights debacle. In November 1987 Alfonsín sent a bill to Congress calling for a series of reforms that included changing the criminal code, introducing the writ of certiorari and per saltum, expanding oral proceedings, and increasing the number of justices from five to seven (Baglini and D'Ambrosio 1993: 44). To pass the bill, however, the Radicals needed the support of the Peronists, who had just won the majority of seats in the Senate. As a counter-offer to the Radicals, the Peronists instead proposed increasing the number from five to nine, presumably also stipulating a role in the selection of new justices.

In the midst of these negotiations the justices voiced their objections in legal journals, with one of the justices, Augusto Belluscio, even threatening to resign (Verbitsky 1993). Thus, although the pending expansion of the Court did not necessarily imply that the individual justices would be removed, it signaled to the justices that the incumbents and opposition alike was interested in altering the Court's composition and in potentially seeking to reduce the influence of its current members. As popular support for the Alfonsín government declined precipitously, it also became increasingly clear that the judicial reform would lie exclusively in the hands of the Peronist Party, which was widely expected to gain control over both branches of government in 1989.

Complicating further the situation the justices faced was the fact that at least in certain issues the preferences of the opposition were either inchoate or in close alignment with the outgoing government. For example, until the primaries held in July 1988, it was simply unclear which of the two candidates would win the party's nomination. For most of the 1987–8 period it looked as though Menem would not win the nomination and that Cafiero would have been the most likely future president. The policy positions of the Renovation wing of the PJ, led by Antonio Cafiero, were quite similar to those of the Alfonsín government on economic and social issues. Cafiero was often accused by his competitor, Carlos Menem, of seeking to convert the PJ into "a little liberal or neoliberal party."[22] Although Menem's own campaign was clearly much more traditional Peronist, emphasizing issues of economic inwardness, nationalism, and corporatism, he shared the Alfonsín administration's desire to limit the human rights trials (Levitsky 1999: 177–82).

Once Menem had captured the nomination he quickly put the judicial reform on hold. But in the eyes of the justices, the growing likelihood that Menem and his party would gain control of both branches made the possibility that such an increase could be forestalled forever highly unlikely. According to former Chief Justice of the Supreme Court Jorge Bacqué, during the presidential campaign Menem met with the members of the Court several times, assuring them that he would not seek to increase the number of justices (Larkins 1998: 440). That the justices believed him, however, seems highly doubtful. The series of meetings themselves suggest that the justices were increasingly uneasy about their own fates and the fate of the institution. Paraphrasing the Argentine journalist Horacio Verbitsky, the clear implication was not that Menem would leave the Court alone once he was elected, but rather that he wanted to stall the reform so that he alone could choose all four of the new justices (1993: 23).

Finally, there is further evidence that immediately prior to assuming office Menem began using a carrot and stick approach with several of the individual justices to get them to resign. For example, Menem allegedly offered an ambassadorship to Carlos Fayt in exchange for his resignation – an offer to which Fayt responded by sending Menem a copy of his book, *Law and Ethics*, with a message saying simply, "Beware I wrote this" (Verbitsky 1993: 38). With other justices, the strategy was far less congenial. For example, following the suicide of Justice Belluscio's mistress, who had thrown herself out of a Paris window after leaving Belluscio a note – "Augusto, you have humiliated me" – the Peronists made the scandal public and threatened Belluscio with impeachment.[23] Thus, although no formal changes to the Court took place in the period preceding Menem's election, a glimpse behind the scenes reveals that once Alfonsín began to lose power, the future of the Court was increasingly insecure.

---

[22] *Clarín*, May 21, 1988, cited in Levitsky 1999: 178.

[23] As Verbitsky also notes, the irony of Belluscio's situation was that he was the author of the *Manuel de Derecho Familia* (Manual of Family Law), which "extolled monogamous marriage as an ethical and legal ideal and considered marital fidelity a duty even in the case of separation" (1993: 37).

In sum, the initial appointment of new justices by the incoming democratic government in 1983 adhered to the established, informal norm of insecure tenure associated with regime changes. Following the new justices' initial appointments, the primary attention focused on the human rights trials occurring in the lower courts. Hence, during the first years of the Alfonsín administration there was relatively little attention and thus little pressure on the justices of the Supreme Court. However, with the administration's rapid loss of power beginning in 1987 and the proposal for judicial reform on the table, the question of the future of the Court emerged as a topic of growing concern for the justices. Taken together with the fact that there were no well-institutionalized procedures in place for *intra*-regime transitions, the justices on the Court thus reasonably feared that Menem's election put the Court's future once again at risk.

4.4 Judges under the First Menem Government: The Difficulty of Democratic Consolidation

Almost immediately upon coming to office, it became clear that Menem's government would be quite different from what most Argentines expected of a Peronist president. Menem's "bait-and-switch" tactics with the electorate are well known (Stokes 2001).[24] In spite of his traditional Peronist campaign, Menem quickly put together a staunchly neo-liberal economic reform package. Headed by the former vice president of Bunge and Borne, a multinational firm that had long been a symbol for Peronists of Argentina's "sellout" to foreign capital, Menem's economic team proposed an immediate devaluation of the currency (ibid.). In August Menem sent to Congress two bills in which he laid out his plans to dismantle and privatize state-owned industries, cut spending, and eliminate restrictions on foreign investment (Ferreira Rubio and Goretti 1998: 38–9; Levitsky 2003: 145). Meanwhile, the Menem government also issued a stunning number of decrees dealing with salaries, taxation, and public debt.[25] In March 1991

[24] There is some debate over whether the reforms Menem enacted were intended or not before the election took place. According to Palermo and Novaro (1996: 128) and Levitsky (1999), Menem did not plan to move the economy in a neoliberal direction before taking office, but rather switched his policies once he realized the depth of the crisis. Against this view, Stokes presents evidence that Menem knew beforehand but that he purposely misled voters in order to win the election (2001: 72).

[25] To put this into perspective, note that between 1853 and 1989 fewer than thirty such decrees were passed, compared with the 178 decrees passed by Menem between 1989 and 1991 (Ferreira Rubio and Goretti 1998: 43–44; also see Jones 1997).

Menem's Harvard-trained economic minister, Domingo Cavallo, launched the Convertibility Plan, which allowed for the free conversion of the peso to dollar. By the end of the year, the plan worked and inflation had fallen to 1 percent. With pubic approval ratings of over 50 percent, Menem appeared unstoppable.

In the context of these major policy reversals, it is hardly surprising that Menem also reneged on his campaign pledge not to remake the Court. A little less than three months after taking office, Menem sent to Congress a bill to increase the number of justices on the Court from five to nine. The main reason cited by the administration was the inefficiency of the Court, evidenced by the overloaded docket. Yet few doubted that the real motive was political. Menem's then Minister of the Interior Eduardo Bauzá, and the president of the Peronist Party and former governor of the Province of Buenos Aires, Antonio Cafiero, referred openly to the need to "homogenize" the Court with the thinking of the executive branch (Baglini and D'Ambrosio 1993: 47). A widely cited quote from one of the Menem government's top officials, Granillo Ocampo,[26] was that the Court was "Alfonsínista" and that "it is impossible to govern if the Supreme Court is against all the Executive's political initiatives and might declare all the laws implemented by it as unconstitutional" (ICJ 1990: 1, cited in Rogers and Wright-Carozza 1995: 158; Verbitsky 1993). Although at the time there was some speculation that the government feared that the Court would block its efforts to pardon the former military leaders, according to most subsequent accounts the real motivation was the fear that the Court would block the government's economic program (Ferreira Rubio and Goretti 1998: 37). Nevertheless, even supporters of the Menem government have acknowledged that there was very little evidence, based on its pre-electoral behavior, that the Court would have done so (e.g., see Rogers and Wright-Carozza 1995: 158).

During this period, several objections to the administration's court-packing plan were raised. Heading the list was the Court's own resolution, Acordada 44, in which four of the five justices issued a widely publicized

---

[26] Granillo Ocampo was the main architect of the government's court-packing proposal. Trained in the United States, Ocampo modeled his proposal on Franklin Delano Roosevelt's court-packing plan in 1937 (Rubio and Goretti 1998: 37). Ocampo was forced to leave his post as the Secretaria Legal y Tecnica (Legal Adviser to the President) in 1991 due to the Swiftgate scandal. In July 1997, Ocampo was sworn in as the new Minister of Justice, after it was revealed that then current Justice Minister Elías Jassan had lied about his ties with the controversial businessman Alfredo Yabrán (*Clarín*, July 1, 1997).

and strongly worded denunciation of the government's plan. In their resolution, the Court pointed out that increasing the number of justices would hardly accelerate the process of judicial decision making, given that now nine justices rather than five had to review each case. The Acordada also warned against the "risk of triggering a sudden alteration in the application of law and legal scholarship" (cited in Rogers and Wright-Carozza 1995: 159). Domestic and international legal organizations, such as the Colegio de Abogados, the Buenos Aires Bar Association, and the International Commission of Jurists, also strongly denounced the plan. In the words of the Argentine newspaper, *La Nación*:

The Argentine system is designed so that each president receives a Supreme Court that he did not designate and only may do so through natural modifications that occur with the passage of time. For the first time in more than half a century, a constitutional government is in the position of being able to accept this system. It seems, however, that the government is choosing not to accept it and instead is running the risk of reducing the stability and independence of the judiciary. (cited in Verbitsky 1993: 35)

Despite these criticisms, the Peronist majority in the Senate rapidly approved the bill in September, and after some delay in the Chamber of Deputies, the law was finally passed in April 1990.[27] With the passage of the Ley de Ampliación, the government was thus able to appoint four new justices. The passage of the Court-packing plan served to accomplish what Menem's insiders had not managed to achieve prior to assuming office: the resignation of two of the five sitting justices. With the passage of the bill, Justices Caballero and Bacqué immediately tendered their resignations, thereby giving Menem an automatic majority on the bench.[28]

---

[27] Following the passage of the bill, the opposition alleged that irregular procedures were used to get the bill through. For example, when the vote took place there was not a legal quorum present in the Chamber of Deputies. There was no article-by-article vote as the procedures require, which meant that the bill was approved in its final form in forty-two seconds (cited in Rubio and Goretti 1993: 37; see also Baglini and D'Ambrosio 1993).

[28] In a much publicized move, Jorge Bacqué submitted his resignation to the Court immediately on the passage of the court-packing bill (Carrió 1996: 155). According to Bacqué, the fact that he had signed the Acordada 44 meant that he had a "moral obligation" to resign once the bill was passed (interview with Bacqué, April 1998). The details of Caballero's resignation are less clear. According to Verbitsky, there was a deal negotiated with Menem in which Caballero would be appointed an embassador to Geneva, which Caballero reneged on. But, it is not clear what eventually led him to resign (Verbitsky 1993: 38–9).

Given the attention paid to the Court surrounding Menem's court-packing plan, much has subsequently been written about the justices' paltry qualifications and close personal ties with the president (Baglini and D'Ambrosio 1993; Verbitsky 1993; Carrió 1996; Poder Cuidadano 1997; Larkins 1998; Molinelli 1999). For his chief justice, Menem chose Julio Nazareno, a provincial Supreme Court justice from Menem's province, La Rioja, and a former partner in Menem's own law firm (Verbitsky 1993: 60). Three of the other four nominees – Rodolfo Barra, Mariano Cavagna Martínez, and Eduardo Moliné O'Connor – had shockingly little professional experience as judges, but all were open Menem supporters with strong ties to his inner circle. Indeed, Barra reportedly remarked on his appointment to the bench, "My only two bosses are Perón and Menem" (cited in Larkins 1998: 428). Cavagna Martínez is the closest friend of Menem's brother, Senator Eduardo Menem; while Moliné O'Connor is Menem's regular tennis partner and the brother in-law of Menem's secretary of intelligence, Hugo Anzorreguy (Verbitsky 1993).

After the expansion, the Court continued to come under strong criticism (Baglini and D'Ambrosio 1993; Diez et al. 1994; Carrió 1996; Gargarella 1996; Larkins 1998; Octavio de Jesus and Ruscelli 1998; but see Rogers and Wright-Carozza 1995). Almost daily, unfavorable stories of the Court appeared in the news headlines. Phrases such as "*juez adicto*" (addict judge), "*mayoría automatica*" (automatic majority), and "*oficialista*" (officialist) became part of the media's daily vocabulary used to describe the justices on the Supreme Court. The negative image of the judiciary went from 70 percent in July of 1990 to 80 percent in April 1993 (Baglini and D'Ambrosio 1993: 86). In the legal community the perception of the Court has been even worse. In 1992 only 6 percent of lawyers believed that the courts were independent (Abregú 1992).

During this period there have been several requests for impeaching judges at all levels of the judiciary, including the Supreme Court. Between 1990 and 1997, some 170 requests were made by politicians in the opposition against sitting judges at all levels of the judiciary (Poder Cuidadano 1997: 24). Among these petitions, between August 1990 and March 1993 there were a total of thirty-one requests to impeach either individual justices or the entire Supreme Court (Octavio de Jesus and Ruscelli 1998: 27).

Yet because of Menem's party's strength in Congress, threats to impeach the justices were not seen as credible. According to a member of the Chamber of Deputies Impeachment Committee, Melchor Cruchaga, the impeachment committees of both houses were dominated by Peronists who protect judges perceived as loyal to Menem from being investigated (Poder Cuidadano 1997: 27). In the Chamber of Deputies the committee was headed by César Arias, who, along with Granillo Ocampo, was a strong proponent of the initial court-packing plan (Verbitsky 1993). Of the seven-member committee in the Senate, four were Peronists (Poder Cuidadano 1997: 29). In Cruchaga's own words, "The majority of committee members respond to political pressures, which turns many of the impeachment cases into political trials" (cited in Baglini and D'Ambrosio 1993).

In stark contrast to the two previous governments, throughout Menem's first term the judges would have little to fear from the opposition. Following the government's successful fight against inflation from 1991–5, the Peronist Party reaped the benefits at the ballot box, increasing their seats in Congress and in the provincial governments in 1991 and 1993 (Stokes 1999: 171–2). Menem's personal popularity remained consistently high, at around 50 percent (Echegaray and Elordi 2001). Indeed, by 1992 Menem had already held his first summit meeting to plan his reelection (Levitsky 2003: 166).[29] Running for reelection first required that Menem reform the 1853 Constitution, which stipulated a single six-year presidential term. Not since Perón came to power in the 1940s had any other democratic president been able to push through a constitutional reform. The 1993 Pacto de Olivos signed between Menem and Alfonsín to reform the Constitution thus attests to Menem's overwhelming popularity. Public opinion polls showed that 65 percent of the people favored reform and between 50 and 60 percent favored the reelection, which helped Menem to bring the Radicals into the constitutional reform negotiations (Palermo and Novaro 1996: 405).

The Radicals, still led by Alfonsín, lent their support to the reform project in exchange for a limited number of concessions, which included the resignation of two of Menem's most loyal judges (Smulovitz 1995: 80; Palermo and Novaro 1996: 414). Both judges went on to enjoy lucrative and powerful careers under Menem's second administration; hence the quid pro quo should not be framed entirely in the language of sanctions leveled by the opposition at the individual justices. For example, Justice Barra, widely seen as Menem's strongest supporter and advocate, was rewarded by Menem and

---

[29] Even prior to assuming office in 1989, Menem had hinted that he intended to seek re-election (Palermo and Novaro 1996: 403). But it was not until November of 1993 that Menem managed to bring the Radicals to the bargaining table to sign the Pacto de Olivos (Acuña 1995: 125). Among other agreements, the Radicals allowed Menem to run for a second term in exchange for agreeing to create stronger checks on the executive's powers.

appointed the new minister of justice, where he served until it was revealed that he had concealed ties to Nazi organizations in his youth. With the newly reformed Constitution in place, in 1995 Menem won his second term in a landslide election, winning 49.8 percent to 29.2 percent against his closest rival, the leftist FREPASO (Front for a Country in Solidarity) candidate José Bordon.

4.5 Judges under the Second Menem Government: The Path toward Democratic Consolidation?

Shortly after Menem's victory in 1995, however, support for the government and the Peronist party began to wane. Menem's campaign promise to "pulverize unemployment as we pulverized inflation" (Latin American Economic Report, 1995, cited in Stokes 1999: 175) temporarily assuaged voters. But the following year support for the government declined sharply. With unemployment at an unprecedented 18.6 percent, the government's popularity plummeted to under 20 percent in 1996 and 1997 (Levitsky 1999: 257). In the 1997 midterm elections the Peronists were defeated for the first time in a decade. According to exit polls, almost 40 percent of those who changed their votes to support the opposition in 1997 did so because of dissatisfaction with the administration's handling of unemployment.[30] Despite outspending the opposition by more than seven times, the PJ lost its majority in the Congress, giving up fourteen seats in the lower house.[31] Almost immediately after the votes for the midterm elections were counted, the race for the presidency in 1999 began.[32]

After the Pacto de Olivos and Menem's re-election, the image of the Court went from bad to worse. Menem's appointment of Adolfo Vázquez, who was seen as a third-rate jurist, was denounced as a particularly egregious example of the administration's lack of respect for judicial independence. On his nomination to the bench Vázquez openly bragged of his personal friendship to Menem (Larkins 1998: 430). Shortly before the 1997 midterm elections Vázquez went a step further and admitted on the popular television show *Hora Clave* that he never voted against the government.[33]

---

[30] *Clarín*, November 2, 1997.
[31] *Tres Puntos*, December 3, 1997; *Clarín*, October 28, 1997.
[32] *Clarín*, October 26, 28, and 31, 1997.
[33] *Tres Puntos*, September 25, 1997.

Along with a host of corruption scandals involving the justices, Vázquez's admission put the Court directly in the center of the mounting 1999 presidential campaign. Opposition parties across the political spectrum sought to capitalize on the public's disgust with the Court. On the right, Domingo Cavallo, Menem's former economic minister and now leader of the new liberal party, Acción por la República, repeatedly criticized the lack of independence in the Argentine judicial system. One well-known anecdote told by Cavallo was that the former Minister of the Interior Carlos Corach wrote on a napkin a list of the justices controlled by the government.[34] In 1995 Cavallo was sued by Justice Belluscio for libel after Cavallo had publicly declared him to be a "corrupt thief."[35] Cavallo, who was himself subsequently found guilty in a separate criminal case dealing with customs officials during his campaign, claimed that the Menem government trumped up charges against its political opponents and then left the judges to do its dirty work.[36] Playing into citizens' concerns about corruption and lawlessness, Cavallo used his own experience with the courts to make more general claims against the Menem government. According to Cavallo, the justice system that Menem had created not only put at risk the country's economic security by scaring away investors, but also meant that "the rights of the innocent, of the honest, and of the average citizen are not guaranteed by the Argentine judiciary."[37]

From the center-left Alliance coalition, forged between the Radical Party and FREPASO, came increasingly strident demands to remove the justices on the Supreme Court. In 1996 Radicals in the Chamber of Deputies published a book, *Juicio a la Corte* (Impeach the Supreme Court) (Baglini and D'Ambrosio 1993), in which they chronicled over approximately two hundred pages the abuses committed by the Court. Among the charges made in the report, the authors included evidence on the suspect procedures used by the Peronists in the Senate to approve the court-packing plan, the political ties of the members to the executive branch, and the specific decisions made by the Court. As the authors of the report themselves stated, "we do not consider the current justices guilty of misconduct in one, two, or even ten cases; we consider them worthy of impeachment for their total submission [in all cases] to the politicians in power" (ibid.: 36–7).

[34] *Clarín*, July 11, 1997.
[35] *Buenos Aires Herald*, August 14, 1997.
[36] *Clarín*, July 11, 30, 31, August 24, 26, September 30, and October 1, 1997; *Página/12*, July 30, 1997.
[37] *Clarín*, August 24, 1997.

4.5 Judges under the Second Menem Government

During the 1999 election campaign, both the Alliance and the anti-Menem Peronist presidential candidate for 1999, Eduardo Duhalde, came out with nearly identical proposals for changing the Court. According to Duhalde, who had a deep antipathy for Menem, if he were to win the presidency in 1999, he would convoke a constitutional assembly to suspend the constitutional clause prohibiting the justices' removal, declare Menem's justices "*en comisión*" (suspended), and use the Consejo de la Magistratura to select new justices.[38] The Alliance echoed this proposal, asserting that "we would not have put the denunciation of the judiciary at the center of our political discourse if we intended to afterwards continue with the same judges."[39]

In the months following the midterm elections, the opposition continued to make judicial reform a central component of its campaign platform. In an interview conducted less than twenty-four hours after the election with one of the opposition's highest profile candidates, Graciela Meijide Fernández, the topic of the judiciary was at the forefront of the discussion. In her words, "The most scandalous example of institutions is the Supreme Court and the paradigm example is Justice Vázquez, whose main qualification for being appointed to the Court was his friendship with Menem."[40]

During the 1997 midterm elections there emerged considerable speculation over whether Menem would run again for office, but by most accounts Menem's "re-re-election" was never a real possibility (Levitsky 2000). By 1998 Menem had officially conceded defeat and the race narrowed between the Peronist governor of Buenos Aires, Eduardo Duhalde, and the Alliance candidate, Fernando de la Rua. With Menem out of the race, the future looked grim for the Court.

Yet as the presidential campaign progressed it became increasingly clear that the implications for the Court were different depending on which candidate won. As one official close to the Court said, "everyone knows that with de la Rua the [process of dealing with the Court] is going to be more institutional. But with Duhalde everyone is panicked."[41] One reason why the justices feared Duhalde more than the Alliance is that a key part of the Alliance Party's platform itself was to strengthen democratic institutions. As FREPASO leader Chacho Alvarez put it, "if we win in 1999, none of

---

[38] *La Nación*, September 25, 1997.
[39] Ibid.
[40] *Clarín*, October 28, 1997.
[41] *La Nación*, May 15, 1999.

the new members of the administration will be heard making telephone calls to the justices."[42] Given their "pro-institutional" campaign, the Alliance would be hard-pressed simply to dismiss the judges without at least following the impeachment procedures laid out in the Constitution. Given that they would almost certainly not have the requisite two-thirds' majority needed to impeach the justices, even if the Alliance won in October, the threat to get rid of the judges was not entirely credible.

By contrast, Duhalde seemed to be under considerably fewer constraints. Unlike the Alliance, he differentiated himself from Menem not on the basis of respect for democratic institutions but on the basis of Menem's economic policy. Thus, at least early in the campaign, the main incentives the Court faced were not to switch political party loyalties completely, but rather to try to walk a fine line between appeasing Duhalde's faction of the party and making sure that the Alliance would not have an easy time of repeating the strategies of earlier governments.

4.6 Conclusion: An Analytic Narrative of Institutional Insecurity

The present chapter has drawn on a range of historical evidence to portray judges' beliefs and expectations both about their own likely fates and about the fate of the government by which they were appointed. To set the stage for evaluating whether the justices' evolving institutional insecurity led them to engage in strategic defection against the outgoing government, this section concludes with an analytic narrative (e.g., see Bates et al. 1998) that summarizes the various components of the strategic setting judges faced. In line with the various hypotheses laid out in the previous chapter, I structure the narrative by focusing on the following elements of the threat: (1) timing, (2) issues and information, (3) capacity and constraints, and (4) target and motivation.

Timing

Strategic defection depends first and foremost on judges' expectations about the likelihood of facing sanctions at the hands of an incoming government. Testing strategic defection thus requires developing a clear understanding of when such expectations emerged. Taken together, the evidence shows that in all four governments under examination the political opposition

---

[42] *Clarín*, October 15, 1997.

leveled threats against the Court throughout the judges' tenure. But in only three of these periods did the threat of being sanctioned by an incoming government ultimately emerge as a real possibility. Calls for carrying out sanctions against the justices became increasingly credible during the last two years of the military regime (1981–3), during the final two years of both the Alfonsín government (1987–9), and the second Menem administration (1997–9). By contrast, the increasing strength of the first Menem government throughout its first term (1989–95) meant that the opposition's threats leveled against Menem's own appointees never got off the ground. Clearly, in none of the periods did judges know with certainty what would happen. Instead, the story suggests that judges' probability assessments about who would win were changing over time as the judges witnessed unfolding political events.

Issues and Information

In addition to judges' believing that the opposition is likely to come to power, the logic of strategic defection depends on judges having sufficient information about the opposition's preferences. Under the military, this was not a problem. The main issue clearly was human rights, regardless of which opposition candidate won. As the transition gathered steam, the judges knew that their reputations would depend fundamentally on whether they could plausibly claim that they had done what they could to protect human rights under severe constraints imposed by the dictatorship.

By contrast, under the outgoing democratic government of Raúl Alfonsín there was probably no single dividing issue on which the future of the justices would be determined. By the late 1980s, the Peronists looked quite similar to the Radicals on some issues, including the key question of limiting human rights. Still, with Cafiero's loss in the primaries in 1988 and Menem's apparent return to orthodox Peronism in the last year of the campaign, there were plenty of issues dividing the two parties. Thus, in this sense, the justices did face incentives to defect strategically once Alfonsín's government began to collapse and Menem emerged as the front-runner.

In the most recent transition from the outgoing Menem administration to the Alliance opposition there was also a mix of preference convergence and divergence among the various parties. The Alliance shared the outgoing government's commitment to continue with Menem's economic policies; Duhalde did not. On the other hand, the Alliance was much more concerned to promote civil and political liberties than either the outgoing government or Duhalde. For example, during the campaign, the Alliance strongly opposed Menem's modus operandi of playing fast and loose with the constitutional limits on his power, on issues such as executive Need and Urgency Decrees and term limits.

Capacity and Constraints

Strategic defection depends on judges believing that the capacity of the incoming government to carry out sanctions is neither wholly unlimited nor entirely restricted. At the end of the military regime, the judges' views of the capacity of the democratic opposition to dictate the terms of the transition were obviously in flux. Despite the past precedent of automatic removal associated with regime change, up until the Falkland-Malvinas War, the justices could have reasonably expected that the military would have some say in the future government. Only in the final months of the regime did it become clear just how limited an influence the military would have. Even then, however, some respected voices outside the regime continued to call for secure tenure. Moreover, insofar as judges cared about their reputations, there were incentives to engage in strategic defection, regardless of how much influence the military could be expected to retain.

At the end of the Alfonsín government, there was simply no recent precedent for how the Court would be handled. It was out of the question that the incoming government would unilaterally remove the Court. Moreover, with a change from one elected government to another, the Radicals could expect to retain at least some influence in Congress, thus limiting somewhat the range of options available to the Peronists for re-making the Court. For example, the new government was far more likely to get the congressional majority needed for passing a court-packing plan than to get a two-thirds' majority that would have been required to impeach justices. Yet at the same time, the likelihood that the Peronist opposition would gain control over both branches of government clearly enhanced the threat to the justices. Thus, to the extent that the judges had sufficient information about the incoming government's preferences, there would have been reason for them to believe that appealing to the Peronists was a reasonable strategy.

The threat posed by the prospect of an Alliance victory in 1999 was mitigated by the fact that the Senate would still be controlled by the Peronists. Thus, the justices could expect that even if the Alliance captured the presidency, the new president would have a relatively difficult time carrying out impeachments, not to mention selecting new justices. At the same time, however, nearly all of the political parties, including many of the Peronists, had come out strongly in favor of getting rid of the Court. Moreover, there was a huge public demand for cleaning up the judiciary, starting with Supreme Court, particularly in issues that united the various parties against the outgoing government. This, then, meant that the Court could not afford to offer its unqualified support for Menem once he began to lose power.

Target and Motivation

A final set of assumptions underlying strategic defection is that justices under threat are indeed concerned about mitigating sanctions. And, more pointedly, judges under threat believe that strategic defection is the best way to go about improving their fates. Of the three periods in which judges faced a threat from the opposition, the military probably represents the most clear-cut case. First, given the justices' participation in the judicial reform project and their long careers within the federal judiciary, it seems safe to infer that the judges appointed by the military cared about keeping their posts. Second, the fact that the chief justice himself later wrote a 400-page response to the CONADEP report suggests that the judges, particularly those who had served the longest on the Court, also cared strongly about maintaining their reputations. That the support of the professional community also appeared contingent on the judges being able to make the argument that they had done what they could to protect human rights meant that the judges who had served the longest faced particularly strong incentives to defect from the military in this area.

As we move to the Alfonsín era, the story of motivations underlying strategic defection becomes more complicated. First, up until the last few months of the Radical administration, the primary threat that the judges faced was institutional, not individual. Court packing did threaten to reduce the legitimacy of the institution, but individual justices were likely to be affected only insofar as their influence on policy would be reduced. More importantly, in contrast to the military period, the judges could have reasonably feared that neither the Court's institutional reputation nor that of the individual justices would be automatically enhanced by strategic defection. To the extent that members of the professional community or the public valued the Court's relative independence, the judges might well have imagined that defection would produce the opposite effect. Still, to the extent that the judges wanted to maintain their influence on the bench, the risk of not defecting was appearing too loyal to Alfonsín in the eyes of the

Table 4.3 *Institutional Insecurity on the Argentine Supreme Court, 1976–1999*

	Military Court (1976–83)	Alfonsín Court (1984–9)	Menem (1) Court (1989–95)	Menem (2) Court (1995–9)
Emergence of threat	Yes, 1981–3	Yes, 1987–9	No	Yes, 1997–9
Key issues/Incumbents vs. opposition	Divergence over human rights abuses	Divergence over social and economic issues; convergence over human rights trials	Divergence over economic privitizations, presidential power	Mixed divergence over economic privitizations, presidential power
Capacity	Medium to high. Grew as military lost control of the transition	High. Threat of unified incoming Peronist government	Low. Unified Peronist government remaining in power	Medium. Threat of coalition-party Executive/Peronist Congress
Motivations/target	High. Removal and loss of reputation, particularly among longest serving members	Mixed. Court packing, individual removals	Low. Impeachment threats, but not credible	Medium to high. Impeachment threats in varying degrees from all opposition candidates

incoming administration, which clearly wanted a Court that would approve its policies. Thus, it is fair to say that judges during this period faced far more of a trade-off in deciding whether to defect. And as Chapter 6 discusses more fully, it appears that not all judges viewed the trade-off in the same way. Although here it is especially tricky separating motives from behavior, we know that some judges, such as Fayt, Belluscio, and Petracchi, appeared willing to stay on the bench at all costs. By contrast, others, such as Bacqué, resigned the very day after the court-packing law was passed.

Turning to the two Menem governments, a less noble set of motivations seems to have been at play. Under Menem's first government, two judges close to Menem were forced to resign as part of the Pacto de Olivos, but neither would have had any incentive to temper his support for Menem. In exchange for resigning from the bench, for example, Justice Barra was promoted to minister of justice. By the end of Menem's second term, however, all of the judges faced multiple charges of impeachment. Although the most compromised judges were clearly the so-called automatic majority, none of the judges wanted to be subjected to the public humiliation of a trial. From the judges' perspective, staying on the bench under a new government was important for a number of reasons. For some, the bench was an obvious opportunity for corruption. For others, such as Boggiano, who was interested in being appointed to the Hague, it was a stepping-stone. For others, such as Nazareno and Moliné O'Connor, keeping their posts under a new but relatively constrained government allowed them an unprecedented amount of power. From Menem's own perspective, the up side of defection against him was that he could retain an enclave of influence in the future. As I describe in Chapter 6, this later proved especially important for Menem given the corruption charges that he and his administration faced.

As Table 4.3 summarizes, despite constitutional provisions guaranteeing secure life tenure, Argentina's Supreme Court has experienced profound institutional insecurity under three out of four recent governments. In each case, the main source of the threat was the incoming opposition, not the incumbent government. Although the specific issues, amount of information, and motivations of the judges varied across these periods, the majority of judges had both the capacity and the incentives to engage in strategic defection once the incumbent government began to lose power. Having laid out the main dimensions of the insecurity judges faced, we are now in a position to begin to assess how justices responded. This is the task taken up in the next two chapters.

5

The Reverse Legal-Political Cycle

AN ANALYSIS OF DECISION
MAKING ON THE ARGENTINE
SUPREME COURT

Having established empirically the validity of several core assumptions underlying the theory strategic defection, the aim of this chapter and the following is to analyze judicial behavior in Argentina. The next step in evaluating the main propositions of the model depends on examining whether the willingness of judges to support their current government changes in response to judges' evolving beliefs and expectations about the threat they faced. In other words, did judges' behavior change as their information about the political environment changed? Did judges who grew less confident in the ability of the current government to insulate them continue to support the current government? Did they suddenly turn against it? Or did they attempt to shy away from deciding cases altogether?

Beginning with a brief overview of the data and methodology, this chapter provides a systematic quantitative analysis of judicial decision making in Argentina. Specifically, I use original individual-level data on the Argentine Supreme Court to assess whether patterns in judicial decision making adhere to the reverse legal political cycle predicted by the theory of strategic defection. Next, the chapter considers the effects of institutional insecurity and uncertainty on judges' participation. In addition, the data are used to explore the proposition that the target and level of threat judges face affect their willingness to act strategically. Finally, I consider several competing hypotheses regarding changes in the court's composition, legality, and the mix of issues being decided by the Court.

5.1 Data and Methodology

To begin to evaluate empirically the several hypotheses generated from the theory of strategic defection, I compare the behavior of justices under periods of relative institutional security to their behavior under periods of relative insecurity. Inferences about strategic defection are thus based not simply on the total percentage of anti-government decisions, which may be affected by any number of factors, but on whether the willingness of judges to rule against the government *changes* relative to changes in their political environment (Helmke 2002). This chapter analyzes original data on individual Argentine Supreme Court Justices' decisions and participation between 1976 and 2000, contained in the Argentine Supreme Court Decisions Database (ASCD; see Appendix B). These data include over 11,000 individual judicial decisions for all cases involving either the government as a party or a presidential decree involving the government in power when the decision was made.[1] Each decision is coded dichotomously, according to whether the judge voted in favor or against the government.[2]

According to the theory of strategic defection, changes in judges' behavior depend on changes in judges' beliefs and expectations about the threats they face. To model this dynamic process, I generate a series of dichotomous timing variables that serve as proxy variables for judges' expectations.[3] Based on the previous chapter's narrative, the earliest points at which such changes could be expected to occur under each of the four governments were the following: Under the military, the earliest plausible beginning for the transitional period would have been two years prior to the collapse of the government. Under each of the three democratic governments, the midterm legislative elections serve as the earliest cutoff points for establishing the transition. Starting with each of the two-year periods, I then adjust the cutoff points at eighteen, twelve, six, and three months to examine the effects of change on judicial behavior under different relative amounts of certainty and information. These cutoff points yield a series of independent

---

[1] The total number of observations included in the data set is 11,423, with 2,346 individual decisions under the military, 2,240 individual decisions under Alfonsín, 2,731 individual decisions under Menem's first government, 3,438 individual decisions under Menem's second government, and the remaining 668 decisions under the first year of Fernando De la Rua's government.

[2] Decisions decided against the state on the merits that make important concessions to the government are coded as "partially against." Decisions decided in favor of the state that make important concessions to the other litigants are coded as "partially for." Because less than 1 percent of the cases contain partial decisions, here I recoded the "partially against" as "against," and the "partially for" as "for."

[3] The theoretical justification for treating timing variables as dichotomous is that it is not the elapsing of time per se that increases the probability of anti-governmental decisions but, rather, the judges' perceptions that the government will lose power. Dummy variables model the changes in judges' perceptions as discontinuous.

transition variables – *final 24 months, final 18 months, final 12 months, final 6 months, final 3 months* – which allow me to assess patterns in individual decision making and participation over time as judges' perceptions and their information shift in accordance with changes in the political environment.[4]

5.2 Timing

The core timing hypothesis predicts that judges who lack institutional security will increasingly decide cases against the incumbent government in anticipation that it is likely to lose power. The second related hypothesis is that judges under threat may increase their support for the government when they expect that the incumbents will retain power. Given the evidence presented in the previous chapter regarding the growing weakness of the military, Alfonsín, and second Menem governments, the specific prediction is that judges during each of these three periods should increase their willingness to decide cases against the government starting in the final two years of each government. By contrast, the relative strength of the first Menem administration suggests that the justices lacked similar incentives to defect at the end of Menem's first term. Thus, evidence would be consistent with both timing hypotheses if anti-government decisions increased at the end of the first two governments and the fourth government but decreased at the end of the third government.

Figure 5.1, showing trends in anti-government decisions by year across each of the four governments, clearly fits with reverse legal-political cycle patterns predicted by the timing hypotheses. Under the military regime in the years through 1980, judges ruled against the government on average in 36 percent of cases. But in the final two years of the dictatorship, once it became likely that a transition would occur, judges increased their percentage of anti-government rulings considerably, to almost half of all decisions going against the government. Likewise, under the Alfonsín government, anti-government rulings also began at a relatively low level of approximately 37 percent and then rose by approximately 10 percentage points

---

[4] For each dummy variable I assign a value of 1 to all decisions falling within the periods of the transitions (see Appendix B). All other decisions take a value of 0. Given that each of the dependent variables used for coding judges' decisions and participation is dichotomous, logit is the appropriate estimation technique. To account for individual-specific effects, each model includes dummy variables for each judge on the Court at the time the decision was handed down.

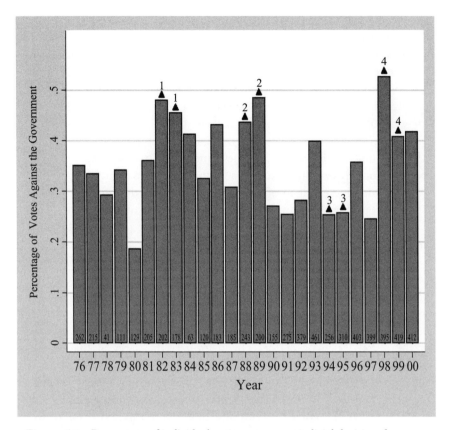

Figure 5.1 Percentage of individual anti-government judicial decisions by year.

as the government became increasingly weak. Similarly, under the second Menem government, there is a dramatic increase in anti-governmental decisions at the end of Menem's last term. On average, decisions against the government rose from around 30 percent of decisions going against the government in the first two years of Menem's second term to nearly half of all decisions in the final two years.

Note further that in two of the three transitional periods, anti-governmental decisions spike relatively early in the pre-transitional period. For example, under the military, anti-governmental decisions peak at 48 percent in 1982, and under Menem's last administration, the peak at 52 percent occurs in 1998. This trend underscores the intuition that insofar as defection serves as a signaling device to incoming governments, judges stand to benefit the most by switching sides as early as possible, provided they have sufficient information about the likely next government.

By contrast, during the first Menem government (1989–95), when the justices did not face a credible threat, there was no increase in anti-government decisions. Instead, consistent with the second hypothesis, the patterns in the individual-level data show that as Menem became increasingly popular and as it became more likely that he would stand for a second term, the percentage of anti-government decisions declined. Under Menem's first administration, the percentage of anti-government rulings began at roughly the same level as under the early years of the two previous governments, increased to 40 percent in 1993, but then fell to roughly 25 percent during the last two years of Menem's first administration. This was a period of notable success of Menem's economic policies and the increasing likelihood of Menem's bid for re-election.

Beginning with the military period, the logit results overwhelmingly confirm the initial trends supporting the timing hypotheses (see Table 5.1). Consistent with the prediction that judges increasingly decide cases against weak governments, every transitional coefficient for the military period is negative in the expected direction and most are statistically significant at the $p < .05$ level or better. The marginal effects reveal that in the final twenty-four months, eighteen months, and twelve months prior to the regime transition, the likelihood of the justices voting against the government increased by 20, 21, and 7 percentage points, respectively. The coefficients for the last six-month and three-month period prior to the regime transition are also negative, but fall short of statistical significance. This, however, is undoubtedly an artifact of lumping the previous transitional period effects into the pre-transitional period. Indeed, as the last coefficient (-0.61) shows, when the last three months are isolated and compared directly with the pre-transition period, the effects are negative and once again statistically significant. Compared with the first five years of the dictatorship, justices in the final three months of the transitional period were more likely to vote against the government by 15 percentage points.

Moving to the democratic government of Raul Alfonsín yields similarly impressive results. All of the coefficients are in the expected direction and, with the single exception of the six-month transition variable (-0.39), all are statistically significant. Indeed, even without excluding the interim period, justices in the final three months of the Alfonsín regime were significantly more likely to rule against the government than they had been more than

5.2 Timing

Table 5.1 *Individual Supreme Court Justices' Anti-government Votes by Time to Transition*

	Final 24 months	Final 18 months	Final 12 months	Final 6 months	Final 3 months	Final 3 vs. pre-24 months
Military government, 1976–83						
Constant	0.51*	0.49*	0.49*	0.49*	0.49*	0.49*
	(0.24)	(0.24)	(0.24)	(0.24)	(0.24)	(0.24)
Transition	−0.81***	−0.85***	−0.38*	−0.11	−0.29	−0.61*
	(0.15)	(0.15)	(0.17)	(0.22)	(0.26)	(0.27)
Number of observations	1339	1318	1318	1318	1318	1037
Chi-square	.001	.001	.3986	.7690	.6853	.4320
Alfonsín government, 1983–9						
Constant	0.90***	0.75**	0.71**	0.63**	0.63**	0.59*
	(0.22)	(0.22)	(0.22)	(0.22)	(0.22)	(0.28)
Transition	−0.39**	−0.30*	−0.40*	−0.39	−0.59*	−0.62*
	(0.13)	(0.15)	(0.16)	(0.23)	(0.26)	(0.27)
Number of observations	989	837	837	837	837	552
Chi-square	.014	.170	.141	.379	0.207	.311
First Menem government, 1989–95						
Constant	0.45***	0.44***	0.40***	0.44***	0.46***	0.42***
	(0.09)	(0.09)	(0.08)	(0.08)	(0.08)	(0.09)
Transition	0.09	0.10	0.48**	0.49*	0.13	0.28
	(0.13)	(0.13)	(0.17)	(0.23)	(0.24)	(0.26)
Number of observations	1640	1613	1640	1640	1640	1272
Chi-square	.001	.001	.001	.001	.001	.001
Second Menem government, 1995–9						
Constant	0.41**	0.31*	0.21	0.15	0.10	0.48
	(0.16)	(0.16)	(0.16)	(0.16)	(0.15)	(0.20)**
Transition	−0.74***	−0.66***	−0.43***	−0.36**	0.06	−0.34
	(0.10)	(0.10)	(0.11)	(0.14)	(0.17)	(0.18)
Number of observations	1807	1807	1807	1807	1807	1023
Chi-square	.001	.001	.001	.001	.013	.103

* $p \leq .05$.

** $p \leq .01$.

*** $p \leq .001$, two-tailed test.

Note: The unit of analysis is a justice's vote in a (full opinion) decision, coded 0 = against the government, 1 = for the government. Transition is measured as described in column headings. Cell entries are logistic regression coefficients. Dummy variables for each justice are included in each model, but the results are not presented here. Standard errors are in parentheses.

three months before the transition. The willingness of judges to rule against the government increased by approximately 9 percentage points for each cut point, growing to 15 percentage points in the final three months prior to the 1989 presidential election compared with the period prior to the 1987 midterm elections.

Shifting to the decision-making pattern among judges under the two governments of Carlos Menem, the results further accord with the expectations provided by the theory of strategic defection. In particular, the strength of Menem during his first administration provides both a null case for defection and an initial test case for strategic support. As expected, none of the coefficients is negative, confirming the expectation that anti-government decisions would not increase at the end of Menem's highly successful first government. In the midst of Menem's successful run for re-election, the coefficients (0.48) and (0.49) for the final year and final six months before the end of this first term show that justices were significantly *more* likely to support the government in its last year prior to Menem's re-election. The marginal effect of the last year on the justices' behavior was to increase by 11 percentage points the justices' willingness to hand down a favorable governmental decision. Although teasing out the differences between strategic and sincere behavior on the full court for this period is difficult, the fact that the justices under Menem increased their pro-governmental decisions in the final year before his re-election fits well within the long-standing suspicion that insecure tenure amplifies the willingness of judges to curry favor with the government, but only when governments themselves are seen as likely to remain in power.

As predicted, under the second Menem government the reverse legal political cycle re-emerges. The probability of handing down an anti-government decision increased dramatically among all justices in the last two years of Menem's second government by 17 percentage points in the last two years and 8 percentage points in the final six months.[5] Overall, then, for each of the four governments examined, the systematic evidence on changes in patterns of judicial behavior overwhelmingly supports both the core timing hypothesis of strategic defection and its converse, strategic support.

---

[5] That the coefficient for the final three months did not achieve statistical significance could indicate that the judges were changing their behavior in response to a slightly reduced threat as the campaign of the Court's most vociferous critic, Eduardo Duhalde, ran into trouble.

5.3 Importance

I now turn to the second set of hypotheses, which predicts that when judges defect, they will do so in the most important cases. All of the decisions analyzed in the chapter are based on full opinion cases.[6] Thus, the data already deal with a subset of cases considered sufficiently relevant by the justices to warrant a full opinion. To provide additional measures of case importance, I constructed four dummy variables. The first variable, *Decree*, provides a rough measure of importance based on political rather than legal criteria. Because these cases involve only decrees passed by the sitting government, this measure distinguishes decisions that deal with timely political issues from those decisions involving the government as a litigant that, as result of case backlog, may be less important by the time the cases reach the Supreme Court. The second variable, *Salient Decree*, takes account of the fact that not all decrees passed are necessarily of equal importance (Ferreira Rubio and Goretti 1998). To deal with this concern, I selected a subset of the decree cases that dealt with issues considered to be especially relevant under each of the three governments, including cases involving issues of constitutional interpretation, *amparo* cases,[7] and habeas corpus cases. To address the further concern that the government may not care equally about winning all cases, I constructed *Appeal* as a dichotomous variable that distinguishes cases in which the government lost in the lower court and filed an appeal to bring the case to the Supreme Court. Finally, to measure the judges' level of effort as an indicator of importance, the fourth variable, *Overturn*, distinguishes cases where the judge had to overturn a favorable decision handed down by a lower court in order to rule against the government from decisions where it upheld a negative decision.

Table 5.2 provides descriptive statistics for these various subsets of cases. Among decisions involving decrees and in the subset of salient decree decisions, the descriptive data show large increases in anti-government decisions clustered at the end of the first, second, and fourth transition periods. In

---

[6] The ASCD data set includes both full opinion cases and summary cases in which the government is named as a party or an executive decree is named in a case. In contrast to summary cases, full opinion cases are signed by the individual justices. According to legal experts, all legally and politically salient cases are decided by the court as full opinion cases (interview with an anonymous law clerk, Buenos Aires, April 1998).

[7] The *recurso de amparo* accelerates judicial review to remedy a government's abuse of constitutional guarantees (Rogers and Wright-Carozza 1995: 168).

Table 5.2 *Number and Percentage of Individual Anti-government Judicial Decisions by Year in Decree Cases, in Salient Decree Cases, in Government Appeals Cases, and in Cases Overturning Second-Instance Court*

Year	% against decree	% against salient decree	% against government appeal	% against overturning second instance
1976	– (N = 0)	– (N = 0)	53 (N = 87)	26 (N = 175)
1977	0 (N = 13)	0 (N = 13)	46 (N = 79)	18 (N = 103)
1978	0 (N = 3)	0 (N = 3)	100 (N = 4)	22 (N = 37)
1979	19 (N = 21)	19 (N = 21)	68 (N = 37)	21 (N = 62)
1980	17 (N = 24)	17 (N = 24)	37 (N = 41)	11 (N = 85)
1981	24 (N = 38)	24 (N = 38)	50 (N = 103)	25 (N = 92)
1982*	48 (N = 100)	45 (N = 95)	64 (N = 86)	33 (N = 101)
1983*	51 (N = 75)	48 (N = 71)	66 (N = 82)	29 (N = 93)
1984	13 (N = 32)	13 (N = 32)	74 (N = 19)	27 (N = 44)
1985	17 (N = 29)	21 (N = 24)	55 (N = 40)	12 (N = 50)
1986	58 (N = 47)	64 (N = 42)	57 (N = 75)	32 (N = 77)
1987	25 (N = 103)	27 (N = 98)	53 (N = 49)	29 (N = 93)
1988*	35 (N = 102)	40 (N = 92)	43 (N = 63)	48 (N = 105)
1989*	67 (N = 51)	67 (N = 46)	58 (N = 77)	43 (N = 106)
1990	19 (N = 63)	21 (N = 57)	36 (N = 44)	7 (N = 56)
1991	14 (N = 37)	14 (N = 28)	27 (N = 113)	25 (N = 111)
1992	40 (N = 101)	41 (N = 92)	27 (N = 151)	22 (N = 126)
1993	37 (N = 248)	36 (N = 237)	53 (N = 186)	30 (N = 152)
1994*	30 (N = 178)	30 (N = 178)	26 (N = 70)	22 (N = 101)
1995*	25 (N = 185)	25 (N = 166)	42 (N = 98)	18 (N = 119)
1996	38 (N = 220)	39 (N = 152)	32 (N = 253)	42 (N = 113)
1997	21 (N = 257)	21 (N = 216)	32 (N = 203)	17 (N = 130)
1998*	52 (N = 306)	51 (N = 207)	56 (N = 207)	63 (N = 118)
1999*	37 (N = 239)	44 (N = 172)	48 (N = 226)	36 (N = 146)
2000	33 (N = 61)	33 (N = 61)	57 (N = 220)	27 (N = 137)
TOTAL	35 (N = 2533)	35 (N = 2165))	46 (N = 2613)	29 (N = 2532)

* Indicates a transitional period.

each of the first two groups, the overall number of decisions increased as the cases involving decrees passed by the executive reached the Court, and quite dramatically, so did the percentage of anti-government decisions, as shown by the jump from 24 percent in 1981 to 48 and 51 percent in 1982 and 1983, respectively. A similar trend occurred at the end of the Alfonsín government, with the sole exception of 1986, when anti-government decisions peaked. The evidence of defection is also strong for Menem's second government, with anti-government decree cases rising from an average of 30 percent in the first two years of his second term up to an average of 44 percent in his last two years, and salient decree decisions increasing from an average of 30 to 48 percent across the same period. Further in line with the theory of strategic defection is that anti-government decisions among both groups of decree cases did not exhibit a similar pattern under Menem's first government.

The findings from the three additional categories are, admittedly, somewhat more mixed. In cases where the government clearly had an interest in appealing a negative lower court decision, the percentage of anti-government decisions increased only modestly in the first transition and actually declined to its lowest level in 1988. However, under Menem's second government I did find a substantial increase from an average of 32 percent in 1996 and 1997, up to 56 and 48 in 1998 and 1999, respectively.

The last subset of decisions in which the justices had to overturn a pro-government decision does a better job of supporting the theory of strategic defection, particularly for the Alfonsín and second Menem governments. Under Alfonsín, the percentage of anti-government decisions increased dramatically from an average of 25 percent in the first four years to 45 percent in the government's final two years, and under Menem's second term, the anti-government decisions increased from an average of 30 percent during the first two years to an average of 50 percent in the final two years. Note, however, that as in the full sample, the peaks in defection among important cases tend to occur in the year prior to the actual transition.

Logistic regression models estimated for each subset of cases under the military, Alfonsín, and second Menem government (see Table 5.3) confirm these overall patterns, indicating strategic defection in the most important cases. All of the coefficients of the final twenty-four months for the first transition are negative and significant at the .01 level or better. The likelihood of anti-government decisions increased by 56 percentage points among decree cases, by 55 percentage points among the salient decree cases, by 23 percentage points among government appeals cases, and by 16 percentage points among cases overturning a favorable lower court decision. Consistent with the overall patterns identified in Table 5.2 for the Alfonsín period, three of the four timing coefficients in Table 5.3 are also negative. For this period, the likelihood of handing down an anti-government decision in decree cases, salient decree cases, and cases where the decision

Table 5.3 *Individual Supreme Court Justices' Anti-government Votes by Time to Transition among Decree Cases, Salient Decree Cases, Government Appeals Cases, and in Cases Overturning Second-Instance Court (in a twenty-four-month period)*

	Decree	Salient decree	Government appeal	Overturn second instance
Military government, 1976–83				
Constant	1.10	1.39	0.24	0.85*
	(1.15)	(1.19)	(0.40)	(0.35)
Final 24 months	−2.52***	−2.46***	−0.93***	−0.67**
	(0.64)	(0.64)	(0.24)	(0.23)
Number of observations	176	172	515	748
Chi-square	.001	.001	.085	.059
Alfonsín government, 1983–9				
Constant	1.44	1.30	−0.20	1.51***
	(0.44)***	(0.45)***	(0.40)	(0.35)
Final 24 months	−0.63*	−0.63**	0.25	−0.86***
	(0.26)	(0.27)	(0.23)	(0.20)
Number of observations	263	248	323	470
Chi-square	.067	.130	.777	.001
Menem second government, 1995–9				
Constant	0.40	0.41	0.26	0.44
	(0.21)	(0.24)	(0.23)	(0.28)
Final 24 months	−0.70***	−0.78***	−0.72***	−1.05***
	(0.13)	(0.15)	(0.14)	(0.18)
Number of observations	1125	836	952	582
Chi-square	.001	.001	.001	.001

* $p \leq .05$.
** $p \leq .01$.
*** $p \leq .001$, two-tailed test.
Note: The unit of analysis is a justice's vote in a (full opinion) decision, coded 0 = against the government, 1 = for the government. Cell entries are logistic regression coefficients. Cell entries are logistic regression coefficients. Dummy variables for each justice are included in each model, but the results are not presented here. Standard errors are in parentheses.

of the lower court had favored the government increased by 12, 12, and 16 percentage points, respectively, during the final two years of the Alfonsín government. Finally, for the second Menem government each and every one of the coefficients supports the view that when judges defect, they do so in the most important cases.

5.4 Participation

Having analyzed patterns in individual judicial decisions, this section turns to examine how judges' expectations and beliefs about the threats they face shape their participation. Taken together, Chapters 2 and 3 suggested two possible alternatives for how judges might choose to react to uncertainty about the preferences of the future government. On the one hand, following a more conventional notion of courts under constraints, judges under threat can simply avoid deciding the case and instead follow a strategy of "wait and see" until they know which type of government is likely to come to power. According to this view, in between the time when the current government begins to lose power and a new government is elected, judges will deal with uncertainty by ducking. On the other hand, the signaling model presented in Chapter 3 argues that avoidance – even under uncertainty – is not necessarily the best way to go. Judges who stay on the sidelines may successfully avoid the suckers' payoff (e.g., judges defect, but lose their posts anyway if the current government retains power), but it also means that they potentially miss the opportunity to exploit the incoming government's uncertainty over the judges' own preferences. Assuming judges want to avoid sanctions, the signaling argument therefore implies that among those judges who are under threat, participation should not decrease and may instead increase.

To begin to adjudicate between these two views, the remainder of this section focuses on three distinct forms of participation: individual justices' abstentions, separate opinion writing, and the court's collective decision over whether to accept appeals.[8] Although each of these forms of participation begs further research, the initial results suggest greater support for the signaling approach and less support for the conventional view.

Abstention

Starting with abstention, the results offer, at best, mixed support for the idea that judges respond to uncertainty by limiting the number of decisions that

---

[8] Information is contained in the ASCD data set, which includes dummy variables for whether a judge participated in the case (*Abstain*), whether the judge issued a separate concurrence (*Concur*) or a separate dissent (*Dissent*), and whether the Court's majority decided to accept the litigants' appeal (*Appeal*). As in the previous section, the independent variables are a series of timing variables that serve as proxies for capturing systematically the judges' expectations about which government is likely to come to power. Similarly, I use logit to estimate the impact on judicial decisions and participation.

Table 5.4 *Individual Supreme Court Justices' Abstentions by Time to Transition*

	Final 24 months	Final 18 months	Final 12 months	Final 6 months	Final 3 months	Final 3 vs. pre-24 months
Military government, 1976–83						
Constant	−3.03***	−3.07***	−3.19***	−3.24***	−3.27***	−2.98***
	(0.24)	(0.24)	(0.24)	(0.24)	(0.24)	(0.24)
Transition	−0.45	0.06	0.70*	1.21***	1.61***	1.25***
	(0.34)	(0.34)	(0.34)	(0.34)	(0.35)	(0.35)
Number of observations	1271	1232	1232	1232	1232	926
Chi-square	.197	.327	.063	.003	.001	.001
Alfonsín government, 1983–9						
Constant	−0.55***	−0.59***	−0.52***	−0.51***	−0.50***	−0.55***
	(0.11)	(0.12)	(0.11)	(0.11)	(0.11)	(0.13)
Transition	0.19	0.23	0.05	−0.02	−0.18	−0.09
	(0.12)	(0.14)	(0.15)	(0.24)	(0.28)	(0.29)
Number of observations	2240	1930	1930	1930	1930	1340
Chi-square	.001	.001	.001	.001	.001	.001
First Menem government, 1989–95						
Constant	−1.25***	−1.26***	−1.25***	−1.27***	−1.27***	−1.21***
	(0.07)	(0.08)	(0.07)	(0.07)	(0.07)	(0.08)
Transition	0.02	0.08	−0.02	0.34*	0.34	0.30
	(0.12)	(0.12)	(0.14)	(0.17)	(0.19)	(0.21)
Number of observations	2731	2704	2731	2731	2731	2155
Chi-square	.052	.050	.052	.015	.015	.009
Second Menem government, 1995–9						
Constant	−0.52***	−0.57***	−0.60***	−0.60***	−0.61***	−0.58***
	(0.11)	(0.11)	(0.11)	(0.10)	(0.10)	(0.14)
Transition	−0.27**	−0.22*	−0.17	−0.28*	−0.44*	−0.59**
	(0.09)	(0.09)	(0.10)	(0.13)	(0.17)	(0.18)
Number of observations	3438	3438	3438	3438	3438	1890
Chi-square	.000	.000	.000	.000	.000	.000

* $p \leq .05$.

** $p \leq .01$.

*** $p \leq .001$, two-tailed test.

Note: The unit of analysis is a justice's participation (full opinion) decision, coded 0 = did sign the opinion (participated), 1 = did not sign the opinion (abstained). Transition is measured as described in column headings. Cell entries are logistic regression coefficients. Dummy variables for each justice are included in each model, but the results are not presented here. Standard errors are in parentheses.

they sign (see Table 5.4). Under the military, for example, abstention does increase significantly in the last year and a half prior to the transition. Given the discussion of the climate of uncertainty over which party would win, the results for this period would thus tend to support the ducking hypothesis.[9] Moving to the Alfonsín government and Menem's first government, however, none of the coefficients for abstention achieves significance.[10] Finally, in direct contrast to the ducking hypothesis, the results for the second Menem government show that justices were even *more* likely to participate in the final two years as the government begins losing power.

Appeal Acceptance

One possibility, of course, is that looking for ducking-related behavior once the Court has already agreed to decide the case is not an entirely fair test. Perhaps the relevant question is not whether an individual justice ultimately decides to participate in a decision (which may result from any number of factors), but whether or not the Court decides to accept the appeal. As scholars of U.S. judicial politics have long noted, the Court's decisions over how to fill its own docket provide ample opportunities to study strategic behavior (Perry 1991; Epstein and Knight 1998; Maltzman, Spriggs, and Wahlbeck 2000).

In the context of Argentina, one possibility is that judges engage in strategic ducking by rejecting appeals whenever they are under attack. Although never examined systematically, this has been the gist of arguments made by various Argentine legal experts, who point to the Court's use of the political questions doctrine as a way of avoiding controversy under the last dictatorship (Garro 1983; Larkins 1996). In contrast, the signaling view suggests that precisely because judges do face a threat, they will be reluctant to turn down the chance to decide cases.

---

[9] Re-estimating the models using the same subsets of important decisions as in Table 5.3, however, the effects virtually disappeared. Only the six-month variable achieved significance, and even this effect was entirely eliminated when I controlled for the changing mix of cases.

[10] In separate regression models, restricting the category to subsets of important decisions showed a significant increase among abstention only under Menem's first government, when Menem was strong and likely to remain in power. Among the four periods considered, this is arguably precisely when judges faced the least amount of uncertainty. After 1994, the justices knew that Menem was eligible to run and that he was enormously popular. Given that he had been in power since 1989, the justices also knew relatively well the government's preferences.

Table 5.5 *Supreme Court's Appeals Acceptances by Time to Transition*

	Final 24 months	Final 18 months	Final 12 months	Final 6 months	Final 3 months	Final 3 vs. pre-24 months
Military government, 1976–83						
Constant	1.14***	1.16***	1.26***	1.52***	1.48***	1.23***
	(0.17)	(0.17)	(0.14)	(0.14)	(0.13)	(0.18)
Transition	0.28	0.63**	0.73*	−0.42	−0.22	0.02
	(0.24)	(0.26)	(0.31)	(0.33)	(0.38)	(0.40)
Number of observations	435	411	411	411	411	218
Chi-square	.229	.013	.014	.211	.564	.963
Alfonsín government, 1983–9						
Constant	0.52***	0.41***	0.54***	0.72***	0.70***	0.43***
	(0.10)	(0.11)	(0.10)	(0.09)	(0.09)	(0.12)
Transition	0.70***	0.85***	0.55**	−0.16	0.15	0.41
	(0.18)	(0.19)	(0.20)	(0.29)	(0.32)	(0.33)
Number of observations	675	575	575	575	575	355
Chi-square	.000	.000	.005	.584	.630	.201
First Menem government, 1989–95						
Constant	0.78***	0.78***	0.70***	0.86***	0.83***	0.78***
	(0.09)	(0.09)	(0.08)	(0.07)	(0.07)	(0.09)
Transition	0.26	0.24	0.76***	0.34	0.78**	0.83**
	(0.14)	(0.14)	(0.17)	(0.23)	(0.27)	(0.27)
Number of observations	979	970	979	979	979	637
Chi-square	.064	.097	.000	.131	.002	.001
Second Menem government, 1995–9						
Constant	1.94***	1.98***	2.09***	2.04***	2.04***	
	(0.09)	(0.08)	(0.08)	(0.07)	(0.07)	
Transition	0.13	0.06	−0.30*	−0.25	−0.36	
	(0.13)	(0.14)	(0.14)	(0.18)	(0.22)	
Number of observations	2196	2196	2196	2196	2196	
Chi-square	.309	.672	.044	.164	.114	

* $p \leq .05$.
** $p \leq .01$.
*** $p \leq .001$, two-tailed test.
Note: The unit of analysis is the aggregate-level Court decision of whether to accept an appeal or not, coded 0 = not accept, 1 = accept. Transition is measured as described in column headings. Cell entries are logistic regression coefficients. Dummy variables for each justice are included in each model, but the results are not presented here. Standard errors are in parentheses.

Although further analysis at the individual level is needed, the preliminary results, shown in Table 5.5, suggest that, with the only exception occurring in the last twelve months of Menem's second government, there has been no decrease in the Court's willingness to accept appeals as a transition approaches across any of the four governmental periods. Rather, for several of the variables the sign is in the opposite direction and significant, indicating that the overall effect of insecurity is to increase the Court's willingness to accept appeals.

Separate Opinions

Finally, perhaps the most compelling test of strategic ducking versus strategic defection comes from examining the individual-level data on the justices' willingness to issue separate opinions. In an institutional context such as Argentina's, where judges are notoriously buried under enormous caseloads (which involve drafting decisions on as many as fifty cases per day),[11] writing a separate opinion is costly simply in terms of the sheer time involved. More important still is that by signing a separate opinion the justice is also reducing – if not sacrificing entirely – the possibility of relative anonymity that is ostensibly provided for authors of the majority opinions.[12] Given the forgoing discussion, separate opinion writing in Argentina should thus be anathema for judges who want to duck and a panacea for those who want to signal.

The most general question is thus what, if any, effects do changes in the political environment have on judges' willingness to write separate opinions? A more specific set of questions emerges over the interaction between the outcome of the majority opinion and judges' choices to issue a separate opinion. Although clearly there are limits to what we can conclude in the absence of a substantive understanding of the opinions (e.g., does a separate concurrence indicate a stronger or weaker position on an issue than the majority opinion?), certain patterns should be more consistent with the logic of strategic defection than others. For example, in terms of separate dissents, evidence weakly consistent with the logic of strategic defection would be if judges under threat did not increase their dissents from anti-government

---

[11] Interview with an anonymous law clerk in the Supreme Court, Buenos Aires, April 1998.

[12] In Argentina, the norm of signing majority opinions is to list justices by name alphabetically and according to seniority, rather than by the author of the opinion (Carrió 1996). As the following chapter documents, however, judges in recent Argentina routinely violate the norm of anonymity by "leaking" to the press who is writing the opinion for a given case.

Table 5.6 *Justices' Separate Dissents by Time to Transition*

	Anti-government dissent, 12 months	Pro-government dissent, 12 months
Military government, 1976–83		
Constant	−18.05***	−3.76***
	(1.04)	(1.01)
Transition	0.61	1.20***
	(0.33)	(0.33)
Number of observations	463	755
Chi-square	.006	.001
Alfonsín government, 1983–9		
Constant	0.03	−0.77**
	(0.37)	(0.28)
Transition	0.66**	0.93***
	(0.24)	(0.23)
Number of observations	332	505
Chi-square	.011	.001
First Menem government, 1989–95		
Constant	0.17	−0.63***
	(0.13)	(0.11)
Transition	0.39	−0.53**
	(0.30)	(0.19)
Number of observations	523	1117
Chi-square	.813	.023
Second Menem government, 1995–9		
Constant	0.43	−0.90***
	(0.23)	(0.23)
Transition	−0.52**	0.26
	(0.17)	(0.14)
Number of observations	665	1142
Chi-square	.007	.052

* $p \leq .05$.
** $p \leq .01$.
*** $p \leq .001$, two-tailed test.
Note: The unit of analysis is a justice's dissent in a full opinion case, coded 1 = did dissent, 0 = did not dissent. Transition timing is measured as described in column headings. Cell entries are logistic regression coefficients. Dummy variables for each justice are included in each model, but the results are not presented here. Standard errors are in parentheses.

decisions and did not decrease their likelihood of issuing a dissent with pro-governmental decisions. Stronger evidence in line with strategic defection would be if judges significantly reduced their willingness to dissent from anti-governmental decisions and significantly increased their willingness to dissent from pro-governmental decisions.

Overall, the results show that separate opinion writing increases when judges are under threat. In contrast to the ducking hypothesis, judges under the military and Alfonsín's government were significantly more likely to issue a dissenting opinion in the final year of each government (see Table 5.6). Moreover, several of the results are in line with both the weaker and stronger hypotheses related to the theory of strategic defection. With the exception of the Alfonsín government, there is no significant increase in dissents with anti-governmental decisions for the periods when the incumbents are likely to lose power. In accordance with what we would expect, there is a significant decrease in dissents from pro-governmental decisions only under the first Menem government. Most strikingly of all, under the last two years of the military there is a significant increase in dissents from pro-governmental decisions, while during the second Menem government, the likelihood of a justice dissenting from an anti-governmental decision decreased significantly. Thus, taken together, the initial evidence on participation is consistent with the idea that judges respond to increasing insecurity not by avoiding decisions but by using them to signal their compatibility with an incoming government.

5.5 Target of the Threat

According to the theory of strategic defection, judges behave strategically in order to attempt to influence the incoming government's decision over whether to impose sanctions. Thus far, I have tested empirically various implications of the theory by assuming that all judges serving under a particular government face the same sanctions. But this may not necessarily be the case. As we saw in the last chapter, for example, sometimes sanctions do get directed at the entire court, but sometimes some justices are clearly under more pressure than other judges. Under the military government, all of the justices sitting on the bench faced equally the threat of removal under a democratic government. However, given the timing of the Dirty War and the human rights abuses committed by the military, the longest serving judges faced the greatest risk in terms of their reputations.

Moving to the first Menem government, the three held-over justices appointed earlier by Alfonsín (Justices Belluscio, Fayt, Petracchi) arguably would have faced more pressure than Menem's own appointees to bring their decisions in line with the government as Menem gained strength and popularity during his first term. By contrast, compared with the held-over judges and Justice Bossert, who had been favored by the Radicals in the negotiations in 1994, the so-called automatic majority (Boggiano, Lopez, Moliné O'Connor, Justices Nazareno, and Vázquez) arguably faced the larger burden of having to convince the opposition that they were independent from Menem at the end of the 1990s.

Distinguishing the behavior of judges who are most at risk also helps to reduce ambiguities in drawing inferences about strategic versus sincere behavior that arise in testing strategic accounts in settings where information about judges' underlying preferences often hinges on the appointing president (cf. Iaryczower et al. 2002). As mentioned earlier, given the mixed composition of the Court under both Menem governments it is somewhat problematic to interpret all judges' behavior in the same way. That the behavior of Menem's own appointees at the end of 1994–5 is included in the forgoing analysis makes it relatively more difficult to know whether increased support was strategic or simply sincere. Likewise, including the justices' decisions not considered part of the "automatic majority" makes it harder to defend the inference that increased defection in 1998–9 was entirely strategic.

To improve the quality of our inferences, this section therefore replicates several of the previous tests by examining changes in behavior only among subsets of judges most at risk. Specifically, for the military period, I confine the analysis to the three longest serving judges who remained on the bench until the end of the transition (Justices Gabrielli (1976–83), Rossi (1976–83), and Guastavino (1980–3)). For the first and second Menem governments, I restrict the analysis to the three held-over judges and the five members of the "automatic majority," respectively. Bringing together the timing, importance, and participation hypotheses, Table 5.7 contains the results for each subset of justices.

Starting with the likelihood that anti-governmental votes will increase at the end of weak governments, the coefficients for both decree and salient decree cases are negative in the expected direction and significant among the subset of judges under the military. The coefficient for salient decree is negative and significant among the "automatic majority" at the end of Menem's second government. Similar to the results for the full court under

5.5 Target of the Threat

Table 5.7 *Subset of Individual Supreme Court Justices' Anti-government Decisions by Time to Transition among Decree Cases, Salient Decree Cases, Abstention, Pro-government and Anti-government Dissent (in a twenty-four-month period, among subsets of justices most targeted)*

	Decree	Salient decree	Abstention	Pro-government dissent	Anti-government dissent
Military government, 1976–83					
Constant	2.59***	1.77***	−3.03***	−3.57***	−2.68***
	(0.68)	(0.41)	(0.24)	(0.41)	(0.37)
Transition	−2.50***	−1.56***	−0.45	2.04***	1.87***
	(0.65)	(0.37)	(0.34)	(0.42)	(0.37)
Number of observations	126	175	1271	474	295
Chi-square	.000	.000	.196	.000	.000
First Menem government, 1989–95					
Constant	0.84**	0.18	−1.37***	−0.56**	0.21
	(0.33)	(0.28)	(0.14)	(0.20)	(0.25)
Transition	0.01	0.48	−0.08	−0.08	−0.14
	(0.33)	(0.29)	(0.18)	(0.25)	(0.32)
Number of observations	164	205	993	356	218
Chi-square	.761	.339	.005	.713	.651
Second Menem government, 1995–9					
Constant	0.73	1.34***	−1.23***	−0.47**	−0.28
	(0.62)	(0.25)	(0.14)	(0.18)	(0.30)
Transition	0.21	−0.67**	−0.18	0.47**	−0.63**
	(0.47)	(0.20)	(0.13)	(0.16)	(0.22)
Number of observations	96	490	1878	696	360
Chi-square	.810	.007	.000	.030	.017

* $p \le .05$.
** $p \le .01$.
*** $p \le .001$, two-tailed test.
Note: The unit of analysis for columns 1 and 2 is a justice's vote in a (full opinion) decision, coded 0 = against the government, 1 = for the government. The unit of analysis for column 3 is a justice's participation (full opinion) decision, coded 0 = did sign the opinion (participated), 1 = did not sign the opinion (abstained). The unit of analysis for columns 4 and 5 is a justice's dissent in a full opinion case, coded 1 = did dissent, 0 = did not dissent. Transition timing is measured as described in column headings. Cell entries are logistic regression coefficients. Dummy variables for each justice are included in each model, but the results are not presented here. Standard errors are in parentheses.

Menem's first government for the twenty-four-month period, among the subset of held-over judges the signs are positive though not significant.

Turning to the results on participation, none of coefficients for abstention shows that the judges most under threat for each of the three governments are ducking. Somewhat puzzling are the results for dissents with anti-governmental decisions. As stated above, we should expect judges under threat to reduce the number of dissents with anti-governmental decisions. Under the second Menem government, this is precisely what we see happening. But under the military government the results point in the other direction, with justices increasingly willing to dissent from anti-governmental cases.

More encouraging is that under both the military and the second Menem government, the likelihood that judges would issue a separate dissent with a pro-governmental decision rose significantly as the threat against judges increased. Also in line with what we would expect, however, there are no significant effects during the first Menem government (when increasing dissents with pro-governmental decisions would have been the wrong signal to send to Menem's increasingly powerful government). Note that the lack of a significant decline among dissents with pro-governmental decisions under Menem's first government suggests that the previous results may fit more with a sincere rather than strategic explanation for the decline in pro-government dissents during this period.

5.6 Rival Hypotheses: Composition, Legality, and the Mix of Cases

Finally, I turn to address three of the most obvious competing explanations for the observed increase in anti-governmental rulings in three out of the last four governments. The first alternative explanation is that changes in the composition of the Court during a government's term account for the observed increase in anti-governmental decisions. The second is that changes in judicial decisions are driven by changes in the legality of the cases coming before the government. A third related, but distinct, alternative explanation is that changes are driven by changes in the mix of issues coming before the court. Producing evidence against these alternative explanations does not prove the validity of the strategic defection argument. But it certainly adds to the plausibility of the interpretation that judges under threat engaged in strategic defection to minimize the sanctions they faced from future governments.

Composition

Because the composition of the Court remained stable during Alfonsín's government and Menem's second government, a compositional explanation for the observed increase in anti-governmental decisions is relevant only for the military period and the first Menem government. Between 1976 and 1983 there were no fewer than ten different compositions of the Supreme Court (Molinelli et al. 1999: 703). Of the twelve justices who sat on the bench during this period, only two remained during the entire military regime (Justices Gabrielli and Rossi) and only four sat on the bench during portions of both the pre-transitional and transitional periods (Black, Justices Gabrielli, Guastavino, and Rossi). For the first Menem period, Justices Bacqué and Oyanarte left the bench in 1990 and 1991, respectively. In 1993, Justices Barra and Cavagna Martinez left as part of the Pacto de Olivos. Thus, only seven out of nine justices (Belluscio, Boggiano, Fayt, Levene, Moliné O'Connor, Nazareno, and Petracchi) served on the bench during both the pre- and post-transitional periods.

To deal with the possibility that later appointees account for the observed changes in rulings against the government, I re-estimated several of the previous models to examine the impact of timing and case importance for the two subsets of justices who served during both periods for each of the two governments.

Similar to the findings for the full set of judges' decisions under the military, the coefficients for each subset of cases are statistically significant (see Table 5.8). Justices increased their anti-government decisions in the last two years of the military government by 41 percentage points in decree cases, by 39 percentage points in the salient decree cases, by 21 percentage points in government appeals cases, and by 11 percentage points in overturning cases. Although the marginal effects are slightly lower than they were in the full court models (Table 5.2), they suggest that the increase in anti-government decisions cannot be explained away by the changing composition of the Court at the end of the dictatorship. As expected, under Menem's first government, none of the results indicates that strategic defection is occurring.

Legality

A second alternative explanation is that the increase in anti-government decisions at the end of weak governments is driven by changes in the legality

Table 5.8 *Individual Supreme Court Justices' Anti-government Decisions by Time to Transition among Decree Cases, Salient Decree Cases, Government Appeals Cases, and in Cases Overturning Second-Instance Court (in a twenty-four-month period, with a stable court composition)*

	Decree	Salient decree	Government appeal	Overturn
Subset of four military-era justices, 1976–83				
Constant	2.34***	2.34***	0.05	1.36***
	(0.60)	(0.60)	(0.13)	(0.14)
24-month	−2.34***	−2.26***	−0.89***	−0.59**
transition	(−0.63)	(0.63)	(0.23)	(0.22)
Number of	148	144	354	480
observations				
Chi-square	.001	.001	.001	.008
Subset of six Menem-era justices, 1989–95				
Constant	0.52	0.15	0.12	1.16***
	(0.28)	(0.25)	(0.23)	(0.27)
24-month	−0.10	0.37	0.27	−0.34
transition	(0.24)	(0.21)	(0.26)	(0.24)
Number of	323	404	400	392
observations				
Chi-square	.567	.019	.146	.095

* $p \leq .05$.
** $p \leq .01$.
*** $p \leq .001$, two-tailed test.
Note: The unit of analysis is a justice's vote in a (full opinion) decision, coded 0 = against the government, 1 = for the government. Cell entries are logistic regression coefficients. Dummy variables for each justice are included in each model, but the results are not presented here. Standard errors are in parentheses.

of the types of cases coming before the court. Put simply, the concern is that if governments at the end of their terms acted less legally, then the increased rulings against the government may be due to changes in the cases themselves, not strategic defection.[13] Under the military, this alternative account is relatively easy to deal with. As the next chapter describes more fully, the military committed the most egregious human rights violations in the mid-1970s and cases began immediately coming to Court, thus it is highly unlikely that the cases being decided at the end of the military regime involved governmental actions that were less legal. By contrast, it is less straightforward ruling out ex ante the possibility that either

[13] I thank Greg Caldeira for making this suggestion.

Alfonsín or Menem acted less legally as their respective administrations lost power. In particular, the economic and political crises erupting in the final years of Alfonsín's government underlines the importance of this alternative explanation.

Although obviously there are no objective direct measures of legality, the ASCD data set allows us to begin to get at these questions indirectly by examining opinions at the lower levels of the federal judiciary. Although not uniformly so, under democracy the second-instance courts – particularly the administrative courts (*contensiosas administrativas*) – are widely considered to be more independent than the Supreme Court.[14] The decisions reached by these lower courts can thus serve as a rough proxy measure for the legality of the cases coming before the Supreme Court. In other words, if the rulings of the lower courts in the same groups of cases later decided at the Supreme Court remain constant over the same period of time, then the alternative explanation that the legality of the cases is changing appears less plausible.

To test this, I estimated four models for the Alfonsín and second Menem administrations. In Table 5.9, the first model in each pair uses the majority opinion of the second instance as the dependent variable; the second models in the pair treat as the dependent variable the individual-level votes among Supreme Court justices among the subset of cases in which the lower instance ruled. In contrast to the results at the level of the Supreme Court among the same group of cases, the results in Table 5.9 show that neither of the coefficients for the lower level courts' decisions is significant. Thus, to the extent that the lower court judges were relatively more insulated under both democratic governments, but did not increasingly decide cases against the government, the pattern of anti-governmental decisions observed at the level of the Supreme Court does not fit with the decreasing legality explanation.

Mix of Cases

A third alternative explanation posits that regardless of the legality of the government's actions, the mix of cases coming before the Court may have

---

[14] One possible reason for this is that given that most cases are accepted on appeal to the Supreme Court, executives have had fewer incentives to gain control over the second instance. This logic also fits with the Menem administration's support for the Court's adoption of the per saltum doctrine.

Table 5.9 *The Effects of Transitional Periods under Alfonsín and Menem's Second Government on Decisions in the Second Instance Compared with the Supreme Court*

	Second instance, Alfonsín	Supreme Court, Alfonsín	Second instance, Menem 2	Supreme Court, Menem 2
Constant	0.33***	0.78**	−0.61***	0.33
	(0.07)	(0.25)	(0.06)	(0.18)
24-month	0.02	−0.36**	−0.07	−0.84***
transition	(0.11)	(0.15)	(0.09)	(0.11)
Number of	1546	793	2142	1534
observations				
Chi-square	.831	.046	.429	.000

* $p \leq .05$.
** $p \leq .01$.
*** $p \leq .001$, two-tailed test.

Note: The units of analysis are the aggregate-level votes for the second-instance Court, coded 0 = against the government, 1 = for the government, and a justice's vote in a (full opinion) decision, coded 0 = against the government, 1 = for the government, for the Supreme Court. Cell entries are logistic regression coefficients. Dummy variables for each justice are included in each model, but the results are not presented here. Standard errors are in parentheses.

changed to include issues that were of a type more likely to be decided against the government. To examine this possibility, I re-estimate the basic timing models for each governmental period where we would expect strategic defection to occur, including all of the nineteen issue variables contained in the database for each model.[15]

The results in Table 5.10 show that a change in the mix of cases does not erase the timing effect predicted by the theory of strategic defection. Consistent with the strategic argument, controlling for the issue categories has virtually no effect on the results for the military regime and the second Menem government. Both coefficients for the final twenty-four months remain negative and significant at the $p \leq .001$ level.

For the Alfonsín government, the first model shows that the transition effect disappears but also that several issues (*Amparo, Military (other), Customs, Emergency Powers, Federal-Provincial, Procedures,* and *Public Administration (hire/fire)*) were significantly more likely to be decided against

---

[15] The vast majority of cases (85%) include only one or two issues.

5.6 Rival Hypotheses

Table 5.10 *Individual Supreme Court Justices' Anti-government Votes, Controlling for a Changing Mix of Cases*

Independent variable				
Constant	0.68*	0.77**	1.23***	1.00***
	(0.29)	(0.29)	(0.23)	(0.21)
Final 24 months (military)	−0.83*** (0.17)			
Final 24 months (Alfonsín)		−0.13 (0.16)		
Final 24 months (Alfonsín) subset			−0.31* (0.14)	
Final 24 months (Menem2)				−0.96*** (0.11)
Military (hire/fire)	−0.44	0.24		−0.78***
	(0.43)	(0.26)		(0.25)
Military (other)	0.28	−1.00***		−0.78***
	(0.23)	(0.29)		(0.24)
Amparo	1.23***	−1.02***		−0.97***
	(0.32)	(0.28)		(0.16)
Monetary Claims	−0.19	−0.04		−0.11
	(0.15)	(0.18)		(0.13)
Constitutional Issues	0.81***	0.61**		−0.26*
	(0.22)	(0.22)		(0.12)
Customs	−1.05**	−1.92**		1.13***
	(0.31)	(0.56)		(0.32)
Emergency Powers	0.25	−1.09*		−2.14***
	(0.98)	(0.56)		(0.43)
Federal-Provincial	−1.55*	−0.49		1.14***
	(0.73)	(0.28)		(0.33)
Habeas Corpus	−0.99**			1.06
	(0.33)			(1.11)
Interpretation	0.09	0.04		−0.00
	(0.15)	(0.17)		(0.13)
Judiciary	0.59	−0.12		−0.86**
	(0.47)	(0.42)		(0.31)
Jurisdiction	−0.35	1.30**		0.67*
	(0.47)	(0.43)		(0.29)
Procedures	−0.14	−1.23***		
	(0.27)	(0.29)		
Property	−0.54			−1.07***
	(0.35)			(0.28)

(continued)

Table 5.10 (*continued*)

Independent variable				
Public Administration	−0.49*	−0.72*		−1.22***
(hire/fire)	(0.22)	(0.32)		(0.41)
Public Employees	−0.50*	0.30		−0.84***
(other)	(0.24)	(0.29)		(0.23)
Taxes	−0.83**	0.07		−0.50***
	(0.25)	(0.31)		(0.15)
Issue Group			−1.23***	
			(0.16)	
Number of	1335	971	989	1802
observations				
Chi-square	.001	.001	.001	.000

* $p \le .05$.
** $p \le .01$.
*** $p \le .001$, two-tailed test.
Note: The unit of analysis is a justice's vote in a (full opinion) decision, coded 0 = against the government, 1 = for the government. Cell entries are logistic regression coefficients. Dummy variables for each justice are included in each model, but the results are not presented here. Standard errors are in parentheses.

the government.[16] Thus, I constructed a new dummy variable (*Issue Group*), which subsumes all of the issues with negative and significant coefficients. Inconsistent with the alternative explanation, the coefficient from the second timing variable (−0.31) is negative and again significant at the $p \le .05$ level. Although somewhat less impressive than the findings from the first and fourth transitions, the data thus show that when controls for cases of a type more likely to be decided against the government are introduced, the justices still increased their decisions against the government during the second transition period by a margin of six percentage points.

5.7 Conclusion

Taken together, the evidence offers overwhelming support for the view that judges under threat behave strategically. Specifically, the data show

[16] To deal with the separate question of whether the effects of the changing political environment obtained across different issues, I ran separate logistic regressions for each issue category with the votes of justices as the dependent variable and the twenty-four-month timing variable as the independent variable. Although the timing variable achieved statistical significance in some issue categories and not in others, in none of the issue categories did the justices increase their support for the outgoing government.

systematically that anti-governmental decisions increased significantly whenever judges began to sense that the current government was losing power and decreased when the incumbents grew strong. Moreover, in line with the mechanism underlying strategic defection, judges also concentrated defection in the most important cases. Bolstering further the signaling view, patterns of participation, appeals acceptance, and separate opinion writing cast considerable doubt on the conventional notion that judges under attack automatically duck to avoid controversy. Finally, by introducing a series of controls, I was able to rule out the three competing explanations regarding composition, legality, and changes in the types of issues that might otherwise account for these observed trends.

6

The Dynamics of Defection

HUMAN RIGHTS, CIVIL LIBERTIES, AND PRESIDENTIAL POWER

> Everything is subject to appeal, thus everything is subject to impeachment.
> Anonymous Argentine Supreme Court Justice[1]

The findings of the previous chapter contrast sharply with the conventional wisdom that courts under attack rarely challenge the government of the day. In accordance with the theory of strategic defection, the last chapter found substantial evidence of a reverse legal-political cycle in which judges under dictatorship and democracy alike defect from the government once it begins to lose power. That I was also able to rule out several competing hypotheses lent further credibility to the theory of strategic defection. To delve more deeply into the mechanisms underlying the strategic defection account and its consequences for the rule of law, this chapter develops a qualitative picture of the Argentine Court's behavior over the last two decades.

For each of the four governments, I examine further the validity of the strategic account by focusing on the Court's handling of the most important and visible issues. Overall, the case studies presented below strongly confirm the expectation that judges under threat defect in the most controversial cases of the day. They also suggest support for several additional hypotheses regarding issue convergence and concentration. I conclude by examining whether defection worked and with a brief epilogue that applies the lessons of the previous chapters to the Court's role in the midst of Argentina's recent political and economic crisis of 2001–2.

[1] *La Nación*, June 12, 2002.

6.1 The Military Court and Human Rights

The previous chapter established a strong relationship between the looming transition and the justices' increasing willingness to rule against the government. Across the board in cases dealing with the government or with decrees passed by the junta, we saw that the level of anti-governmental decisions increased significantly once the junta began to lose its grip on power. Without a doubt, however, in the eyes of the democratic opposition, the single most important issue area that the Court dealt with during this period was human rights. Thus, if the theory of strategic defection is correct, we should observe very clear changes in the Court's jurisprudence in this key area of cases once the military regime began to unravel.

Throughout the 1970s, the Court had repeatedly supported the regime's anti-subversion policies. Between 1976 and 1980 there were 5,487 petitions for writs of habeas corpus submitted to the federal courts by families seeking information about the whereabouts of members believed to have been imprisoned by the military (CONADEP 1984: 401). During this period only *one* request for habeas corpus was granted by the Supreme Court. In the much publicized case of Jacobo Timerman, editor-in-chief of the Buenos Aires newspaper *La Opinión*, the Supreme Court granted a writ for Timerman's release in 1979 (Timerman 1982). As Argentine legal experts have pointed out, the Timerman case was a clear exception to the rule at the time and had no spillover effect on thousands of other similar cases.[2] The Court did make some attempt during the first few years of the military regime to obtain information about the fate of the *desaparacidos*, in cases such as *Zamorano* (1977) and *Perez de Smith et al.* (1977).[3] But in the overwhelming majority of cases the Court either simply denied that it had jurisdiction to hear the case or, as in *Tizio* (1977), reversed lower court rulings that had issued writs of habeas corpus. In this case and others, the Court denied the writ by arguing that the courts could not question the executive's assertion that the detainee was being held in connection with subversive activities (Garro and Dahl 1987: 294; Carrió 1996: 112).

[2] Interview with former Second Instance of Appeals Court Judge Jorge Torlasco, Buenos Aires, March 1998.
[3] For example, in the case *Perez de Smith et al.* a writ of habeas corpus was filed on behalf of 1,542 people believed to have been taken by the armed forces. Although denying that the Court itself lacked jurisdiction to hear the case, the Court implored the junta "to strengthen the investigation regarding the whereabouts of persons whose disappearance is brought to the attention of the courts, so that judges would be in a position to exercise their constitutional powers" (translated and cited in Garro and Dahl 1987: 297–8).

In 1981, as the military began losing power and the possibility grew that the justices would be blamed for failing to protect human rights adequately, the Court began to shift course. In its decision in *Moya* (1981), the Court modified its earlier strategy for dealing with habeas corpus cases. Rather than reject outright the petition or merely request information from the government, as it had in the past, the Court switched its jurisprudence and demanded that the military either allow Moya to leave the country or place him under house arrest. While house arrest certainly was not the same as giving the prisoner liberty, the decision represented a decisive break with the Court's earlier rulings.[4] Since 1976, with the *Ercoli* decision, the Court had argued that the military could suspend the so-called right of option during states of siege provided for in Article 23 of the 1853 Constitution.[5] What *Ercoli* effectively meant was that anyone detained by the military could not exercise his or her constitutional right to leave the country to avoid arrest and detention.

In *Moya* the Court reversed itself to rule that the conditions necessitating the suspension of this right no longer obtained. Thus, it ordered that Moya must be allowed to exercise fully the right of option granted by the Constitution to leave the country if he so wished. The other significant move by the Court in *Moya* was not simply to restore an option previously eliminated, but also to create one. This was the Court's so-called *libertad vigilada* (house arrest). The Court argued that this would allow the government to keep track of persons suspected of subversion but no longer permit the government to hold them in prison indefinitely.

Moreover, unlike *Timerman*, *Moya* did not remain an isolated case. *Moya* set a precedent that was later applied to approximately 900 similar cases between 1981 and 1983.[6] Although it is true that the detainees were not fully released under such conditions, the change in the Court's handling of habeas corpus cases was significant for the detainees and for the sitting government. Indeed, at the time of the decision there was considerable speculation that the military, which continued to hold people accused of subversion in detention, would refuse to implement the decision (Gabrielli 1986: 98).

---

[4] But for a different interpretation, see Gabrielli 1986.
[5] In *Ercoli* the Court found that the "Acta Fijando el Proposito y los Objectivos Basicos para el Proceso de Reorganization Nacional" (which, among other things, suspended the right of option) was constitutional (Carrió 1996: 95–6).
[6] For example, see *Gordillo Arroyo, Podesta, Feldman,* and *Perelmeter* (cited in ibid.: 113).

6.1 The Military Court and Human Rights

Table 6.1 *Military-Era Supreme Court Justices' Anti-government Decisions in Habeas Corpus Cases by Time to Transition (1 = for government; 0 = against government)*

Constant	0.70 (0.14)***
Time 1	−0.42 (0.10)***
Habeas	0.11 (0.35)
Transition*Habeas 1	−0.87 (0.42)*
Number of observations	1339
Significance of chi-square	.0000

* $p < .05$.
** $p < .01$.
*** $p < .001$.
Note: Entries are probit coefficients. Standard errors in parentheses.

Systematic evidence that the Court defected against the miliary in human rights cases at the end of the regime is also contained in the ASCD database. I examine statistically the impact of the transitional period on the justices' willingness to rule against the government in habeas corpus cases, which are included as one of the nineteen issue variables contained in the database. Similar to the statistical models presented in the previous chapter, I used logit analysis to estimate the effect of being in a transitional period (*Time 1*) on the likelihood of a justice handing down an anti-governmental decision in habeas corpus cases (*Habeas*), with a dummy for judges and an interaction term (*Transition*Habeas 1*) to examine whether the effect of habeas cases on the government's willingness to hand down anti-government decisions varies with an increase in the threat that judges face.

The analysis shows that once the Court began to defect it was more likely to defect in habeas corpus cases than in other types of cases (see Table 6.1). This interpretation rests especially on the coefficient (−0.87) for the interaction term, which is in the expected direction and significant at the $p < .05$ level. Note that the coefficient for the *Habeas* term alone is indistinguishable from zero. In other words, in non-transitional periods habeas corpus cases were no more or less likely than all other types of cases to be decided against the government. The Court's sensitivity to habeas corpus cases began only with the unraveling of the military dictatorship. Taken together, these case studies and systematic data show not only that the military-era Court defected at the end of the dictatorship, but also that the justices did so especially in the area most important to the democratic opposition, that of human rights.

Following *Moya* the trend in the majority's opinions was to expand even further the rights under habeas corpus protection. In *Spadoni*, decided in March 1983, the Court ordered the immediate release of a detainee held under the state of siege, even though he had not sought to exercise his right of option. In his commentary on the case, the Argentine constitutional law scholar Bidart Campos underlined the importance of the case:

This sentence (*Spadoni*) has in the history of the Court since 1976 as much significance as *Zamorano, Timerman,* or *Moya*. That is because the Court tells us that in this case the beneficiary of the writ is not someone who has requested to leave the country to end his detention.... Here the right of option was neither invoked nor exercised: The writ was granted directly and liberty was fully recovered within our national territory.[7]

A potential alternative explanation worth considering is that the change in the Court's jurisprudence was simply a response to the end of the Dirty War. That is, in the absence of an urban guerrilla threat, the Court no longer saw the need for draconian measures. But if this were the judges' primary motivation, then the jurisprudence should have changed some two years before in 1979 when, by almost all accounts, the war had ended.

Bolstering further the strategic defection interpretation of these switches are the justices' self-conscious attempts to improve their image by presenting these very decisions as evidence that the Court had acted as a brake on the military. The former Chief Justice Adolfo Gabrielli's book, *La Corte Suprema y la Opinion Pública (The Supreme Court and Public Opinion)*, which was published in 1986 during the height of the trials of military officers, offers a litany of cases that is designed to document the judiciary's protection of human rights throughout the military era. The book refers explicitly to the cases discussed above to refute the charges made by human rights groups that the justices had succumbed to the military or had merely provided a veneer of legality for the dictatorship by issuing opinions that challenged the military in rhetoric but not in fact. For example, citing the arguments made by the conservative legal group FORES and by Bidart Campos, Justice Gabrielli states:

That the role of the judiciary was quite different from how the CONADEP report describes it is apparent by the fact that the report itself constantly refers to "exceptional" decisions made by the Court. But these decisions which are inconsistent with the [CONADEP] report were not the exception, but rather the rule.... The functioning of the judiciary and especially the Supreme Court during the de facto

---

[7] *El Derecho*, May 12, 1983, cited in Gabrielli 1986: 130, my translation.

government has served to partially soften the effects of "inconveniences" produced by regime instability. What is certain is that the Court has shown concern for freedom and for human rights, and in many cases, has executed its role as protecting the Constitution and in defending and restoring constitutional rights. (Gabrielli 1986: 491, 494; my translation)

Whereas Gabrielli's book attempts to depict the Court as having protected human rights *throughout* the dictatorship, other evidence suggests a different interpretation. Most notably, between 1976 and 1980 the Court received thousands of letters from families of the disappeared. But according to one source close to the Court whom I interviewed, the modus operandi of the Court during these years was simply to "throw the letters in the trash."[8] After 1981, however, the Court's handling of letters seems to have been much improved. Gabrielli's book concludes by publishing several of the letters he received from families of disappeared persons whom the Court had released. In one letter written in 1982 and saved by Justice Gabrielli, the parents of a daughter who had been detained for subversion by the military dictatorship wrote:

Upon learning of the Court's decision to grant the writ of habeas corpus to my daughter, I was naturally overcome with gratitude. It is not easy to express how great is our feeling that this decision represents the highest value that can be summarized only as: Justice. (reprinted in Gabrielli 1986: 507; my translation)

Gabrielli's attempts to document the Court's efforts to protect human rights is thus entirely consistent with the view that the judges during this period cared deeply about their reputations. Once the threat to the justices became salient, these letters as well as the Court's decisions themselves became vitally important evidence for the justices to use to try to convince the incoming democratic opposition that they had done what they could to limit the military in the key area of human rights. Of the many grateful letters that Gabrielli found to include in his book, however, not a single one is dated before 1981.

6.2 The Alfonsín Court and Human and Civil Rights

Judges also faced powerful incentives to defect against the government at the end of Alfonsín's government once it became clear that the Radicals were losing power. However, as Chapter 4 also pointed out, this was

---

[8] Anonymous interview, Buenos Aires, September 1997.

complicated by the fact that among some important issues of the day, it was not always clear that the incumbent and the opposition candidates wholly disagreed. Although the previous chapter showed strong support for the view that judges defected rather than ducked, focusing on the dynamics of the judges' decisions in key cases provides a fresh opportunity to consider the more subtle effects of incomplete information on the Court's behavior. In particular, the Court's handling of the administration's attempts to limit the human rights trials allows us to examine how judges dealt with signaling their independence from the outgoing government in cases where the opposition appeared to share the incumbents' views.

As described in Chapter 4, the main source of judges' uncertainty following the 1987 midterm elections was not whether the Peronists would win but which Peronist candidate would win. Whereas the "Renewalist" wing of the Peronist party, led by Antonio Cafiero, held views similar to those of the Alfonsín administration in many social and economic policies, the Menem wing was much more socially conservative than both the Renewalists and Alfonsín's Radicals. Thus, at least initially, the Court was put in the difficult position of knowing that the Radicals' days were numbered, but not knowing which of the two factions within the Peronist opposition would be in charge of the Court's fate.

Faced with this circumstance, the Court essentially had three options. First, it could have continued to hand down highly visible liberal rulings, on the assumption that the Renewalist faction would dominate. Because the Renewalist wing had policy preferences similar to the incumbent's, the Court could have continued to play the role that it had in the early years of the Alfonsín regime. Substantively, this would have meant that the Court could have continued to make noteworthy strides in furthering the protection of individual and civil rights in numerous cases. For example, in *Dufourq* (1984) and *Aramayo* (1984) the Court limited the validity of de facto laws as binding on democratic governments, which opened up a number of areas for litigation. In *Fiorentino* (1984) the Court overturned previous jurisprudence to declare illegal the practice of obtaining confessions through coercive means and declared inadmissable evidence gathered without a search warrant (*Fallos* 306: 1761, cited in Gargarella 1996: 260; Bacqué 1995: 9). In the cases of *Bazterrica* (1986) and *Capalbo* (1986) the Court expanded greatly the realm of privacy in cases dealing with individual possession of narcotics. Finally, in *Sejean* (1986) the Court overturned the civil marriage law prohibiting remarriage also on the basis of the right to privacy (cited in Carrió 1996: 149). The clear risk to the Court had it continued in this direction was that Cafiero and his Renewalist faction of the Peronist party would lose.

The second option was for the Court instead to switch its jurisprudence and overturn its earlier liberal decisions. Although this was the route the majority of the Court post-1990 ultimately followed, with decisions such as *Fernandez* (1990), *Montalvo* (1990), and *Comunidad Homosexual Argentino* (see Bacqué 1995), there is no evidence that a shift of this magnitude occurred under Alfonsín. Even after Menem's victory in the primaries there were several reasons why such a dramatic change in the Court's jurisprudence would have been risky. First and foremost, the juridical instability that would have resulted would have alienated many of the Court's strongest supporters in the legal and academic community in a way that simply deciding against the government would not. Although these groups would not directly determine the Court's fate, they could potentially help to raise the costs of sanctioning the Court to the incoming government. Second, even though Menem ultimately ran on an orthodox platform, he had previously been a part of the Renewalist faction, making it difficult for the judges to know with certainty where his preferences truly lay.

In line with the ducking hypothesis, the third option for the justices was to instead adopt a lower profile. Although the last chapter found little statistical support for this proposition, a more qualitative view provides a somewhat different picture. For example, a review of the main Argentine legal sources documenting the Court's jurisprudence shows no comparable landmark case decided by the Court after the Radical defeat in the 1987 midterm elections, and certainly not one in which the Court took the side of the Radicals against the Peronists as the Court had done in *Sejean*.[9] Still, it is difficult to rule out the possibility that the absence of landmark decisions simply indicated that the Court had already dealt with the issues that were of the greatest concern to the justices. The fact that there was a steady increase in the number of cases entering the Court during this period through the *recurso extraordinario* suggests that the Court had no shortage of opportunities to find potential landmark cases. Yet the very fact that the Court was willing to take cases that could have potentially put it in the spotlight during this crucial period suggests that adopting a lower profile during Alfonsín's final years was not necessarily the Court's primary goal.

Probably the most convincing evidence against the ducking hypothesis for this period is the timing of the Court's decision in *Camps* (1987) over the

---

[9] On the political disputes over the divorce law see Nino 1993: 324.

highly unpopular law of "Due Obedience" limiting the scope of the human rights trials. According to Nino, earlier in the administration, he and other legal advisers to Alfonsín had tried to get the Court, and specifically Justice Petracchi, to "clarify" the issue of lower level officers' responsibility for human rights abuses committed during the Dirty War. Referring to the period prior to 1987, Nino notes that "Petracchi was sympathetic to the idea, [but] he retreated arguing that the link between due obedience and the issues at hand was too tenuous" (1996: 92). Only after the Alfonsín government began to weaken did the Court take the issue.

The majority decision in the case, however, is noteworthy for another reason. Namely, it allows us to examine how the Court dealt with the problem of issue convergence between the government and the opposition. In spite of the Peronists' pro-human rights rhetoric in the mid-1980s and their harsh criticism of Alfonsín's handling of the trials, the Peronist majority in Congress was crucial to the passage of the law. Indeed, although the justices could not have predicted this at the time, one of Menem's first major acts as president was to pardon the former military leaders. In *Camps*, ruling against the government would thus have been tantamount to also ruling against the Peronist opposition. Given its previous decisions over the issue in cases such as *Videla* (1986), the Court's own preferences seemed to point against both the incumbent government's and the opposition's position.[10] Yet in the majority decision the Court voted to uphold the law.

Although it is difficult to distinguish support for the administration from support for the opposition, the fact that the main argument of the decision upholding the government's policies carefully avoided any references to the executive branch is telling. At no point in the decision did the Court explicitly support Alfonsín's stance toward the issue. Instead, the majority's reasoning was that the Court's duty was to respect the (Peronist-dominated) legislative branch. According to the decision, the Law of Due Obedience "is constitutional because it was based on the congressional power to grant amnesty and the 'necessary and proper clause' of the constitution" (Garro

---

[10] Along these lines, it should be noted that in *Videla* the Supreme Court revised the Appeals Court's categorization of responsibility of subordinate officers. According to the Supreme Court, the burden of responsibility shifts from the subordinate to the superior officer only in cases where the order is "service connected." In other words, by narrowing the scope of responsibility for superior officers, the Court increased the burden of responsibility on lower level officers (see Garro and Dahl 1987: 330–1). So, in contrast to what the government wanted, in *Videla* the Court opened the door for more trials of lower level officers.

and Dahl 1987: 340). Justice Fayt's separate concurrence similarly argued that it was the Supreme Court's duty to "respect the congressional will in light of the seriousness of the situation" (*Camps* cited in ibid.: 340). Only Bacqué, the judge who later resigned once Menem packed the Court, dared to dissent. Thus, although the outcome alone does not help us to distinguish whom the Court is supporting, the reasoning and composition of the majority opinion is consistent with the notion of strategic behavior. Even though the majority decision supported the outgoing government's law, judges who cared about keeping the Court intact were also seeking to ensure that their decision appealed to the incoming party as well.

6.3 The Menem-Era Court and Presidential Power

Throughout Menem's decade in power, the Court was strongly challenged by the political opposition. Yet as I've argued, during Menem's first term (1989–95), there were relatively few sanctions that the opposition could deploy against the justices. Aside from the notorious quid pro quo agreement made between Menem and Alfonsín to replace two justices during the 1994 constitutional reforms, Menem's own popularity, combined with the Peronists' stronghold in both houses of Congress, effectively meant that the opposition had no ability to sanction judges. Thus, out of the hundreds of requests made to impeach judges during Menem's first term, not a single petition resulted in the removal of a judge. Given this context, the increase in support among Menem's own appointees and among the held-over judges accords well with the strategic account.

This, for example, was the period marked by some of the Court's most egregiously pro-Menem rulings. In one of the Court's earliest and most criticized decisions, *Fiscal Molinas*, the majority opinion overruled the first- and second-instance courts to allow Menem to remove without impeachment and to fire the head prosecutor in charge of investigation administrative affairs (Verbitsky 1993). Similarly, the majority opinion in *Peralta* upheld the administration's controversial Plan Bonex, which was based around the presidential decree 36/90 freezing private savings accounts. By legitimizing the power of the executive to legislate, the decision was also widely seen as endangering the separation of powers on which the Argentine Constitution rests (Bagalini and D'Ambrosio 1993; Larkins 1998). In another case, the majority opinion overturned the Court's own jurisprudence regarding the autonomy of provincial elections, thus paving the way for federal government intervention in the gubernatorial election in Corrientes (Bagalini and D'Ambrosio 1993).

At the end of Menem's second term, however, a very different picture emerged. As Menem's power began to wane, a new wave of scandals involving various justices on the Supreme Court erupted. Almost daily the headlines reported new evidence of corruption among one or several of the members of the Court. These scandals catapulted the question of the judiciary to the top of Menem's opponents' agenda. The decline of Menem's own popularity along with a constitutional ban on his immediate "re-re-election" meant that the justices could no longer count on remaining protected. The Peronists' defeat in the 1997 midterm elections and the bitter fight for leadership of the Peronist party between Menem and Eduardo Duhalde put the justices' future into doubt for the first time. In accordance with our expectations, the previous chapter thus found strong systematic support that the Court – including Menem's most loyal supporters – responded by defection.

Nevertheless, as I described above in Chapter 4, the justices also were well aware of the fact that the capacity of any new government to carry out sanctions would likely be far more limited than it had been during the previous periods. Whichever candidate won the presidency in 1999, he would clearly need the cooperation of other parties to sanction the justices formally. For example, even if the Alliance won the presidency, the Senate, at least until 2001, would remain in the hands of the Peronists. In the immediate post-election period this meant that the Alliance would still have to rely on the anti-Menem Peronists in Congress to impeach the justices. As a result, this period thus provides an excellent opportunity for examining the additional theoretical implications for issue concentration that emerge in the context of multiple sanctioning players. Precisely because multiple sanctioning players were expected to be involved in deciding the judges' fates, we should thus see the judges under Menem pooling their defection specifically in issues where the preferences of the various opposition players converge. By contrast, in issues in which only one or the other group's interests were clearly at stake, we should see the justices far less willing to defect. Put simply, if the strategic defection view is correct, then during this period the Court should have remained loyal to Menem on issues where the opposition groups did not share a common interest and should have defected on those issues where the two groups did share a common interest.

In the pre-election period no other issue coming before the Court united the Alliance opposition and the Duhalde camp as clearly against the Menem government as did the question of Menem's so-called re-re-election. Thus, it is precisely in this case where we should begin to see Menem's support among the justices crumble. The facts of the case and how it reached the Supreme Court are as follows. In the early months of 1998, Menem announced, "If the people ask me to and the Constitution permits it, I will run for a third term."[11] The outcry from both political parties was immediate. Basing their arguments on the Constitutional reform of 1994, which explicitly prohibited the president from running for a third term, the Alliance strongly denounced Menem's re-re-election effort. Radical party leader Raúl Alfonsín and the prominent Radical deputy, Rodolfo Terragno, swiftly proclaimed that the issue was "legally impossible."[12] Among the anti-Menem Peronists, Duhalde's supporters in Congress quickly vowed that if Menem proposed a second reform of the Constitution to allow him to run again, the anti-Menem Peronists in the lower house would block it.

Throughout his presidencies, Menem's main strategy for dealing with his opponents was to use the Court. Menem's hope was that he could use a favorable decision from the Supreme Court regarding his eligibility to run for office as a way of garnering public support for his re-re-election efforts. At the time, surveys reported that nearly 80 percent of Argentines disagreed with Menem's re-re-election plans (Levitsky 2000). Low popular support, combined with the strength of the Alliance and of the opposition within the Peronist Party, meant that Menem could not credibly threaten to hold a plebiscite (as he had threatened to do in 1994)[13] or count on Congress to provide a quorum for reforming the Constitution. As *La Nación* reported, "Over the next six months Menem would have to work day and night, Sunday to Sunday, to make credible the question of his re-election." According to his strategists, the key for accomplishing this feat lay with the Court. Menem's closest supporters claimed: "There is no other possible route: the Court is the only way."[14]

In early 1998 the Menem administration approached the Court, asking the justices to issue a resolution that proclaimed unconstitutional the ban on

---

[11] *La Nación*, February 16, 1998.

[12] Ibid.

[13] Indeed, it was Duhalde, not Menem, who ultimately threatened to hold a plebiscite the following September. According to press accounts, it was widely believed that Menem would have lost the plebiscite by a landslide, which in turn would have weakened his subsequent bid for the nomination in his party's primaries in April 1999 (*New York Times*, July 28, 1998).

[14] *La Nación*, March 8, 1998.

Menem's running for a third term. Menem loyalists within the party began presenting writs of *amparo*[15] before the lower tribunals, arguing that the grandfather clause included in the 1994 Constitution that effectively barred Menem from a third term in office constituted unfair discrimination. The clause in question had been included at the behest of the Radicals in the Pacto de Olivos specifically to prevent Menem from running for a third term and stated: "The mandate of the current president at the moment of the sanctioning of the reform shall be considered as his first term."

Spearheading the Menem administration's legal assault on the re-re-election ban was none other than Rodolfo Barra, the same justice who had been asked by Menem to resign from the Court so that the Radicals would approve the constitutional reforms in 1994. As described in the previous chapter, Barra was later promoted by Menem to become the minister of justice. In 1998 Barra claimed that the ban on Menem's run for a third term rested on whether the 1994 Constitution was a reformed version of the 1853 Constitution or whether it could be considered a new Constitution. If the 1994 Constitution were considered a new constitution, as Barra argued it was, then Menem's 1995 election must be considered his first term in office, not his second. Thus, by Barra's logic, Menem could stand for election in 1999 without violating the two-term limit and without needing to reform the Constitution.

It should be noted that by nearly all other accounts, Barra's argument was completely without juridical merit. Article 1 of the law passed to sanction the 1994 Constitution specifically referred to the need to "partially reform" the Constitution. In no part of the reform law was the Constitution ever referred to as a "new" Constitution. Even such Menem stalwarts as his brother, Senator Eduardo Menem, and José Roberto Dromi, a lawyer and one of Menem's earliest key economic advisers, agreed that the 1994 Constitution was only a reformed version of the 1853 Constitution.[16]

In the midst of the growing controversy over Menem's re-re-election bid, the justices and their futures stood at the center of the political battle. Even the *New York Times* noted the significance for the Argentine Court, declaring that "the [re-re-election] case will be a test of the independence

---

[15] The *recurso de amparo* was introduced into Argentine jurisprudence by the Court in the mid-1950s and was formally added to the Constitution as part of the 1994 reforms. Essentially, the writ of *amparo* is an injunction granted by the Court to stop the state from violating basic constitutional rights and guarantees (interview with Justice Moliné O'Connor, Buenos Aires, May 1998).

[16] *Clarín*, May 17, 1998.

of the judiciary."[17] The Court faced a difficult choice. On the one hand, deciding against the government would mean that the justices were foreclosing their only possibility for Menem to serve another term and thus to keep themselves protected from future sanctions. As one local newspaper reported, the administration made this clear to the justices by warning them, "If you do not sign the resolution [permitting the re-re-election], you are signing your own death warrant."[18] Although such a warning was only figurative, it drove home the idea that the justices' protection depended on the Menem government remaining in power.

On the other hand, if the Court allowed Menem to stand for a third term and he lost, the consequences for the justices would be even more disastrous. One of the justices on the Court observed, "If we vote for a third term, we had better hope that [Menem] wins next year. Because if we allow him to run and he does not win, I can already imagine the hoards on the Plaza Lavalle and in the entrance of Tribunales who will be demanding our heads."[19]

Given the increasingly low probability of Menem actually winning a third term, however, it quickly became apparent that the Court's best option lay with refusing to support Menem. Almost immediately the Court made it very clear that it would do what it could to avoid deciding the question. Here, given the preferences of the government, the Court's very visible strategy of ducking was tantamount to defection. Even among the most loyal justices (Nazareno, Moliné O'Connor, Vázquez, López, and Boggiano) support for issuing a ruling declaring the ban unconstitutional rapidly evaporated. In stark contrast to their usual support for the government, Justices Nazareno and Moliné O'Connor leaked to the press that they would not back the government unless some popular support for the re-election emerged.[20] Another Menem loyalist, Antonio Boggiano, who allegedly hoped for a seat in the Hague, left for a long vacation in Europe.[21]

Meanwhile, a coalition between the Alliance members and Duhalde's supporters in the Senate emerged over the question of impeachment proceedings. In particular, the anti-Menem coalition threatened to impeach Justice Vázquez immediately if he supported the re-re-election bid. At the

---

[17] *New York Times*, March 1, 1999.
[18] *La Nación*, March 8, 1998.
[19] *Clarín*, May 17, 1998.
[20] *Clarín*, March 28, 1998.
[21] *La Nación*, May 5, 1999.

very least, the opposition could ask Vázquez, who had publicly proclaimed his personal loyalty to Menem, to recuse himself from deciding the case on the grounds that he was partial. Given the reluctance of Nazareno, Moliné O'Connor, and Boggiano to handle the case, the loss of Vázquez meant that Menem's so-called automatic majority had all but vanished. As one justice stated, "This Court often votes 5–4 in cases that involve the interests of the government. The only issue on which the Court will vote 9 to 0, you can be sure, is to avoid resolving the [re-re-election] case."[22]

Ultimately, the strategy of the Court to avoid deciding the case worked, and Menem dropped his bid for a third term. As the elections approached, the Court pursued a course of strategic defection in several other high-profile cases as well. In 1999 the Court voted to limit the discretion of the executive to rule by decree laws.[23] It curried favor with state employees by ruling against the state to increase the pensions to military officers in retirement. And it declared the Menem administration's decree unconstitutional in the IVA case.[24] Less than two months before the election the Court unanimously rejected the government's appeal to the Court that it hear three cases involving key members of the administration in an alleged Croatian-Ecuadorian illegal arms deal. *Clarín* remarked:

The Court's stock of good will towards the government, clearly shown by several justices in the last years, seems to be coming to an end. After having let Menem know this past February that the political climate would not permit a third term, the Court refuses to venture into a case like the arms deal.[25]

By contrast, in cases where the interests of the Alliance and Menem's opponents within the Peronist Party clearly diverged, the Court had far more leeway to remain loyal to Menem. This can be seen in several cases involving freedom of expression in which the Court ruled in favor of the government. In the high-profile case *Menem v. Verbitsky* (1999), the Court's loyal majority accepted Menem's appeal and overturned a lower court decision in favor of the Argentine journalist Horacio Verbitsky, whom Menem had sued for libel. The issue of freedom of expression was an important concern for the Alliance, whose members, along with the Organization of American States and the International Commission of Human Rights,

---

[22] *Clarín*, May 17, 1998.
[23] It should be noted, however, that the Court's ruling would end up affecting the next president, Fernando De la Rua, far more than Menem.
[24] *Clarín*, September 15, 1999.
[25] *Clarín*, August 20, 1999.

strongly criticized the decision.[26] But the issue was far less important for Duhalde, who had never been a strong advocate of a free press.

Even in other election-related cases, when the interests of only one of Menem's opponents were involved, the Court continued to favor the Menem government. In a case involving the Peronist governor of Córdoba, José Manuel de la Sota, the Supreme Court overturned the Provincial High Court of Córdoba to rule against the Alliance's demand for separate ballots. Remarking on the decision, Fernando de la Rua, the Alliance presidential candidate, stated that "now we have to be elected by the Court, which is a barbarity."[27] Duhalde, in contrast, who would benefit from de la Sota winning, said nothing.

Similarly, when only Duhalde's interests were at stake, the Court also remained loyal to Menem. This is illustrated most clearly by the case *Parque Norte* (1999), brought on appeal to the Supreme Court by Congressman César Arias, an ultra-Menemist. The original case dealt with Duhalde's allegations of irregularities in the internal Peronist Party elections held in July 1999 that had given Menem control over the party leadership until 2002. The Supreme Court reversed both the first instance court and the court of appeals, which had ruled in favor of Duhalde, and asserted that results of the internal elections should stand and that Menem should maintain the leadership of the party. For its part, the Alliance did not contest the ruling.

6.4 Conclusion: Did Defection Work?

Building on the findings of the previous chapter, the case studies presented in this chapter have allowed me to explore more deeply the dynamics of strategic defection among the most important and contentious political issues of the day. Under each of the governments, I have shown how the threat that judges face resulted in profound changes in the Court's jurisprudence. As the military lost its grip on power, judges adopted a far more liberal stance in human rights cases, particularly in cases involving writs of habeas corpus. As Alfonsín's support began to crumble, the Court's earlier zeal for establishing a liberal jurisprudence in human and civil rights cases was overshadowed by the Court's key decision to back the law limiting the scope of human rights trials. And as Menem's decade of governance drew to an end, the so-called automatic majority suddenly began to limit Menem's

---

[26] *La Nación*, April 4, 1999.
[27] *La Nación*, October 8, 1999.

prerogatives, particularly in issues, such as the so-called re-re-election case, that unified the opposition against the incumbent government.

Moreover, beyond providing evidence of instability in the Court's jurisprudence across these periods, the case studies also strongly support the strategic interpretation that the justices were well aware of the threats they faced and that they saw their decisions as a mechanism for mitigating such threats. Under the military, the Court thus not only moved in a more liberal direction, but the chief justice saved and published glowing letters from families whose children or spouses had been freed by the Court's efforts. Under Alfonsín, the Court was in a difficult position of knowing the views of the incoming opposition and thus refused to deal with the issue of limiting the human rights trial until the opposition-led Congress signed the law. To deal with the problem of issue convergence, the majority opinion supporting Alfonsín's position was framed entirely in reference to the opposition-led legislature's right to limit the trials. Finally, under Menem, the justices' very public commentary contained in the nation's leading newspapers and their sudden unwillingness to support Menem suggests that the justices were highly conscious of the threat that they faced and the consequences of their decisions.

Having thus confirmed empirically the links among judges' ex ante beliefs and motivations and their behavior, I conclude by considering the separate question of how strategic defection ultimately played out in each of the periods. Specifically, did incoming governments pay attention to judges' earlier decisions, and if so, how well did the strategy of defection work?

While there is little doubt the Court's decisions in the cases described above were closely tracked by opponents and supporters of the court alike, the evidence that defection ultimately worked to stave off sanctions against the Court is, admittedly, harder to gauge. Determining strategic defection's success requires examining the outcomes that did occur as much as it demands exploring the counterfactual scenarios that did not occur. In other words, in examining this part of the theory it is important not simply to ask whether defection paid off, but also to raise the more speculative question of what might have happened in its absence.

Under the military, for example, we know that despite the outgoing government's best efforts, the Court was promptly removed as soon as the country returned to democracy. In terms of the model, the military's ultimate inability to preserve enclaves of influence can be translated simply into extremely low costs to the incoming government of removing its successors' judges. To keep the military Court, the incoming government would have to have had extremely high priors in terms of the judges' compatibility with the new government. Thus, while it is plausible that judges mistakenly assumed that removal would be harder for the democratic opposition, as time wore on and they saw the power of the military collapse, strategic behavior was most likely driven by a concern with maintaining their reputations, rather than their posts.

From a counterfactual perspective, the evidence that judges' reputations survived intact is more positive. Despite the continued criticism of the military court by various human rights groups, two decades later the dominant view among elites is that the Court did what it could to protect human rights in a difficult situation. For example, according to Andrés D'Alessio, the Dean of the University of Buenos Aires and a well-known former member of the Federal Appeals Court that tried the former military leaders under Alfonsín, the military court was conservative, but also highly professional. In D'Alessio's judgment, "very early on the military realized that it would have a problem with [controlling] this Court. It kept the Court because it appeared legitimate to the international community."[28] Although D'Alessio cited favorably such early decisions as *Perez de Smith* (1976) and *Timerman* (1979) it is hard to imagine him reaching such a conclusion in the absence of later cases such as *Moya* (1981) and *Spadoni* (1983), which he also emphasized as clear evidence of the Court's willingness to challenge the military.

Moreover, although there is no systematic post-career information available for the military-era judges, several justices have gone on to distinguished careers as law professors. Most notably, Pedro Frías played a major role in the constitutional reforms in his home province of Córdoba. Frías recently appeared on a list of candidates with impeccable credentials published in *La Nación* to fill the slot recently abandoned by former Chief Justice Julio Nazareno. The contrast could hardly be starker with the former military leaders, who have had no professional career since the end of the regime and, indeed, are often assaulted on the streets of Buenos Aires.

Turning to the Alfonsín-era Court, the evidence that Menem paid attention to the Court's decisions is also undeniable. The answer of whether defection worked to save the Court, however, is also less straightforward.

[28] Interview with Andrés D'Alessio, Buenos Aires, March 1998.

On the one hand, given Menem's immediate proposal to pack the Court once he assumed office, one possibility is that the Court did not do enough to convince Menem of its compatibility. Indeed, as we have seen in certain high-profile decisions, some judges were not necessarily willing to behave strategically. For example, Bacqué's dissent in *Camps* suggests a pattern of behavior more in line with the third separating equilibrium in which judges simply value the issue outcome more than the value of the post. Moreover, to the extent that the two governments' preferences converged in important areas, even the judges who were willing to behave strategically had a very difficult time using decisions to appeal to the incoming government. In such cases, ruling against the outgoing government ultimately would have been tantamount to pooling in the wrong direction. Menem did not want to inherit a court utterly loyal to Alfonsín, but he also did not want to confront a Court that would rule against him (Verbitsky 1993; also see Rogers and Wright-Carozza 1995). Thus, whereas defection may have been the only message that the judges could send, it may, in certain cases, have ultimately been the wrong one.

On the other hand, that the majority of justices appointed by Alfonsín ultimately did manage to break the norm of insecure tenure and keep their posts under Menem suggests that defection was more successful at the individual level. Once the Court had been packed, the held-over judges did dissent with Menem's majority in several high-profile cases,[29] but they also proved their willingness to go along with the government by supporting some of Menem's most important policies. As we have seen in Chapter 2 for example, Petracchi was the author of the *Aerolineas Argentinas* majority opinion shortly after Menem took office. This decision created the doctrine of per saltum and allowed Menem to privatize the national airlines. Along with Justice Fayt, Petracchi also supported Menem's highly controversial decision to pardon the former military leaders in 1990. Justice Fayt is widely reputed to have been the author of the *Peralta* (1990) decision, which, as mentioned above, upheld the constitutionality of Menem's Plan Bonex, converting by decree private savings into government bonds. Indeed, to the extent that strategic defection enabled these three judges to survive under Menem, their reputations suffered almost as much as those of Menem's

---

[29] For example, following the Acordada 44, which strongly disagreed with Menem's plans to stack the Court, the justices who stayed on the bench held Menem's decree removing the attorney general unconstitutional in *Fiscal Molinas*.

own appointees. By the end of Menem's first term, the impeachment charges brought against the Court by Radicals in the Lower House included several charges for misconduct against *all* of the judges, not just Menem's appointees.

Turning to the end of the Menem era, during the 1998–9 campaign, the justices – especially, though not exclusively, the "automatic majority" – were under severe attack from presidential candidates across the political spectrum. Yet despite De la Rua's repeated vows to clean up the judiciary and "purify" the Supreme Court throughout the campaign, not a single justice was removed or added to the Court during De la Rua's time in office. To the contrary, shortly after taking office, De la Rua's discourse immediately shifted to respecting the independence of the Court.

Just why De la Rua did not ultimately attempt to punish any of the members of the Supreme Court lends itself to different interpretations. According to cynics, De la Rua simply realized that it was not so bad to live with a politically savvy Court. As *La Nación* later put it, "very quickly, the government discovered the convenience of being able to count on a supportive court that validated all of the economic adjustments."[30] In terms of the model, then, it did not really matter what De la Rua's prior beliefs about the Court were as long as it was also subservient to his government. By another account, however, one could argue that in a context of relatively high removal costs driven by divided government, strategic defection did make a difference, such that even judges with otherwise bad reputations could survive by defecting. Although impossible to verify, in a counterfactual scenario where the judges remained purely loyal to Menem it is more likely that De la Rua would have had both the incentives and capacity to get rid of the members of the Court.

6.5 Epilogue: The Court and the Collapse of Argentina

Two years after the country's most mundane transfer of power in the twentieth century, Argentina collapsed into economic and political chaos. In the midst of massive social protests and violence, on December 20, 2001, De la Rua resigned as president. Over the next few weeks, as Argentina plunged further into an economic disaster, culminating in the largest debt default

---

[30] *La Nación*, February 3, 2002.

in history, the country experienced a rapid succession of presidents. On January 1, 2002, Eduardo Duhalde, who had lost to De la Rua in 1999, was appointed by Congress to lead the country as the fifth interim president. As the new government fought to regain control over the economy, massive pot-banging demonstrations, known as *cacerolazos*, continued unabated.

Among the most visible targets of these demonstrations were the members of the Supreme Court. It is hard to overstate the depth of the anger expressed at the Court during this period. Along with Congress, Menem, and De la Rua, the public held the Supreme Court justices responsible for contributing to the collapse of the country. Week after week, hundreds of protesters gathered outside tribunales and the private homes of the justices to demand their resignations. In expressions of rage and disgust, protesters carried signs with phrases including "Argentines: We have already thrown out Cavallo [De la Rua's economic adviser] . . . Now, it is time for the Supreme Court"; "Supreme Ones and Corrupt Ones"; "Supreme Court: Don't you have any shame? The people do not want you"; and "Argentina reclaims justice: Get out Supreme Court." In one particularly symbolic gesture, protesters drove a hearse with a coffin in front of the Court with a sign that read, "The death of justice."[31] In another public display, nine actors dressed up in prisoners' garb with the names of each judge slung around their necks and posed on the steps of tribunales. For the first time since the human rights trials, the justices began receiving death threats.

Almost immediately on taking office, Duhalde began to move against the Supreme Court. Two days after being sworn in, the headlines reported that the new administration was studying plans to renovate the Court. According to government sources, the administration initially considered reducing the Court from nine to five and calling for resignations of individual justices.[32] Leading the list of the justices targeted were Julio Nazareno and Adolpho Vázquez, who had recently signed the *Yoma* (2001) majority opinion freeing Menem from corruption charges, despite their well-known personal ties to the former president. Meanwhile, the minister of welfare called on the Court to help with the national economic crisis by slashing its budget by 13 percent.[33] Normally exempt from paying taxes, the judges were also asked to give up this privilege.

---

[31] *La Nación*, February 14, 2002.
[32] *La Nación*, January 3, 2002.
[33] *La Nación*, January 21, 2002.

When it became clear that none of the justices was willing to bend to these pressures, Congress began to move forward with the impeachment process of the entire Court. The charges that would be leveled at the judges included allegations of misconduct in several of the Court's most high-profile cases dealt with during the last decade including the Israeli Embassy investigation, the "re-balancing" of the telephone rates, the decision to free Menem, and the Court's decision to use the doctrine of *per saltum* to validate the highly unpopular banking freeze, known as the "*Corallito.*"[34]

On February 1, 2002, one day after the impeachment process began, the Court handed down a second decision on the banking restrictions in the case of *Smith*. In a 6–0 vote with three abstentions,[35] the Court reversed its earlier ruling and held that the freeze on bank deposits ordered by the government to prevent the collapse of the financial system was unconstitutional. Although the court averred that it could not be the judge of whether an economic crisis existed, it asserted the right to examine the reasonableness of the measures used by the government to confront the crisis. In the harshly worded opinion that followed, the Court declared that the government's policy did not merely limit the right to private property, it annihilated it.[36]

The Court's decision was a striking departure from its past rulings. As commentators quickly pointed out, many of the same members of the Court who now claimed that the government had gone too far in restricting individual property rights in the interest of the common good had given carte blanche to Menem's government in an economic crisis twelve years earlier. In sharp contrast to the *Smith* opinion, the majority reasoning in *Peralta* (1990) had upheld an executive decree (36/90) freezing bank accounts and mandatorily issuing government bonds in exchange on the basis that "individual rights and guarantees can be protected only to the extent that the country's overall well-being is ensured" (cited in Rogers and Wright-Carozza 1995: 57). Now, in the midst of an arguably far worse economic

---

[34] A complete list of the charges against the Supreme Court justices and the justices' defenses are posted on the Web site of Lower House at http://www.diputados.gov.ar.

[35] The majority opinion was signed by Justices Nazareno, Moliné O'Connor, Vázquez, and Boggiano. López was the reputed author. Justice Fayt issued a separate concurrence distinguishing the decision from *Peralta*. Justices Petracchi and Bossert were recused from the case because they had funds trapped by the *Corallito*. Justice Belluscio abstained.

[36] *La Nación*, February 2, 2002.

crisis, the Court's majority struck a very different balance between these two concerns.[37]

While the ruling applied only to the concrete case of Carlos Smith, a depositor from Corrientes, the threat of subsequent decisions and the collapse of the financial system instantly threw Duhalde's interim government into turmoil. Scheduled to unveil his new economic plan that day, the president instead attacked the Court's decision and warned of the dire consequences that it would produce. "Don't be fooled," Eduardo Duhalde told the country, "I could care less if one or two banks go under, [but] if the Corralito explodes like a time bomb then no one is going to get their savings."[38] While Duhalde dismissed the decision as politicized and proclaimed the Court "thoroughly discredited," the head of the impeachment commitee, Sergio Acevedo, vowed to work, "morning, noon, and night, to prepare the charges against the Court before the month's end."[39] The attempt to impeach the justices, however, would ultimately prove one of the biggest failures of Duhalde's presidency. Nine months after the process began, Congress voted to drop all charges and the Court remained intact.

Several factors played a role in the Court's ability to weather the crisis. Despite the huge public outcry to remove the justices, the IMF had made it known relatively early on that it disapproved of Duhalde's efforts to do away with the Court. As it turned out, the congressional strategy of getting rid of all of the justices at the same time also resulted in enormous delays and sloppiness. For example, Justice Bossert complained that the committee did not understand the reach of many of the Court's decisions or the norm of recusal and misrepresented the individual actions of the justices.[40] As a result of these and other errors, elite opinion gradually turned against the

---

[37] The decision was defended on the following grounds. Despite the fact that the Court had ruled just weeks earlier against the depositor in *Kipper*, the policies in question in that case referred to temporary exchange controls taken in the final days by De la Rua's government (Cavallo 2002). The issue at stake in *Smith* dealt instead with the government's right permanently to convert savers' U.S. dollars into pesos at an arbitrary rate. In the latter case, the government had thus gone much further, and the Court was simply acting as a legitimate check on excessive governmental power. In short, according to this argument, the Court's apparent inconsistency between the two cases rests on a misunderstanding of the issues involved in different government policies.

[38] *La Nación*, February 2, 2002.

[39] Ibid.

[40] For example, in *Fayt* (1997), Bossert had issued a dissent from the majority opinion, declaring unconstitutional mandatory retirement for judges at age seventy-five (*La Nación*, October 15, 2002).

process. In an op-ed piece entitled, "The Responsibility Is Everyone's," the verdict was clear:

From the beginning the executive's approach to the Court has been mistaken: It was a mistake to try to impeach the entire Court. . . . Now, because Congress won't close the trials, not only do we maintain this conflict among the branches of government, but we transfer the problem to the future.[41]

Yet to fully understand why the judges kept their posts, we must also consider the Court's own actions throughout this period. Starting with the *Smith* decision, the majority of justices made it clear that they would do everything within their power to stay on the Court. As several commentators were quick to point out, the fact that Court's decision came once the impeachment process had already begun suggests a highly calculated move by the justices to blackmail the government into dropping the impeachment charges. In the words of the FREPASO deputy, Nilda Garre:

The Court's decision was not made to protect those with savings, but to extort the powers of the state, especially the Congress, that initiated the proceedings against several members of the Court. Surely, Menem's famous automatic majority, which recently allowed him to go free for having put into place the economic policies under which we all now suffer, is again functioning in the service of their boss [Menem] and his project of destabilizing institutions.[42]

As thousands of *amparos* against the banking freeze and "pesification" (converting dollars into pesos) were making their way to the Supreme Court, it soon became very clear that the Court would have the last word on Duhalde's plans for economic recovery. Although one of the justices complained that "everything is subject to appeal, thus everything is subject to impeachment,"[43] from the government's perspective, the situation seemed just the opposite. The Court was using the mounting number of cases against the government as a sword of Damocles over Duhalde's head. Thus, almost as soon as the impeachment proceedings began, the government began a series of back-room negotiations with the justices. By mid-July, Duhalde had fired his minister of justice and called for the end to the impeachment proceedings. Chief Justice Nazareno responded to this positive gesture by simply saying, "This Court had lived with various presidents. It is not a hostile Court."[44] Although it would take another several

[41] *La Nación*, September 18, 2002.
[42] *La Nación*, February 3, 2002.
[43] *La Nación*, June 12, 2002.
[44] *La Nación*, July 20, 2002.

months to get the quorum needed to dismiss the charges, the judges had clearly won.

Stepping back from this narrative, the strategic situation that the judges faced during this period was both more exaggerated and different from what it had been in the past. Although the Court had long been unpopular, never before had there been such public demand to remove it. Over 90 percent of the population was in favor of getting rid of the justices. In this context, *not* re-making the Court carried enormous political costs. Indeed, this was one of the key reasons that the Radicals were so reluctant to provide a quorum to dismiss the charges. In the Court's favor, however, few presidents had been as weak as Duhalde. One consequence was that, as the impeachment process dragged on, it became increasingly clear that even if the judges were removed, Duhalde would have a difficult time getting the opposition to allow him to construct the Court that he wanted.[45] To put it in terms of the model, while the political costs to removal were thus probably lower than they had ever been, the costs to re-selection were far higher. In this sense, Duhalde's presidency offers a concentrated version of the lame duck dynamic of incumbent presidents who are unable to punish judges once they defect.

The situation that the Court faced, however, was more than simply an exaggerated version of the past. It was also fundamentally different in several important respects. Most notably, in the original model judges appointed by one government anticipate political changes driven by exogenous events and seek to use their decisions to appeal to the incoming government. In this story, by contrast, judges had no particular allegiance to the outgoing government. Nor, given the events of the time, could they have had any prior beliefs about who the next president would be. They were reacting to events as they unfolded. That said, once the new government was in power, the judges faced a clear choice of whether to support the new president or not. That in *Smith* the judges declared the outgoing government's decree unconstitutional is incidental. The real loser was clearly the new government.

One interpretation of the judges' strategy is that, once Duhalde came to power, they saw no chance of success in being able to convince the new

---

[45] Moreover, given the Court's severe legitimacy problems, the pool of available judges was also far shallower than it had been in the past. For example, as Carlos Arslanian's refusal to accept Duhalde's subsequent attempt to appoint him to the bench shows, few respected jurists wanted to be associated with the Court (*La Nación*, October 23, 2002).

government that the Court would be compatible. Given the long-standing enmity between Duhalde and Menem, the judges knew that their fates were sealed, so they simply faced no incentives to support Duhalde. In support of this interpretation is that the Court handed down *Smith* once the impeachment proceedings had already begun. Cast in theoretical terms, this interpretation fits with the judicial dependence equilibrium in which judges who know that they are going to be punished face no incentives to switch their votes.

Yet what is far more striking about the story is the fact that the judges were most definitely committed to stay on the Court. Refusing to support the government was thus not an acceptance of an inevitable fate, it was an active attempt to change the outcome. In this situation judges' decisions not only went against the new government's preferences but were used in an attempt to bring down the new government. As a spokesman for the Court bluntly put it at the time, "Kill or be killed: that was the situation. And they decided to shoot first."[46] Although certainly in the past defection did not help incumbent presidents, in each of the previous periods exogenous events were far more important in bringing about their demise. Defection began only after the presidents grew weak. In this period, by contrast, defection was not a response to presidential weakness, it was the goal. As the press put it, the *Smith* decision represented an attempted judicial coup against the government. Political change was thus not merely an external factor shaping judges' decisions, it was endogenous to their decisions.

By the end of Duhalde's presidency, the Court seemed unstoppable. In response to the Court's split decision to overturn the government's "pesification" plan converting dollars into pesos, the first lady, Chiche Duhalde, bitterly complained, "Our country is governed by the judiciary, the only branch that is not chosen by the people, that is lamentable."[47] Yet with the inauguration of the popularly elected president, Nestor Kirchner, in May 2003, the situation has once again changed for the Court. Within a month of being sworn in, Kirchner appeared on public television demanding Congress to reopen the impeachment proceedings.

Having learned from Duhalde's experience, however, this time around the process would be very different. In addition to gaining the support of the IMF, the Impeachment Committee decided to proceed one justice at a time. Their first target was the symbol of the Menem era, Chief Justice

---

[46] *La Nación*, February 2, 2002.
[47] *La Nación*, March 6, 2003.

Julio Nazareno. Of all of the justices facing multiple allegations in the previous trials, at a total of forty-four charges, Nazareno had faced the highest number. Although Kirchner is clearly politically stronger than Duhalde and the economic situation is far less dire, a key component in ensuring the success of the impeachment has been the new president's decision to limit his own discretion in appointing new judges. According to the opposition, their willingness to proceed beyond impeaching Nazareno would be determined by how inclusive the selection process proved to be. In a highly publicized move, Kirchner thus issued Decree 222, which mandates public transparency and participation in the judicial candidate selection process. Facing an inevitable vote to impeach him, the threat of additional criminal charges, and the possibility of losing his pension, Nazareno resigned. Next, in December 2003, Justice López agreed to submit his resignation, while the Senate voted to remove the Court's vice president, Moliné O'Connor. With the earlier appointment of Justice Maqueda[48] and the possibility of additional impeachments and resignations,[49] the era of the automatic majority had finally come to an end.

---

[48] Once the impeachment charges were dropped, the least compromised justice, Gustavo Bossert, tendered his resignation, claiming "moral exhaustion." To replace him, Duhalde ultimately appointed Juan Carlos Maqueda. Although the choice was broadly criticized as purely political, Maqueada's position as the provisional Peronist leader of the Senate meant that his confirmation was virtually guaranteed. Maqueda was sworn in as a new justice on December 30, 2002.

[49] With Justices Nazareno, López, and Moliné O'Connor gone, the rumor is that Vázquez is next. Meanwhile, Justice Boggiano, long intent to be appointed to the Hague, has already shown signs of defection against his former cohort, and in his late seventies, Justice Fayt is close to retirement.

7

Conclusion

BROADER LESSONS AND
FUTURE DIRECTIONS

Without effective institutional protections, judges face uncertain futures. For generations of scholars, such institutional insecurity has meant that judges will refuse to stand up to the government of the day. Under dictatorship, the conventional view is that only the most heroic or altruistic judges dare to uphold the law against an authoritarian regime. Under democracy, the continued absence of effective guarantees in many Latin American countries implies that court-executive relations are strictly a one-way affair. Executives regularly find ways to manipulate and control courts; courts are loath to limit the power of executives.

As the Argentine experience suggests, however, the facts do not always support these expectations. Judges under the military Proceso did little to assuage brutal state-led repression, but then commanded the military leadership to free "subversives." Judges under the new democracy devoted their lives' work to arguing for the protection of human rights, but then limited the scope of the trials prosecuting former military leaders. Throughout the 1990s, members of the Court's so-called automatic majority repeatedly declared their loyalty to Menem but ultimately ruled against his bid for a third term. And in the midst of one of the worst economic crises in Latin American history, judges upheld decree laws designed to manage the economic crisis in one moment, only to strike them down a few months later.

Casual and expert observers alike have long suspected that the Argentine Supreme Court's behavior is politically driven and, indeed, criticize it on that very basis. Yet to date, there has been no overarching explanation of why political constraints lead judges to support the government in some instances, but not in others. To make sense of this puzzle, this study has developed a systematic theoretical framework that recasts fundamentally the connection between the choices judges make and the constraints they face. Building on the simple but powerful separation-of-powers approach, the book's main thesis is that, under certain conditions, institutional constraints may instead lead judges to rule against the current government. I refer to this phenomenon as strategic defection. In sharp contrast to dominant sincere and strategic views of judges in the American politics literature, strategic defectors rule against the current government not because they are independent but precisely because they are not. In the remainder of this chapter, I summarize the book's main conclusions, extend its arguments to court-executive relations in other Latin American countries, and explore its more general implications for the study of comparative law and political institutions.

7.1 Strategic Defection and the Reverse Legal-Political Cycle

Why would judges who lack effective institutional guarantees ever rule against the government? Why would judges appointed by a government loyally support it in one moment, and abandon it in the next? To answer these questions, I began with the basic observation that the dynamic of inter-branch relations depends on assumptions about the inter-temporal conflict of interest judges face. When the main threat against judges stems from the current government, judges face incentives to support the government of the day, even if they do not share its preferences. This is the message of much of the American politics literature that treats judges as strategic decision makers, interpreting laws passed by former legislatures in light of current majorities. When the primary threat instead emerges from a future government, however, judges may face incentives to rule against the current government, even though they share the current government's preferences. This has been the situation in contemporary Argentina where, because presidents have been able to hand-pick their own courts, threats aimed against judges generally stem from the opposition. In this context, the capacity of incumbents and future governments to threaten sitting judges credibly has also been inversely related. Once the threat from the opposition was sufficiently credible, the current government was often incapable of applying effective counter-pressure to keep its judges loyal.

The logic of strategic behavior hinges on establishing a plausible connection between the choices judges make and the constraints they face. In the American politics literature this connection is clear: Judges adjust their decisions in order to avoid having them overturned. In exporting this approach to settings where sanctions involve removal, the loss of reputation, or, worse, establishing the connection between constraints and behavior is, perhaps surprisingly, less straightforward. A central motivation for the formal model developed in Chapter 3 was, therefore, to establish a theoretical foundation linking judges' choices under one government to their fates under a new government. Relaxing standard assumptions of complete and perfect information, I showed that in contexts where institutional guarantees are not automatically respected, judges can use their decisions as signals to exploit incoming politicians' uncertainty.

Taken together, the model provided a unified framework for exploring the implications of altering various assumptions about motivations, information, and institutions. In terms of judges' goals, an obvious but important condition for strategic behavior was that judges place a higher value on avoiding sanctions *relative to* deciding cases in accordance with their sincere preferences. Note that satisfying this condition need not imply that judges have no principles nor that in seeking to avoid sanctions, judges necessarily care about furthering the same goal. Judges with any number of motivations – career, policy, reputation – may make this trade-off, depending on the circumstances. Considerable effort was then made in the empirical portions of the book to provide independent evidence about judges' goals and priorities for each of the various periods. Although the overwhelming majority of judges undoubtedly cared about their decisions, in most periods the surrounding evidence – independent of the judges' decisions – suggested that they were even more concerned about the sanctions they faced.

The other two core conditions sustaining strategic defection involved the interaction of politicians' and judges' beliefs and strategies. The first of these was that incoming politicians are sufficiently uncertain about the type of judge they face relative to the costs of punishing judges. The other core condition was that judges be sufficiently certain about which party or type of government is likely to come to power. The model then used these conditions to generate several intuitive and counter-intuitive insights into the nature of court-executive relations.

First and foremost, the model implied a reverse legal-political cycle in which judges strategically defect once governments grow weak. Specific predictions were rendered about the trajectory of anti-governmental decisions during a transitional period and also why judges concentrated their defection in certain types of cases. Moreover, insofar as judges used their decisions as signals to mitigate the sanctions they faced, the study also served

155

to highlight an important tension with the common assumption that judges duck to avoid controversy. That Argentina's judges were sometimes all too willing to enter the political fray was explained as a competing rational response, rather than simple foolhardiness.

Quantitative and qualitative evidence from Argentina strongly supported the theory of strategic defection. Using timing as a proxy for judges' beliefs, statistical evidence revealed dramatic patterns of change in judges' behavior at the end of each government. In accordance with the theory, under three of the last four governments, judges increasingly ruled against the government as soon as the opposition began to garner strength. By contrast, when the incumbent government remained strong, judges increasingly supported the government. In most of these periods, changes in judges' behavior were even more pronounced among the most politically salient cases. Although there was some scattered evidence of judges delaying decisions or avoiding making landmark decisions, there was no systematic pattern of ducking under any of the governments. Controlling for various competing explanations, including changes in the Court's composition and the legality and mix of cases, further bolstered the strategic account. Qualitative evidence surrounding the Court's handling of such hot-button issues as human and civil rights and presidential authority provided additional support for the key mechanisms underlying the strategic account.

Moving from theory to reality, however, the situation also became considerably more complex than the model depicted. Specifically, despite the stable equilibrium outcome predicted by the theory, in the real world defection instead functioned more as a wager, not a guarantee of judicial success. For example, in some situations, we saw that despite judges' best attempts, strategic defection did not ultimately prevent them from being removed. Yet although one would eventually expect repeated removal to eliminate the incentives for strategic behavior, Argentina's chronic instability before and after the transition to democracy created a profound sense of uncertainty about what each of the various incoming governments would do. In the midst of such uncertainty, judges' behavior was based on the hope that defection afforded the best chance of avoiding sanctions at the hands of the next government.

From a normative perspective, the findings of this study cast new light on concerns about the rule of law in Latin America. Whereas scholars have long lamented the absence of the rule of law in the region (Stotzky 1993; Hammergren 1998; O'Donnell 1998; Domingo 1999; Mendez, O'Donnell, and Pinheiro 1999), the logic of strategic defection provides a clear mechanism linking institutional and jurisprudential instability. At the same time, however, the added twist is that, under certain conditions, defection can arguably substantively improve the conditions under which citizens live.[1] During the last dictatorship, for example, strategic defection made a vital difference in the lives of those who suffered at the hands of the last dictatorship. While there is no question that the Argentine Supreme Court should have done more to protect human rights throughout the military dictatorship, neither should we dismiss the importance of the change in the Court's decisions that gave relief to at least some of the military's victims.

Or consider the role that defection played in restricting Menem's bid for power. By prohibiting Menem to run for a third presidential term and by limiting presidential decree power, Menem's once subservient Court ended up shoring up the Constitution. For example, in a case dealing with state subsidies, the court's majority upheld the lower courts' rulings, striking down one of Menem's 1996 decree laws.[2] The ruling was widely interpreted as a shrewd move by the Court both to distance itself from the perception that it was utterly subservient to Menem and, at the same time, to set a new precedent that would constrain the incoming government of De la Rua, who was then leading in the polls. From the perspective of juridical stability, the decision clearly clashed with the majority's earlier opinions.[3] But it also served to undermine a questionable precedent that gave the president nearly unlimited power and curtailed the legislative authority of Congress.

Where, then, does this leave us? Clearly, strategic defection is no substitute for judicial independence, particularly if such independence is exercised by judges whose values we share. Under the conditions that result in strategic defection, the willingness and capacity of the judges to check

---

[1] As liberal theorists have long warned, legalism, not liberal democracy, may result when laws are upheld for their own sake (Shklar 1986). For an application of this idea to Chile, see Hilbink 1999.

[2] *La Nación*, August 25, 1999.

[3] In *Peralta* (1990), for example, the majority overturned lower court injunctions against the government's economic stabilization plan and granted the executive the power to decree the freezing of private savings accounts in the context of economic emergencies. In *Aerolíneas Argentinas*, also known as *Fontenla* (1990), the Court similarly overturned the first-instance court to uphold an executive decree privatizing the national airlines. This decision was made despite the fact that the issue was still being debated in the Congress (Carrió 1996). Thus, over the past two decades the conclusion many legal experts have drawn is that the rule of law has been seriously undermined by the Court's shifting jurisprudence (Bacqué 1995; but also see Rogers and Wright-Carozza 1995).

the government of the day hinges on judges' calculations about politics, not on their considered judgments about the legality or illegality of the government's actions. Whether strategic defection thus leads the Court to defend human rights or the separation of powers depends entirely on the nature of the conflict between the outgoing government and its likely successor. Indeed, as the analysis of the Court's behavior during Menem's first term suggests, if a law-defying government is likely to stay in power, then a constrained Court will only exaggerate such tendencies. Thus, although the dynamics of defection can inadvertently lead to normatively desired outcomes, they may also lead in the opposite direction.

7.2 Strategic Defection in Comparative Perspective

This study fits with part of a growing trend of comparative politics that seeks to adapt rational choice approaches to analyze political institutions in developing parts of the world. Specifically, the study develops a modified version of the separation-of-powers approach to examine inter-branch relations in contexts marked by high stakes and incomplete information. While there is always some trade-off between the tractability of formal models and their ability to represent the real world, altering assumptions to match reality need not require abandoning the rigor and elegance provided by such an approach. Indeed, in the case of the separation-of-powers theory, such a theoretical approach may actually function much *better* in countries such as Argentina.

Examining how courts function abroad also helps to move our understanding beyond the parochialism of the U.S. Supreme Court and toward a more general understanding of judicial behavior. Along these lines, the pattern of inter-branch relations that obtains in such contexts differs markedly from the classic pattern described in the American politics literature. According to the classic story, the standard legal-political cycle involves anti-governmental decisions clustering at the beginning of new governments until new justices are appointed. This is the implication of Dahl's seminal article on the U.S. Supreme Court (1957), in which judges act sincerely and inter-branch harmony is driven by politicians' control over selection. By contrast, in institutionally unstable situations where judges face uncertain futures, anti-governmental decisions cluster at the end of weak governments. In this reverse legal-political cycle, such decisions are made by the very judges whom the government previously appointed, who are willing to overturn their own jurisprudence to minimize the threat of future sanctions.

That problems of judicial independence and institutional insecurity also vary considerably within Latin America provides an excellent opportunity for beginning to examine further these two legal-political cycles. While some countries look a great deal like Argentina in terms of ineffective judicial guarantees, others provide judges with a far more stable environment. Such differences, it should be underlined, do not necessarily correspond to the formal protections judges enjoy. As we have seen from the case of Argentina, secure life tenure may be written in the Constitution, but it has hardly been respected in practice. In any application of the theory of strategic defection, therefore, it is crucial to go beyond the formal rules to examine the actual constraints and incentives that judges face. As a first step in that direction, this section considers patterns of inter-branch relations in Venezuela, Chile, and Mexico. Though still only preliminary, the results of this exercise strongly confirm the main thrust of the strategic account. Namely, only in institutionally insecure environments do we see a marked change in the willingness of judges to support their government. This is the case of contemporary Venezuela and in Mexico after the PRI (Partido Revolucionan'o Institucional) lost power. Where judges are relatively insulated, as in Chile, or where other factors mitigate incentives to rule against the government, as in Mexico under PRI hegemony, there is no discernible pattern of strategic defection.

Venezuela

Contemporary Venezuela provides an ideal setting for extending the strategic defection account. Elected by a landslide victory in 1998, President Hugo Chávez was quick to seize control over the other branches of government. Shortly after being sworn into power, Chávez won a popular referendum granting him the power to convene a Constituent Assembly to draft a new constitution. The powers granted to the Assembly included intervening in and dissolving judicial institutions. Extensive purges were carried out at all levels of the judiciary. The key target of the assembly was the Supreme Court of Justice, which Chávez and his supporters "considered (probably correctly) to be emblematic of the corruption and biases of the old partyarchy" (Coppedge 2003).

To accomplish its goal of "purifying" the judicial system, the assembly formed a special emergency judicial council. Heading up the commission was a close ally of Chávez, Manuel Quijada, who warned, "The objective is that the substitution of judges take place peacefully, but if the Courts refuse

159

to acknowledge the assembly's authority, we will proceed in a different fashion" (Rohter 1999). Shortly thereafter, the Supreme Court ruled in a split vote that the assembly's assumption of judicial powers was constitutional. As one of the former judges complained at the time, "The Court committed suicide to avoid being assassinated."[4]

In December of 2000 the old Supreme Court was dissolved and renamed the Supreme Tribunal of Justice. According to the new Constitution, the justices were to be chosen by an independent screening committee and approved by the new single-chamber assembly for a term of twelve years. That Chávez's Movimiento V Republica (MVR) Party controlled the Assembly with 121 of the 131 seats left little doubt as to the administration's ability to create the Court that it wanted.

At least during the first few years of Chávez's term, the new Court did little to stem the excesses of the government's self-proclaimed "revolution." Given the media's critical stance toward Chávez, the Court took a particularly illiberal stance in cases dealing with the freedom of the press. For example, the Court denied the right of reply to a journalist, Elias Santana, who was demanding air time to respond to Chávez's criticism on the weekly radio program *Alo Presidente*. According to legal experts at the time, the decision by the Court "opened the door to judicial censorship."[5] The Supreme Court defended its position, arguing that the complaints by the press were "part of an organized campaign to discredit the government."[6] In March 2002, the Court restricted further the freedom of the press by eliminating the principle of double jeopardy and allowing cases against journalists to be reopened on the grounds of public interest. Both decisions were widely criticized within the international legal community.[7]

During the time of the second decision, however, Chávez's grip on power was becoming increasingly tenuous. As a result of continued low living standards, the president's popularity had plummeted from 80 percent in

---

[4] Whether the two judges who managed to stay on the new Court, Antonio Ignacio Ramirez Jimenez and Ivan Guillermo Rincon Urdaneta (the Chief Justice), were among those who voted for the Constituent Assembly is not clear, but it raises the interesting possibility that a limited form of strategic defection may have been occurring despite the fact that the dissolution of the former Court during this period was virtually inevitable.

[5] *Miami Herald*, July 14, 2001.

[6] Ibid.

[7] Inter-American Press Association, October 12–16, 2001, http://216.147.167/publications/report_Venezuela 2002.cfm.

1999 to 24 percent by February 2002. Chávez's attempts to take over the state-owned oil company Petroleos de Venezuela, S.A. earlier that January had triggered a series of strikes, crippling the country economically. These events culminated in a coup against the government on April 12, 2002. Although the interim government led by Pedro Carmona lasted only two days before Chávez was restored, it brought the vulnerability of the government and its institutions into sharp relief. On seizing power, Carmona had immediately dissolved both the assembly and the Supreme Court. Once a much weakened Chávez was reinstated, the conditions were ripe for strategic defection.

By almost all popular accounts, the Court did dramatically shift against Chávez in the immediate post-coup period. As members of his own party counseled Chávez to resign, the Supreme Court suddenly declared unconstitutional seventeen of the forty-nine laws issued by Chávez as part of the government's Empowerment Law passed the previous fall. According to previous newspaper reports, these laws had been strongly opposed by the business community (which had supported the anti-Chávez coup) as violating the right to private property, the right to engage in assembly, and the right to collective bargaining.[8]

Without a doubt, however, the best evidence that Chávez's court was deserting him came in a series of rulings by the Court in August 2002 over prosecuting the military officers responsible for staging the coup. In a 11–8 vote, the Court ultimately voted to dismiss the charges due to a lack of evidence. With protesters threatening to storm the Court, Chávez urged Congress to "review the dossiers of the judges who 'made that absurd and aberrant decision.' "[9] In statements strikingly parallel to Duhalde's outrage over the *Smith* decision, Chávez told supporters that the Court was totally discredited but that "we have to swallow the decision, the way you swallow fish bones."[10] The justice minister, Diosdado Cabello, claimed that the Supreme Court ruling was "the second phase of an attempt to achieve a so-called institutional coup, including the trial of the head of state."[11] Meanwhile, encouraged by the Court's new direction, the opposition began bringing a series of charges against Chávez, including misappropriation of

---

[8] Inter-American Press Association, March 18, 2002, http://216.147.167/publications/mid_infvenezuela2002.cfm.

[9] "Venezuela: Chávez heads popular protest against Supreme Court Decisions," August 28, 2002. http://www.greenleft.org.au/back/220/506p12c.htm, accessed March 2003.

[10] Http://www.socialistaction.org/news/200209/looms.html, accessed March 2003.

[11] "Venezuela: Chávez heads popular protest against Supreme Court Decisions."

public funds, accepting illegal campaign contributions, and taking responsibility for protesters killed during the April opposition marches.[12]

Yet even despite the decline in his popularity, Chávez still wielded far more power than his Argentine counterpart. As tensions mounted in Venezuela during the course of the year, the Court came under severe attack by Chávez's supporters. By December, the Supreme Court decided to suspend work in protest against political harassment from the Chávez government. This decision came a week after the Chávez-dominated assembly voted to impeach the Court's vice president, Alberto Martini, on the grounds that he was not qualified. Later that month, the Court appeared to strike a compromise with the government, ordering Chávez to restore control over the Caracas police force to the mayor, but also helping Chávez to break the oil strike. By 2003, the opposition fragmented and the Court voted to postpone a national referendum that could have brought Chávez down. Whether the Court will defect or return to its original position of subservience is thus intimately linked to Chávez's future prospects for remaining in power.

Chile

If Argentina and Venezuela provide textbook cases for examining the logic of strategic defection, Chile offers a clear counterexample. For most of the twentieth century, Chile has been revered as having a stable rule of law and an independent, nonpoliticized judicial system. With the exception of the Allende government (1970–3), since 1925 democratically elected leaders have respected the constitutional guarantees of life tenure, salary protection, and nonpoliticized appointment process (Prillaman 2000: 139).

By most accounts, such independence persisted despite the coup in 1973 (Correa Sutil 1997; Hilbink 1999; Prillaman 2000). Unlike many other Latin American military governments, General Pinochet left the Supreme Court fully functioning and intact during his seventeen-year dictatorship. Although the endurance of the Court despite the dictatorship could perhaps be read as a sign of successful strategic defection prior to the coup, there is little indication that the judges under Allende changed their jurisprudence once his government began to lose power. The Court had been highly conservative before Allende came to power and remained so throughout Allende's aborted government. With the Court repeatedly striking down

---

[12] Http://www.petroleumworld.com/storyT318.htm, accessed March 2003.

Allende's efforts to distribute land, for example, there was no sharp change in the Court's commitment to protect property rights once Allende began to lose power (Prillaman 2000: 139).

Following the coup, the Court was generally sympathetic to the Pinochet government, but it was not a mere pawn of the regime. At the beginning of the dictatorship, for example, the Supreme Court declared its power to exercise judicial review in several cases involving the decree laws passed by the Pinochet government. In a series of cases involving the firing of state employees, the Court asserted that the administration's decree laws had violated property rights contained in the 1925 Constitution. Ultimately, the military, not the Court, was forced to modify its position (see Barros 2002: 96–103).

Yet, as occurred in Argentina under most of the dictatorship, the Chilean Supreme Court did very little to address the human rights abuses committed by the state under the dictatorship. Although the general neglect of human rights during this period was not strictly the fault of civilian courts, whose jurisdiction had been severely limited by the state of siege and the creation of special military tribunals, the Supreme Court adopted a very conservative stance toward the demand for justice. For example, during the first decade of the regime, the Court accepted a mere ten petitions for habeas corpus out of a total of more than 5,400 (Prillaman 2000: 140). According to Barros,

Although the Chilean Supreme Court of 1974 defended its faculty of reviewing legislation, when it came to directly confronting the exception in its repressive and coercive dimensions the court backed off. In late 1973 and throughout 1974, in some of the most controverted decisions in its history, the court repeatedly abdicated its constitutional mandate to supervise and correct "all the tribunals of the Nation," declaring itself incompetent to rule on complaints [*recursos de quejas*] regarding the military tribunals in a time of war. (2002: 132)

Moreover, given the heavily bureaucratized structure of the judicial system, the high court served as a highly effective sanctioning device for lower court judges who may have been less inclined to support Pinochet (Hilbink 1999). Along these lines, the Constitution of 1980 actually strengthened the functional autonomy of the high court, granting it even greater control over the judiciary's budget and appointment and removal processes (Prillaman 2000: 141).

In 1988 Chileans voted "no" in the plebiscite over whether Pinochet should continue for another eight years. Although the vote registered a clear, if surprising, defeat for Pinochet, the military government remained in firm control of the transition process. The ability of the outgoing dictatorship to create effective enclaves of influence is widely seen as one of the most distinctive features of the Chilean transition (Siavelis 2000; Boylan 2001). These protections also carried over into the judiciary. Although the democratic opposition expressed an interest in re-making the Court, the overwhelming majority of justices were very well insulated throughout the protracted transition. For example, under Alywin (1990–4), the government sought to impeach three justices for neglect of judicial duties and to increase the size of the Court. While Congress did ultimately convict one justice in 1993, the court-packing plan failed entirely. That the composition of the Court began to change during this period was strictly due to retirements for age- and health-related reasons (Prillaman 2000: 146).[13]

The relative incapacity of the democratic opposition to credibly threaten the Court during the transitional period suggests that there should have been no sharp change in the Court's jurisprudence at the end of the dictatorship. A recent statistical analysis comparing Argentine and Chilean Supreme Court decisions shows some support for the view that Chile's judges strategically supported the government but no evidence of strategic defection (Scribner 2003). Particularly in the area of human rights, the most striking feature of the Court's jurisprudence before and after the dictatorship was its unwavering conservatism (Hilbink 1999). Among liberal democratic observers, the Chilean Court thus provides an object lesson of the problems associated with Courts exercising too much independence (Fiss 1993; Hilbink 1999). Although the Chilean Court eventually has moved in a more liberal direction with decisions such as *Chequepan*, *Contreras*, and *Espinoza*, such decisions occurred well after the transition had already taken place. Even then, the Court moved in a liberal direction only gradually. Despite years of domestic and international legal challenges,[14] it was not until 2000

---

[13] In 1997 a scandal involving the chief justice, who had allegedly accepted bribes from narco-traffickers, helped to convince more moderate forces among the right to bring impeachment charges, and the justice was forced to resign. It was not until 1998 that a mandatory retirement age of seventy-five was introduced and the Court was expanded from seventeen members to twenty-one (Prillaman 2000).

[14] In October 1998, Pinochet was arrested in London for human rights abuses against foreign citizens on the request of the Spanish Judge Baltasar Garzon. Over the next sixteen months, Pinochet was held in London pending a decision over his extradition. In a highly controversial decision, the U.K. Home Secretary Jack Straw decided to release Pinochet due to his physical condition (http://news.bbc.co.uk/1/hi/uk/663886.stm, accessed March 2003).

that the Supreme Court finally agreed to strip Pinochet of his immunity, thus paving the way for the former dictator's prosecution for human rights abuses.[15]

Mexico

For most of the twentieth century, Mexico provides a clear case in which judges lacked secure tenure in practice, but in which their incentives to defect were limited by the strength of the ruling Partido Revolucionario Institucional (PRI) and by a very different set of career objectives. For example, prior to 1994, the formal provisions ensuring Supreme Court justices life tenure were routinely violated by incoming presidents.[16] According to data on tenure rates gathered by Magaloni and Sánchez (2001), the average length of appointment at the level of the Supreme Court was ten years, with most judges retiring at age sixty-three. Between 1934 and 1994 around 40 percent of all judges lasted less than five years, with most turnovers occurring according to the presidential term (ibid.: 6). As in Argentina, therefore, most Mexican presidents appointed a majority of judges to the bench.

Unlike their Argentine counterparts, however, most Mexican justices were not necessarily aiming to stay on the bench. The fact that the rules prohibited consecutive re-election of all offices meant that under the PRI the Supreme Court was effectively turned into simply another political post. More than half of all justices serving on the Court between 1934 and 1994 had a non-judicial career before and *after* serving as a justice (ibid.).[17] Although comparable data for Chile and Venezuela remain to be compiled, similar data for Argentina tell a very different story. Although roughly a

---

[15] On July 1, 2002, in the so-called Caravan of Death trials, the second chamber of the Chilean Supreme Court of Justice held in a 4-1 vote that Pinochet was mentally unfit to serve trial and dismissed the charges against him (http://www.web.amnesty.org/library/Index/ENGAMR220062002?open&of=ENG-CHL, accessed March 2003).

[16] The 1917 Mexican Constitution established life tenure for judges appointed after 1923. This provision was modified under Cárdenas (1934–40) and reinstated from 1944 to 1994 (Magaloni and Sánchez 2001: 5).

[17] According to Magaloni and Sánchez, 38 percent of Supreme Court justices had a judicial career before serving as a Supreme Court justice; 26 percent had a former political career; and 33 percent had a career in a state or federal bureaucracy. After leaving the bench, 38 percent went on to serve as governors; 26 percent went on to serve as senators, another 26 percent to fill federal posts in the executive branch; and 5 percent were elected as deputies (ibid.: 6).

third of justices appointed since Péron had prior political experience, less than 10 percent went on to political posts after serving on the bench (see Molinelli et al. 1999: 678–84).

Under these circumstances, the decisive factor limiting judges' incentives to defect was that the regime was controlled by a single hegemonic party. Thus, according to Sánchez and Magaloni:

The Mexican Supreme Court was subservient to the president because most justices tended to follow *partisan* careers before or after leaving the Court, creating strong incentives to please the leader of the party, namely the president, as a means to further their political ambitions. (2001: 6)

That said, there is some evidence during this period that judges did rule against the government. For example, in his classic study, González Casanova (1970) finds that, among cases involving the president of the Republic decided between 1917 and 1960, claimants won in approximately 34 percent of all disputes. In a similar analysis focusing on cases where the government was a party in labor or criminal *amparo* petitions, Schwarz (1977) finds that the percentages for and against the government are roughly even (cited in Larkins 1996: 616–17). Because these are aggregate figures, however, we have no way of knowing whether the mix of anti-governmental decisions varied over the course of the regime or over the course of a particular administration. Moreover, without knowing more about issues or the preferences of the various actors, it is impossible to interpret such rulings as evidence of strategic defection.

Indeed, while it could be that intra-party disputes during this period led judges to defect against outgoing presidents, it seems far more likely that such cases were simply politically unimportant to sitting presidents. The consensus of the literature during this period is that justices rarely decided politically salient cases against the government. One scholar writes:

undoubtedly the reason that the executive has been able to allow this judicial control over its activities is that, in reality, the court does not interfere in basic policy questions decided by the executive. Even if the law of amparo did not specifically exclude all political matters from its jurisdiction, there is a great deal of evidence that judges at all levels of courts would hesitate long before they would be willing to act against a major policy decision of the president. (Scott 1949, cited in Verner 1984: 485)

This pattern of self-limitation and compliance highlights an additional important consequence of the strategic defection account. That is, because Mexican judges faced little incentive to defect to appeal to an incoming opponent government, they likewise faced little incentive to enter the political fray (cf. Staton 2003). As a result, in Mexico under the PRI, judges who lacked legitimacy could avoid deciding high-profile cases, without worrying that they were also giving up a chance at survival that only costly decision making could afford. Thus, compared with Argentina, the Mexican judges' career paths, combined with the relative stability of the PRI throughout much of the twentieth century, helps to explain both the relative subservience and passivity of the Mexican courts.

During the 1990s, the emergence of a true political opposition in Mexico, coupled with the 1994 constitutional reforms giving the Supreme Court a more important role, have unquestionably changed the rules of the game for the justices. On the one hand, judicial reforms requiring a super-majority to appoint and remove judges appear to have put an end to the pattern of tenure instability.[18] To the extent that judges are relatively well insulated, the incentives to defect would thus seem to be relatively muted. Aggregate results presented by Magaloni and Sánchez (2001) suggest preliminary support for the null hypothesis. In their analysis of 165 decisions involving constitutional controversies handed down during 1994–2000 the Supreme Court ruled in the PRI's favor in an overwhelming majority of cases. Likewise, in the period from 1994 to 1997, the Supreme Court defended the PRI's interests in cases dealing with public security (Yamin and Noreiga 1999, cited in Rios-Figueroa 2003) and electoral rules (Fix-Fierro 1998).

On the other hand, a closer analysis suggests that once the opposition took control over the Congress in 1997, the Court's loyalty to the PRI began to shift. In a recent systematic study of more than 300 court cases involving the PRI, Rios-Figueroa (2003) finds that the likelihood of judges ruling against the PRI jumps from a mere 7 percent of all cases decided in the period between 1994 and 1997 up to 44 percent in the period between 1997 and 2000. Once the PAN won the presidency, the probability of an anti-PRI ruling increased to 51 percent. While such behavior can be viewed as support for the view that judges are more able to hand down decisions against a fragmented government (Rios-Figueroa 2003), the pattern is also consistent with the logic of strategic defection.

Sorting out fully the causal mechanisms that distinguish the two accounts must await further research, but the fact that the justices' preferences were

---

[18] Note that following the European model, under the new 1994 Constitution the term length for Supreme Court justices has been changed from life to a non-renewable fifteen-year term.

likely in line with the PRI's during this period (ibid.), begs the question of why they sided with the opposition. While the fragmentation hypothesis tells us only that judges facing a weak government may rule against it without fear of being overturned, the strategic defection account provides a logic for why judges do so, despite the fact that they share the government's preferences. If the strategic defection account is the right one, then the stability of the Court during this period may instead be endogenous to the pattern of anti-PRI decisions handed down once the PRI began to lose power.

In sum, the theory of strategic defection provides a generic logic for understanding court-executive relations that potentially extends well beyond the borders of Argentina. Applying that logic to other contexts, however, requires careful scrutiny of the incentives and information that judges possess. In Venezuela, judges appointed by Chávez were heavily criticized by the opposition as being lackeys of the government. In line with the core defection hypothesis, once Chávez's power began to crumble, judges previously loyal to the government suddenly began to defect. Although more research on judges' beliefs and expectations awaits, systematic patterns in the Mexican Supreme Court's post–PRI era rulings suggest another potential example of strategic defection. By contrast, in Chile and in Mexico during the era of PRI hegemony no pattern of defection appears to have occurred. In terms of the model, the Chilean case instead fits most closely with the judicial independence equilibrium in which the costs of violating judges' tenure were deemed too high by the incoming democratic government. Under the classic period of single-party rule in Mexico, however, the lack of defection was most likely driven by the judges' career concerns with respect to the party leadership. Thus, just as judges with principled goals are not always sufficient for preventing strategic defection, judges motivated by less noble concerns are also not always sufficient for inducing it.

7.3 Further Implications, Future Directions

The systematic theoretical framework developed to examine the effects of institutional instability on judges' and politicians' behavior opens up several areas for future research. First and foremost, the logic of strategic defection can and should be applied to other institutionally unstable environments both within Latin America and beyond. Indeed, efforts in this direction have already begun (Tate et al. 2002; Scribner 2003). Nevertheless, a few words of caution are in order. In particular, evaluating the theory in other contexts will only be as successful as scholars' efforts are to the portray *actual* constraints that judges face. While it is daunting enough to gather systematic data on judicial decisions cross-nationally, it is arguably much more difficult to identify systematically the beliefs, goals, and preferences of the actors involved, particularly in large-*n* analyses. Yet without such information on the main independent variables, we cannot fully test the strategic defection account. Cooter and Ginsburg's (1996) excellent comparative work on judicial discretion in advanced democracies provides one template for multi-country analyses that might be modified to test strategic defection. Witold Henisz's Political Constraints Database (2000), which systematically codes veto players, provides another potentially useful approach. Still, because of the practical trade-offs between depth and breadth, scholars will want to think carefully about the implications of any research design they choose.

On the theoretical side, several issues also merit future attention. First, in terms of the main model developed in the book, the basic assumption was that the costs that politicians incur for punishing judges are substantively variable but exogenously fixed. In other words, the model was agnostic about whether politicians' costs are due to public backlash, congressional disapproval, or difficulties in selecting new judges, but it assumed that such costs were independent from what judges themselves did while on the bench. Yet empirical evidence from Argentina suggested that the constraints that incoming politicians faced were not always purely independent of judges' choices. How judges ruled sometimes helped to shape the costs that incoming governments faced in punishing them. For example, under Menem's second government the Court's decision to defect in the re-re-election case arguably prevented the opposition parties from unifying against the Court under De la Rua. An emerging wave of formal theoretical literature (Carruba 2001; Staton 2003) has begun to explore how to endogenize such costs. But because most of these models are solely limited to the question of establishing the judiciary's legitimacy, it is not entirely clear whether they can easily support an equilibrium in which judges defect. For example, Staton's (2003) model shows that a single decision can have an enormous impact on the Court's legitimacy but essentially rules out the possibility that strategic judges can convince the public that it is objective. Thus, it remains an open question of how precisely to model a situation in which judges' strategic behavior can also help to determine the costs that politicians face in punishing the Court.

Second, as we also saw from the recent debacle of the Court under Duhalde, the fate of the sitting government itself may potentially prove endogenous to the Court's decisions. Another intriguing theoretical modification for the future, then, particularly appropriate for circumstances where politicized courts survive under weak governments, is to move from a sequential game of incomplete information to a bargaining game in which judges and governments jointly determine each other's fates. Here, a useful theoretical analogue could be the standard war crisis model used in the international relations literature to capture the decision of states to go to war (Bueno de Mesquita and Lalman 1992; Signorino 1999). Note, however, that in such a strategic setting, anti-governmental decisions will take on a very different substantive meaning. Rather than judges defecting from governments they otherwise agree with in order to appeal to the next government, ruling against the rulers instead would be a calculated move to get rid of governments that judges do not like.

Returning to the original model, another basic assumption was that politicians care about retaining judges who shared their views but are uncertain about the underlying ideology of the sitting justices. In the American politics literature, the supposition that politicians care about a judges' ideology is de rigueur. Moving beyond the North American context, Chapter 3 drew on the logic of the separation-of-powers model to suggest more generally why a judge's ideology might matter to incoming politicians. Using politicians' uncertainty over the judge's ideology as a starting point, the model then explicated the conditions under which a judge would strategically pool against his or her type to avoid sanctions. Thus, in the stylized world of the model, for example, an incoming liberal politician who knew that a judge ruled conservatively when the dictatorship was strong and liberally once the dictatorship began to unravel might infer that the judge was acting strategically at the beginning, not the end, of the dictatorship. From the judge's point of view, the fact that politicians could draw this inference opens up the possibility of strategic behavior. As long as the judge believes that politicians are sufficiently uncertain about his or her type, then, under certain conditions, strategic defection is a rational best response. In reality, not surprisingly, politicians are not always that gullible. But even in real world situations where strategic defection proves to be a longshot, as long as the judge cares more about avoiding sanctions (β) than the issues (α), switching sides is still a rational best response.

A third avenue for further research is whether these same conclusions hold true if we alter our assumptions about what incoming governments want from a court. For example, it could be that an incoming government cares solely about whether judges are going to block its policies, not about the judges' underlying ideology.[19] In this alternative scenario, it is not immediately obvious whether strategic defection has the same intuitive appeal. Indeed, for incoming governments who merely want compliance from the Court, defection could send incoming governments an ambiguous signal. Judges who rule against the outgoing government may be seen as rats leaving a sinking ship or may simply appear to be independent. In the former case, an incoming government may correctly perceive the judges as pliable in the short run, but would be right to be skeptical about the judges' loyalty in the long run. In the latter case, however, the incoming government would be risking retaining judges who would be willing to rule against it throughout its term.

Yet note that judges who simply stick by the outgoing government also risk sending an unclear message to an incoming government. If judges continue to support the outgoing government, how can incoming politicians distinguish whether a judge is truly compliant or whether he or she simply agrees with the incumbents? While fully answering this question must await future research, it would seem that in order for defection to make sense under this scenario, two conditions would need to be met. First, incoming governments must view the judge's willingness to rule against the government as strategic, rather than as truly independent. In other words, judges should switch to signal compliance, not compatibility. Second, however, the incoming government must then also have sufficiently low discount rates such that it is willing to incur the possibility that the judge will turn against it, too, down the road.

Overall, the story of defection supplies the micro foundations underpinning the familiar observation that presidentialist systems are prone to oscillate between presidential omnipotence and impotence (Linz 1990; Mainwaring 1990; Mainwaring and Shugart 1997; O'Donnell 1999). In the particular institutional arena of court-executive relations, this framework makes sense of the apparent paradox in which the very presidents who seek to exert the most control over courts at the beginning of their terms are left with the least loyal courts at the end of their terms. Because outgoing presidents are unable either to punish or to protect their own judges, they are left with only a series of ad hoc responses, such as delaying

---

[19] I thank John Ferejohn, Barry Friedman, and the participants at the Workshop on Law, Economics and Politics at New York University for suggesting this point.

implementation or refusing to comply with unfavorable decisions,[20] which further undermine the rule of law.

The findings of this study carry also several additional implications for the legal strategies employed by other social and political actors. On the one hand, a major debate in the U.S. judicial politics literature is whether courts can become effective agents of social change (Rosenberg 1991; Schultz 1998; also see Epp 1998). Because secure tenure tends to produce judges who are conservative, or "backward-looking," a primary concern is that judges often do a far better job of defending the status quo, rather than pushing forward a rights revolution. Legal activism, in other words, is not the most productive avenue for those seeking profound social and political change (but see McCann 1994).

By contrast, insofar as courts in institutionally insecure environments are forced to be "forward-looking," a key question is whether social movements should choose a legal course of action, if only to speed up or to reinforce a policy shift in that direction. Indeed, despite the overall lack of confidence in the judiciary, social movements have repeatedly sought redress in Argentina through the judicial system (Brysk 1994). By the same token, the flip side of the defection story is that bureaucratic agents of the executive are also likely to adjust their strategies (cf. Ferejohn and Shipan 1990; Canes-Wrone 2003). In such contexts, the anticipation of strategic defection may be enough to shift the policies pursued by administrative agencies. If it is, then scholars will want to explore who uses the courts and to what ends is embedded in the larger legal-political cycle.

Finally, beyond the realm of court-executive relations, the theory of strategic defection provides a clear and intuitively appealing logic for examining other types of institutional relationships. After all, in such contexts, uncertainty and high stakes are hardly limited to courts. Such problems pervade presidentialist systems in everything from intra-party politics (Levitsky 2003: 158–61) to legislative-executive relations (Mejia-Acosta 2000) to a host of other quasi-independent institutions, such as bureaucracies and central banks. In terms of future research, the theory of strategic defection offers a coherent approach to understanding how cycles of institutional and political instability map onto inter-institutional relations. Again, however,

---

[20] For example, during the military period, both the *Timerman* decision and the *Moya* decision nearly provoked uprisings within the military. In response to the Court's decisions, the junta agreed to free Jacobo Timerman, but stripped him of his citizenship and forced him into exile (Timerman 1981).

in order to be persuasive, any extension of the strategic defection account to other institutional arenas needs to clearly identify the relevant actors' beliefs, goals, and information, grapple with competing accounts, and explicate the logic underlying the mechanism.

To conclude, treating judges as strategic actors puts us in the position of understanding a wide range of important – but heretofore unexplained – behavior and political outcomes. In stark contrast to conventional wisdom, judges who face institutional insecurity do not automatically serve the government in power. Rather, under the right combination of circumstances, such constraints are precisely what provoke courts to stand up to the current government and to do so in the most important and contentious issues of the day. Ultimately, these decisions not only affect the fate of the judiciary, but also establish the quality and stability of the rules under which citizens interact with each other and with their governments.

Appendix A

Overview of the Federal Argentine Judiciary and the Argentine Supreme Court

Organization

The Argentine Supreme Court (Corte Suprema de Justicia de la Nación) stands at the head of a federal judiciary currently composed of a total of 343 first-instance courts (*juzgados*), 42 oral tribunals (*tribunales orales*), and 24 appeals courts (*cámaras*). Article 94 of the 1853 Constitution establishes that the number of lower courts shall be determined by Congress. The organization of the federal courts is regulated by decree law 1285/58, which specifies the areas of specialization for each of the various tribunals. Currently, the lower federal courts are divided into separate tribunals for administrative law (Fuero Contensiosa Administrativa and Fuero Federal de la Seguridad Social), criminal law (Fuero Criminal y Correccional Federal, Fuero Penal Oral Federal de la Capital Federal, Fuero Penal Oral Federal del Interior), civil and commercial law (Fuero Civil y Comercial Federal), and electoral law (Fuero Electoral). The twenty-four Federal Courts of Appeals are located in fifteen of the country's twenty-three provinces.

Jurisdiction and Precedent

The jurisdiction and powers of the federal courts are determined by the Constitution of 1853 – recently reformed in 1994 – the Congress, and through the Supreme Court's own jurisprudence. The Constitution's Articles 94, 100, 101, and 67, section 11, regulate the jurisdiction of the federal judiciary. As in the United States, the main task of the Argentine federal courts is to resolve all "federal questions," which includes all questions of interpretation that emerge from laws passed by the Congress and cases whereby a right of the Constitution has been allegedly violated (Miller et al. 1995: 411; Molinelli et al. 1999). Since 1887 the Court has established through its own jurisprudence the power of judicial review. As in the United States, this power rests ultimately with the Supreme Court but can be exercised by courts at any level of the federal judiciary (Miller 1989; Miller et al. 1995: 2). The norm that has developed is that the lower federal courts and the Supreme Court itself are obligated to follow the precedents established by the decisions of the Argentine Supreme Court. Thus, as Argentine legal scholar Alberto Garay has noted, "in spite of its Roman Law background, in practice the [Argentine] Supreme Court has come to resemble the Common Law countries, much more than the civil law countries" (my translation, Garay 1997: 108). Indeed, not only does the Argentine judiciary follow the basic ideas of common law, but it has throughout its history adopted almost word for word many of the specific legal doctrines developed in the United States, including, for example, judicial review, the doctrine of political questions, the doctrine of institutional *gravedad*, and, most recently, the doctrine of *per saltum* (Miller 1989; Nino 1992; Carrió and Banks 1993; Miller et al. 1995). Unlike European constitutional courts, the Argentine Supreme Court cannot exercise abstract review.

Appeals Procedures

There are two main routes through which the Argentine Supreme exercises jurisdiction: original and appellate. In terms of original jurisdiction, Article 101 of the Argentine Constitution is almost identical to Article 3, section 2, of the U.S. Constitution and establishes that the Argentine Supreme Court has original jurisdiction in all cases dealing with ambassadors, ministers, and foreign councils, as well as in cases in which a province is a party (Bidart Campos 1995). Cases of original jurisdiction constitute a relatively small proportion of the cases that the Argentine Court treats. For example, using the statistics compiled by the Argentine Supreme Court, I calculated that between 1984 and 1997, cases of original jurisdiction comprised only .03 percent of all cases decided by the Court (*Poder Judicial de la Nación* 1996).

The two primary types of appeal are ordinary (*recurso ordinario*) and extraordinary (*recurso extraordinario*), both of which are regulated by Law 48[1]

---

[1] Law 48 was modeled on Section 25 of the U.S. Judiciary Act of 1789 (Miller et al. 1995: 413–14).

promulgated in 1863, decree law 1285/58, and several other federal laws and codes (Miller et al. 1995: 412–13). Ordinary appeals encompass four types of cases: The state is a party when the sum exceeds a specified amount and in cases of criminal extradition, naval embargos, and all criminal cases dealing with sedition or treachery in which the penalty exceeds ten years. Extraordinary appeals are used to remedy violations of constitutional and federal laws and procedures. The basic procedure for both types of appeals is to submit the appeal to the lower court whose sentence is being appealed. If the lower court rejects the appeal, then the litigants may use a third type of appeal, known as the *recurso de queja* (also known as the *recurso de hecho*), which asks the Supreme Court directly to decide whether or not the lower court's decision to reject the appeal was correct (Miller et al. 1995: 412).

Over the last century, and particularly over the last fifty years, the use of both the *recurso extraordinario* and the *recurso de queja* has grown dramatically and now far exceeds the use of *recurso ordinario*. For example, between 1974 and 1983, fully 57 percent of all appeals entering the Supreme Court were via the *recurso de queja* alone (Gabrielli 1986: 393). Between 1984 and 1997, cases coming to the court via the *recurso extraordinario* and the *recurso de queja* constituted over 99 percent of all cases (*Poder Judicial de la Nación* 1996).[2] The increasing reliance on these two mechanisms for appeal has been due to the development of specific doctrines developed by the Court itself in the mid-twentieth century, such as the *doctrina de arbitrariedad*, which deals with cases in which provincial law violates the Constitution or federal law (Miller et al. 1995: 492).

Docket Control

The most dramatic difference between the Argentine Supreme Court and those of the United States and other common law countries more generally is the huge number of cases that the Argentine Court decides annually. For example, between 1974 and 1984 the average number of cases decided annually by the Argentine Supreme Court was between 4,000 and 5,500 (FORES 1988). Between 1984 and 1994, that figure rose slightly to an average of approximately 6,000. But since 1997 it has skyrocketed to over 36,000 (*Poder Judicial de la Nación* 1996; Molinelli et al. 1999: 710). Not surprisingly, case backlog is an increasing problem for the Court. For example in 1989, there

---

[2] For a more complete analysis of the different appeals made to the Argentine Supreme Court, see FORES 1988; Molinelli, Palanza, and Sin 1999: 710–13).

were approximately 1,400 cases in process, 87 percent of which had been in the Court for less than six months (Garrido 1993: 72). A decade later, there were over 50,000 cases "*en tramite*" (pending) in the Supreme Court, with no reliable statistics of the length of time that they have been left unresolved.[3]

While there is no single reason for the huge workload of the Court, a number of factors are responsible.[4] First, until 1990 the Court lacked the equivalent of the writ of certiorari, which would have allowed it to control effectively its own docket.[5] Nevertheless, as the evidence suggests, even after the introduction of the writ of cert in 1990, the Court has hardly done much better. Indeed, the number of cases has grown dramatically since 1990. In the mid-1990s, there have been a number of additional reforms proposed to augment the Court's discretionary power.[6]

An additional reason for the more recent burst of cases stems from the 1994 constitutional reforms, which made the *acción de amparo* a part of the Constitution. Originally developed in Mexico, the *amparo* is a type of injunction or legal remedy whereby the Court uses an accelerated process to ensure the effective exercise of constitutional review against arbitrariness and manifest illegality (Rogers and Wright-Carozza 1995: 168). According to Justice Moliné O'Connor and Chief Justice Nazareno, the addition of the *acción de amparo* to the 1994 Constitution coupled with the fact that there are no class-action suits filed in Argentina has encouraged thousands of individual cases to be filed at the Court by those who oppose what the Menem government has done. As Justice Moliné O'Connor himself put it, "from 1989 until this very day Argentina has made huge changes in almost all areas. . . . In all elections the government has maintained the majority in

---

[3] For example, in the Supreme Court's own statistics for 1996, there were 81,619 cases *en tramite* (in process). However, even though they purportedly used the same data source, other scholars report 80,755 cases *en tramite* (ibid.: 710).

[4] For example, the bulk of these cases in 1997 comes from retirees filing cases in the Court following the Court's ruling in *Chacobar* (1995; interview with the Secretaria Letrada de Estadísticas de la Corte Suprema de la Nacion, Buenos Aires, May, 1998).

[5] In 1990 as part of the same law that increased the number of justices on the Supreme Court, the Procedural Code was modified to allow the Court to exercise discretion in cases dealing with *recurso extraordinario* (Codigo Proceso, sección 6, articulo 280).

[6] For example, in 1993 Justice Boggiano proposed setting a maximum number of cases that could be decided by the Court every year. According to an editorial that appeared in *La Nación*, ideally the Argentine Supreme Court would follow the United States and decide no more than 250 cases every year. As the editorial went on to add, limiting the number of cases would improve the quality of the decisions overall, thereby increasing the prestige of the Court (April 10, 1998).

Congress, thus there has been no way to stop politically what the executive has been doing. The only way to challenge [the government] has been through the Courts."[7] Additional interviews with lawyers and activists from human and civil rights organizations such as CELS, Poder Cuidadano, and Fundación Carlos Nino further confirm that this is indeed the strategy being adopted. In the majority of cases, however, the modus operandi is for the Supreme Court to confirm the lower courts' rejection of the appeal.[8]

Internal Organization and Decision-Making Procedures and Norms

According to the constitutional scholar Alejandro Carrió, the Argentine Supreme Court functions as a typical collegial organization where the work of its members is primarily written. In addition to the nine justices who currently sit on the bench, there are several lawyers and functionaries who work for the Court. Of these, the highest ranked functionaries are the eight so-called *Secretarios del Tribunal*, each of which holds the equivalent ranking of an appeals court judge and specializes in a different branch of the law. Each of the *secretarios* has his or her own staff of attorneys and administrators. In addition to the *secretarios*, each justice has his or her own staff of *secretarios* and *prosecretarios letrados* with whom they work directly. Unlike "clerks" in the United States, the *secretarios* and *prosecretarios letrados* are the equivalent of appeals court judges and first-instance judges, respectively. The Court-packing plan increased not only the number of justices, but also the number of *secretarios* from approximately thirty in the 1980s to over 150 by the mid-1990s (Verbitsky 1993: 75). The administrative business of the Court is mainly handled by the president of the Court, who is elected by a majority of at least five other justices for a three-year term.[9] The Court's *Acordadas* (administrative decisions) are published annually along with the Court's decisions.

The procedures for reviewing cases and ultimately drafting opinions are as follows. Generally, all cases that come to the Argentine Supreme Court arrive first in one of the eight *secretario*'s offices. Which particular office a case goes to is determined by the particular branch of law that the

---

[7] Interview, Buenos Aires, May 22, 1998.
[8] Interviews with Martin Böhmer, May 1998; Martin Abregú, Buenos Aires, April 1998; Carlos March, Buenos Aires, April 1998.
[9] *La Nación*, May 15, 1999.

case deals with. For example, the *secretario* that deals with criminal cases would have received all of the requests for writs of habeas corpus that were filed during the military government. After reviewing the case, the *secretario* drafts an initial opinion, which is then sent to the justices' offices. Once the case arrives in a justice's office, the justice's own *secretarios* then draft their own versions of the opinion, which are then reviewed and signed by the justice.[10]

From the first justice's office to which the case is sent, the case is then circulated, arriving at each of the remaining justices' offices according to a written schedule. The order in which a justice receives the case seems to be determined by the president or chief justice of the Supreme Court, who rules on the case last.[11] In addition the chief justice determines when and whether the attorney general should also write an opinion. The chief justice votes, but cannot break a tie vote in the Court, as can the president of the Senate.

After each justice has had a chance to examine the case, he or she decides (often with the help of his or her clerks) whether to sign, to amend, to concur separately, or to file a dissent with the circulating draft. During the circulation phase, the offices of the justices also exchange written memoranda over the details of the case. The informal norm that has developed is that if the first five justices reject the appeal, the case stops circulating. Once all of the justices have had a chance to review the case, a consensus either has or has not emerged. Depending on the time of year, the justices meet together either weekly or bi-weekly in sessions called *acuerdos* to discuss the case further or to sign the opinion formally. In contrast to the U.S. Supreme Court, the norm is that while all the names of those who agree with the decision appear under the opinion, the actual "author" of the opinion remains anonymous. In practice, however, it seems likely that the legal experts and other justices often do know who the author of the opinion is (e.g., see Carrió and Garay 1991).

Moreover, in contrast in the United States, it should be noted that there are no oral proceedings nor are there any amicus curiae (friends of the Court) briefs admitted during the decision-making process. According to Carrió (1996), this carries several implications for the Court and the litigants involved in the case. On the one hand, lawyers do have some access to the

---

[10] Interviews with an anonymous clerk, March 1998; Hernán Goulco, March 1998; clerks for Justices Bossert and Moliné O'Connor, Buenos Aires, April 1998.
[11] Interview with Justice Gabrielli, Buenos Aires, May 1998.

Court via the so-called *charlas* (chats) that lawyers arrange with the *secretarios* and the justices. However, there is no formal procedure for doing so, which obviously implies several opportunities for clientelism and favoritism to emerge. Also, according to Carrió, *charlas* are quite inefficient: Justices waste time hearing details of cases they have not yet reviewed, while the lawyers spend time running back and forth among the justices' offices, often without even knowing whether a case is still *en tramite* (in process; ibid.).

Appendix B

The Argentine Supreme Court Decisions Data Set

One of the main tasks of field research was to develop and to implement a method for systematically measuring judicial behavior. Ideally, the goal was to construct a data base that would include all cases in which the government had some identifiable interest. The most appropriate method for selecting such cases, however, was not immediately obvious. In contrast to the U.S. Supreme Court, the Argentine Court hands down thousands of decisions every year, many of which have nothing to do with the interests of the government. Thus, coding neither all decisions nor a random sample was appropriate.

Other more refined techniques also proved either unsatisfactory or simply were too difficult to implement given the context. For example, I initially sought to replicate Robert Dahl's method (1957) by examining the Argentine Court's use of judicial review in constitutional cases. Although I was able to gain access to the Argentine Supreme Court's computer system to locate "constitutional cases," it became clear that there was no necessary overlap between these cases and cases in which one could identify the interest of the government. As a result, many of the cases that made the constitutional list did not serve as a very good measure of judicial subservience to the government per se.

A different method, which might have overcome this problem, would have been to use amicus curiae (friends of the court) briefs filed by the government to identify the government's interests. For example, in the United States, amicus curiae briefs have been used by scholars both to identify the preferences of the government as well as to document the information that the justices have about the interests of the government (e.g., see Epstein and Knight 1998: 146–7). In the Argentine case, such briefs could have been used either to supplement the information about the government's preferences in the constitutional cases or as a method of selecting the cases directly. For example, if the government regularly filed briefs in cases it cared about, one could then track the decisions to see whether they went in favor of or against the government's preferences. Unfortunately, in spite of recent efforts to adopt amicus curiae made by various lawyers' associations, this norm does not exist in Argentina (Abregú and Courtis n.d.).

Ultimately, the method that I employed uses the annual indices in each volume of Argentine Supreme Court decisions (*Fallos de la Corte Suprema de Justicia de la Nación*) to select cases that meet one or both of the following criteria: (1) the case names the state as a party and/or (2) the case names a decree passed by the current executive. A series of cross-checks with a list of cases considered politically relevant by Argentine legal experts that I compiled revealed that most of the important cases were selected by this criteria.

The data contained in the Argentine Supreme Court Decisions (ASCD) data base were then gathered in three main waves. During field research in Buenos Aires in 1997–8, I coded cases at the aggregate level decided between 1976 and 1992. I then later coded this same set of cases at the individual level using the collection of *Fallos* at the Ohio State University Law Library in August 1999. I subsequently added the data for 1992–2000 using the collections at the University of Michigan Law Library in 2001 and the Harvard Law Library in 2002. At present, the data set includes over 11,423 individual judicial decisions handed down by the Court between March 24, 1976, and December 31, 2000. Each case was coded according the variables listed in Appendix Table B.1.

Appendix Table B.1 *Argentine Supreme Court Decisions Data Base Codebook*

Case identification variables		
Column no.	Variable name	Variable description
1–6	ID	Case Number
8–13	DATE	Case Date
15	TYPE	0 = Government-as-Party
		1 = Decree
		2 = Both

Issue variables		
17	AFRET	1 = Armed Forces Retire
		0 = Not
18	AFOT	1 = Armed Forces (Other)
		0 = Not
19	CONSTFED	1 = Constitutionality of Statutes, Decrees, Resolutions, Acts
		0 = Not
20	CONSTLOC	1 = Constitutionality of Local Statutes, Decrees, Resolutions, Acts
		0 = Not
21	INTERP	1 = Construction[a] or Nullity of Statutes, Decrees, Acts, and Resolutions[b]
		0 = Not
22	CLAIMS	1 = Claims against or by Argentina
		0 = Not
23	CUSTOM	1 = Customs
		0 = Not
24	PROCS	1 = Federal Civil and Criminal Procedures (Right to Defense)
		0 = Not
25	HABEAS	1 = Federal Habeas Corpus
		0 = Not
26	AMPARO	1 = Acción Amparo
		0 = Not
27	JURIS	1 = Jurisdiction and Competence
		0 = Not
28	FED	1 = Federal-Provincial
		0 = Not
29	JUDGES	1 = Judges
		0 = Not
30	PROPERTY	1 = Right to Property
		0 = Not
31	PUBLICHF	1 = Public Employees (Hiring and Firing)
		0 = Not

The Argentine Supreme Court Decisions Data Set

Case identification variables

Column no.	Variable name	Variable description
32	PUBLICOT	1 = Public Employees (Other)
		0 = Not
33	FEDOT	1 = Review of Other Fed. Admin. Action
		0 = Not
34	TAXES	1 = Taxes
		0 = Not
35	EMERGE	1 = State of Siege and Emergency
		Powers (Article 23)
		0 = Not

Background and lower court outcome variables

37	INSTANC1	0 = Against State
		1 = For State
		8 = Missing
		9 = Not Applicable
38	INSTANC2	0 = Against State
		1 = For State
		8 = Missing
		9 = Not Applicable
39	APPEAL	1 = Recurso Extraordinario
		2 = Recurso de Hecho
		3 = Recurso Ordinario
		4 = Original
		5 = Unknown or N/A
40	PGAPP	0 = Accept Appeal
		1 = Deny Appeal
		2 = Refuse Opinion
		8 = Unclear
		9 = N/A
41	PGOP	0 = Against State
		1 = For State
		8 = Unclear
		9 = N/A

Aggregate Supreme Court decision variables

43	SCD1	0 = Deny Appeal
		1 = Partially Deny
		2 = Accept Appeal
		3 = Partially Accept
		9 = Not Available

(*continued*)

Appendix Table B.1 (*continued*)

Column no.	Variable name	Variable description
Case identification variables		
44	SCD2	0 = Uphold 2nd Instance
		1 = Partially Uphold
		2 = Overturn 2nd Instance
		3 = Partially Overturn
		9 = Not Available
46	SCD3	0 = Against State
		1 = Partially against State
		2 = For State
		3 = Partially for State
		9 = Not Available
48	OPTYPE	0 = Summary
		1 = Full Opinion
49	UNAN	0 = Unanimous
		1 = Not Unanimous
		9 = Not Applicable
50	CONSENT	0 = No Separate Consent
		1 = Separate Consent
		9 = Not Applicable
51	DISSENT	0 = No Separate Dissent
		1 = Separate Dissent
		9 = Not Applicable
52	AUTHOR	0 = Regular Justices
		1 = Conjueces

Individual judge vote variables

53	Horacio H. Heredia
54	Frederico Videla Escalada
55	Adolfo Gabrielli
56	Alejandro R. Caride
57	Abelardo Rossi
58	Pedro J. Frías
59	Elías Guastavino
60	Emilio Daireaux
61	César Black
62	Carlos Renom
63	Julio J. Martínez Vivot
64	Emilio Gnecco
65	Genaro Carrió
66	José Caballero
67	Augusto Belluscio

The Argentine Supreme Court Decisions Data Set

Case identification variables

Column no.	Variable name
68	Carlos Fayt
69	Enrique Petracchi
70	Jorge Bacqué
71	Julio Oyanarte
72	Ricardo Levene
73	Mariano Cavagna Martínez
74	Rodolfo Barra
75	Julio Nazareno
76	Moliné O'Connor
77	Antonio Boggiano
78	Gustavo Bossert
79	Guillermo López
80	Adolfo Vázquez

Coding for individual-level justices

0	Against State
1	For State
5	Abstain
9	Not on Court
3	Summary
4	Not Clear
2	Dissenting from Majority against State
6	Dissenting from Majority for State
7	Separate Concur for State
8	Separate Concur against State

Core Timing variables

TIME to Transition 1
0 = all other (March 24, 1976–Dec. 12, 1981)
1 = decision dated within the twenty-four months prior to the regime
   transition (December 13, 1981–December 12, 1983)

TIME to Transition 2
0 = all other (Dec. 13, 1983–July 6, 1987)
1 = decision dated within the twenty-four months prior to the
   inter-governmental transition (July 7, 1987–July 6, 1989)

TIME to Transition 3
0 = all other (July 7, 1989–April 1993)
1 = decision dated within the twenty-four months prior to the
   inter-governmental transition (May 1993–May 1995)

(continued)

Appendix Table B.1 (*continued*)

Case identification variables

TIME to Transition 4
0 = (June 1995–Nov. 1997)
1 = decision dated within the twenty-four months prior to the inter-governmental transition (Dec. 1997–Dec. 1999)

[a] Interpretation; challenges to validity not based on Constitution; applicability.
[b] Not otherwise included or unless explicitly stated.

Appendix C

Equilibria Proofs

Equilibrium 1: *Judicial Independence*, Separating Equilibrium

$L \setminus \theta; R \setminus \sim\theta$
$R_{LG} = NI, NI; R_{CG} = NI, NI$
Choice $R \in \{I, NI\}$
$\mu(\theta \mid L, LG) = 1$
$\mu(\theta \mid L, CG) = 1$
$\mu(\theta \mid R, LG) = 0$
$\mu(\theta \mid R, CG) = 0$
$c \geq j \geq 0$
$0 \geq r \geq 1$

(1) Liberal government *BR* if sees *L* is *NI* if $Eu(NI) \geq Eu(I)$

$0(1) + -j(0) \geq -c(1) + -c(0)$
$c \geq 0$

(2) Conservative government *BR* if sees *L* is *NI* if $Eu(NI) \geq Eu(I)$

$-j(1) + 0(0) \geq -c(1) + -c(0)$
$-j \geq -c$
$j \leq c$

(3) Liberal government *BR* if sees *R* is *NI* if $Eu(NI) \geq Eu(I)$

$0(0) + -j(1) \geq 0(-c) + 1(-c)$
$-j \geq -c$
$j \leq c$

(4) Conservative government BR is sees R is NI if $Eu(NI) \geq Eu(I)$

$$-j(0) + 0(1) \geq -c(0) + -c(1)$$
$$c \geq 0$$

So, given these conditions, this will be a separating equilibrium.

Equilibrium 2: *Judicial Dependence*, Separating Equilibrium

$L \setminus \theta, R \setminus \sim\theta$
$R_{LG} = I, I; R_{CG} = I, I$
Choice $R \in \{I, NI\}$
$\mu(\theta \mid L, LG) = 1$
$\mu(\theta \mid L, CG) = 1$
$\mu(\theta \mid R, LG) = 0$
$\mu(\theta \mid R, CG) = 0$
$0 \geq j \geq c$
$0 \geq r \geq 1$

This, however, does not fit the assumption that $j > 0$. Therefore, this is not a salient equilibrium.

(1) Liberal government BR if sees L is I if $Eu(I) \geq Eu(NI)$

$$-c(1) + -c(0) \geq 0(1) + -j(0)$$
$$0 \geq c$$

(2) Conservative government BR if sees L is I if $Eu(I) \geq Eu(NI)$

$$-c(1) + -c(0) \geq -j(1) + 0(0)$$
$$-c \geq -j$$
$$j \geq c$$

(3) Liberal government BR if sees R is I if $Eu(I) \geq Eu(NI)$

$$-c(0) + -c(1) \geq 0(0) + -j(1)$$
$$j \geq c$$

(4) Conservative government BR if sees R is I if $Eu(I) \geq Eu(NI)$

$$-c(0) + -c(1) \geq -j(0) + 0(1)$$
$$0 \geq c$$

Equilibrium 3: *Sincere Judiciary*, Separating Equilibrium

$L \setminus \theta; R \setminus \sim\theta$
$R_{LG} = (NI, I); R_{CG} = (I, NI)$

Equilibria Proofs

$\mu(\theta \mid L, LG) = 1$
$\mu(\theta \mid L, CG) = 1$
$\mu(\theta \mid R, LG) = 0$
$\mu(\theta \mid R, CG) = 0$
$j \geq c \geq 0$
$((\beta - \alpha) / 2\beta) \leq r \leq ((\alpha + \beta) / 2\beta)$

(1) Liberal government BR is NI if sees L if $Eu(NI) \geq Eu(I)$, yes if $c \geq 0$

(2) Conservative government BR is I if sees L if $Eu(I) \geq Eu(NI)$, yes if $j \geq c$

(3) Liberal government BR is I if sees R if $Eu(I) \geq Eu(NI)$, yes, if $j \geq c$

(4) Conservative government BR is NI if sees R if $Eu(NI) \geq Eu(I)$, yes, if $c \geq 0$

(5) Liberal judges' BR is L, if $Eu(L) \geq Eu(R)$

$Eu(L) = r(\alpha + \beta) + (1 - r)\alpha$
$Eu(R) = r(0) + (1 - r)\beta$
$r(\alpha + \beta) + (1 - r)\alpha \geq r(0) + (1 - r)\beta$
$r\alpha + r\beta + \alpha - r\alpha \geq \beta - r\beta$
$r\beta + \alpha \geq \beta - r\beta$
$2r\beta \geq \beta - \alpha$
$r \geq ((\beta - \alpha)/2\beta) \equiv r^* \Rightarrow$ Liberal judge will vote L.

So, if this condition holds, liberal judges voting liberally is the best response.

(6) Conservative judges' BR is R, if $Eu(R) \geq Eu(L)$

$Eu(R) = r(\alpha) + (1 - r)(\alpha + \beta)$
$Eu(L) = r(\beta) + (1 - r)0$
$r(\alpha) + (1 - r)(\alpha + \beta) \geq r(\beta) + (1 - r)0$
$r\alpha + \alpha - r\alpha - r\beta + \beta \geq r\beta$
$\alpha - r\beta + \beta \geq r\beta$
$\alpha + \beta \geq 2r\beta$
$((\alpha + \beta)/2\beta) \geq r \equiv r^{**} \Rightarrow$ Conservative judge will vote R.

So, if this condition holds, conservative judges voting conservatively is the best response. This equilibrium holds if these restrictions are satisfied: $r^* \leq r \leq r^{**}$. A particular case of this equilibrium is when the judge places no value of the issue:

$((\beta - \alpha)/2\beta) \leq r \leq ((\alpha + \beta)/2\beta)$

If $\alpha = 0$, then $\frac{1}{2} \leq r \leq \frac{1}{2}$. Another case of this equilibrium is when the judge places a higher value on the issue than on his or her post:

If $\alpha > \beta > 0$, then r^* is negative and r^{**} is positive also holds.

In this case, the separating equilibrium holds.

Equilibrium 4: *Strategic Liberalism*, Pooling Equilibrium

$$L \mid \theta; L \mid \sim\theta$$
$$R_{LG} = (NI, I); R_{CG} = (I, NI)$$
$$\mu(\theta \mid L, LG) = p$$
$$\mu(\theta \mid L, CG) = p$$
$$\mu(\theta \mid R, LG) \leq 1 - (c/j)$$
$$\mu(\theta \mid R, CG) \leq c/j$$

Under these restrictions on prior beliefs, this equilibrium holds: $p \geq 1 - c/j$ and $p \geq c/j$, $r \geq (\beta - \alpha) / 2\beta$ and $r \geq (\beta + \alpha) / 2\beta$. For this to be true, $c/j \leq 1$, therefore $0 < c \leq j$.

(1) Liberal government BR is NI if sees L if $Eu(NI) \geq Eu(I)$

$$0(p) + -j(1 - p) \geq -c(p) + -c(1 - p)$$
$$0 - j + jp \geq -cp - c + cp$$
$$-j + jp \geq -c$$
$$jp \geq -c + j$$
$$p \geq (j - c)/j$$

If $p \geq 1 - (c/j)$, then the Liberal government will not punish judges who vote L.

(2) Conservative government BR is I if sees L if $Eu(I) \geq Eu(NI)$

$$p(-c) = (1 - p) - c \geq p(-j) + (1 - p)0$$
$$-pc - c + pc \geq -pj$$
$$-c \geq -pj$$
$$p \geq c/j$$

If $p \geq c/j$, then the Conservative government will punish judges who vote L. So, on the equilibrium path, where these two conditions hold simultaneously, Liberal governments will not punish and Conservative governments will punish judges who vote liberally.

Off the equilibrium path:

(3) Liberal government BR is I if sees R if $Eu(I) \geq Eu(NI)$

$$(-c)\mu(\theta \mid R, LG) + (-c)(1 - \mu(\theta \mid R, LG)) \geq 0(\mu(\theta \mid R, LG)) + (-j)$$
$$(1 - \mu(\theta|R, LG))$$

Equilibria Proofs

$$-c\mu(\theta|R, LG) - c + c\mu(\theta|R, LG) \geq -j + j\mu(\theta|R, LG)$$
$$-c \geq -j + j\mu(\theta|R, LG)$$
$$j - c \geq j\mu(\theta|R, LG)$$
$$(j - c) / j \geq \mu(\theta|R, LG)$$
$$\mu(\theta|R, LG) \leq (j - c) / j$$

If $\mu(\theta|R, LG) \leq 1 - (c/j)$, then the Liberal government will punish judges who vote R.

(4) Conservative government BR is NI if $Eu(NI) \geq Eu(I)$ if it sees judges voting R.

$$\mu(\theta|R, CG)(-j) + (1 - \mu(\theta|R, CG))0 \geq (-c)(\mu(\theta|R, CG)) + (-c)$$
$$(1 - \mu(\theta|R, CG))$$
$$-j\mu(\theta|R, CG) \geq -c\mu(\theta|R, CG) - c + c\mu(\theta|R, CG)$$
$$-j\mu(\theta|R, CG) \geq -c$$

If $\mu(\theta|R, CG) \leq c/j$ then the Conservative government will not punish judges who vote R.

So, off the equilibrium path, where these two conditions hold simultaneously, Liberal governments will punish and Conservative governments will not punish judges who vote conservatively.

(5) Liberal judges will vote L (same proof as Equations 3 and 5)
Result: $r \geq (\beta - \alpha) / 2\beta$
(6) Conservative judges will vote L

$$Eu(L) \geq Eu(R)$$
$$r(\beta) + (1 - r)(0) \geq r(\alpha) + (1 - r)(\alpha + \beta)$$
$$r\beta \geq r\alpha + \alpha - r\alpha - r\beta + \beta$$
$$r\beta \geq \alpha - r\beta + \beta$$
$$2r\beta \geq \alpha$$
$$r \geq (\beta + \alpha)/2\beta$$

So, this equilibrium holds if conditions 5 and 6 on judges' prior beliefs are satisfied. Conservative judges will act strategically and vote L if sufficiently certain that the new government will be liberal.

Equilibrium 5: *Strategic Conservatism*, Pooling Equilibrium

$$R \setminus \theta; R \setminus \sim\theta$$
$$R_{LG} = (I, NI); R_{CG} = (NI, I)$$
$$\mu(\theta \mid R, LG) = p$$
$$\mu(\theta \mid R, CG) = p$$

$$\mu(\theta|L, LG) \geq 1 - (c/j)$$
$$\mu(\theta|L, CG) \geq c/j$$

Under these restrictions on prior beliefs, this equilibrium holds: $p \leq 1 - c/j$ and $p \leq c/j, r \leq (\beta - \alpha)/2\beta$ and $r \leq (\beta + \alpha)/2\beta$. Steps 1–4 are the same as the proof of Equation 4.

(5) Liberal judges will vote R if $Eu(R) \geq Eu(L)$

$$r(0) + (1 - r)\beta \geq r(\alpha + \beta) + (1 - r)\alpha$$
$$\beta - r\beta \geq \alpha r + \beta r + \alpha - \alpha r$$
$$\beta - r\beta \geq r\beta + \alpha$$
$$\beta \geq 2r\beta + \alpha$$
$$\beta - \alpha \geq 2r\beta$$
$$(\beta - \alpha)/2\beta \geq r$$
$$r \leq (\beta - \alpha/2\beta$$

(6) Conservative judges will vote R if $Eu(R) \geq Eu(L)$

$$r(\alpha) + (1 - r)(\alpha + \beta) \geq r\beta + (1 - r)0$$
$$r\alpha + \alpha - r\alpha - r\beta + \beta \geq r\beta$$
$$\alpha + \beta \geq 2r\beta$$
$$r \leq (\alpha + \beta)/2\beta$$

So, this equilibrium holds if conditions 5 and 6 on judges' prior beliefs are satisfied. Liberal judges will act strategically and vote R if sufficiently certain that the new government will be conservative.

References

Abregú, Martín. 1992. "Cría Cuervos." *No Hay Derecho* 3, no. 8 (December).

Abregú, Martín, and Christian Courtis. n.d. "Perspectivas y posibilidades del *amicus curiae* en el derecho argentino." In Separata del Libro, *La aplicación de los tratados sobre Derechos Humanos por los tribunales locales*, pp. 387–402.

Acuña, Carlos. 1995. "Algunas notas sobre los juegos, las gallinas y la lógica política de los pactos constitucionales (Reflexiones a partir del pacto constitucional en la Argentina)." In *La Nueva Matriz Política Argentina*. Buenos Aires: Nueva Visión.

Acuña, Carlos, and Catalina Smulovitz. 1995. "How to Guard the Guardians: Feasibility, Risks, and Benefits of Judicial Punishment of Past Human Rights Violations in New Democracies (Some Lessons from the Argentine Experience)." In A. James McAdams, ed., *Transitional Justice and the Rule of Law in New Democracies*. Notre Dame, Ind.: University of Notre Dame Press.

Alfonsín, Raúl Ricardo. 1993. "The Function of Judicial Power during the Transition." In Irwin P. Stotzky, ed., *Transition to Democracy in Latin America: The Role of the Judiciary*. Boulder, Colo.: Westview.

Alt, James E. 1991. "Leaning into the Wind or Ducking Out of the Storm? U.S. Monetary Policy in the 1980s." In Alberto Alesina and Geoffrey Carliner, eds., *Politics and Economics in the Eighties*. Chicago: University of Chicago Press.

Alvarez, Irma. 2000. "Suspendan 83 Jueces u Destituyen a 28." *El Universal*, March 30, 2000. Cited in Michael Coppedge, "Popular Sovereignty versus Liberal Democracy in Venezuela." In Jorge I. Domínguez and Michael Shifter, eds., *Constructing Democratic Governance*, 2nd ed. Baltimore, Md.: Johns Hopkins University Press, 2003.

Ames, Barry. 1999. "Approaches to the Study of Institutions in Latin American Politics." *Latin American Research Review* 34: 1.

Bacqué, Jorge A. 1995. "Corte Suprema de Justicia de la Nación: Cambio de Jurisprudencia en Materia de Derechos Individuals." *No Hay Derecho* 6, no. 12: 9–17.

Baglini, Raúl, and Andrés D'Ambrosio. 1993. *Juicio a la Corte*. Buenos Aires: n.p.

Banks, William C., and Alejandro D. Carrió. 1993. "Presidential Systems in Stress: Emergency Powers in Argentina and the United States." *Michigan Journal of International Law* 15, 1 (fall).

Barros, Robert. 2002. *Constitutionalism and Dictatorship: Pinochet, the Junta, and the 1980 Constitution*. New York: Cambridge University Press.

Bates, Robert H., et al. 1998. *Analytic Narratives*. Princeton, N.J.: Princeton University Press.

Baum, Lawrence. 1992. "Membership Change and Collective Voting in the United States Supreme Court." *Journal of Politics* 54: 3–24.

Baum, Lawrence. 1999. *The Puzzle of Judicial Behavior*. Michigan: University of Michigan Press.

Baum, Lawrence. 2001. *The Supreme Court*, 3rd ed. Washington, D.C.: Congressional Quarterly Press.

Becker, David G. 1999. "Latin America: Beyond Democratic Consolidation." *Journal of Democracy* 10, no. 2 (April).

Bickel, Alexander M. [1962] 1986. *The Least Dangerous Branch: The Supreme Court at the Bar of Politics*. New Haven: Yale University Press.

Bidart Campos, German J. 1980. "Hábeas corpus: Finalidad y prueba." *El Derecho*, September 11. Cited in Adolpho R. Gabrielli, *La Corte Suprema de Justicia y la opinion pública, 1976–1983*, p. 319. Buenos Aires: Abeledo Perrot, 1986.

Bidart Campos, German J. 1995. *Tratado Elemental de Derecho Constitcional Argentino*, vol. 6: *La Reforma Constitucional*. Buenos Aires: Sociedad Anomina Editora Comercial, Industrial y Financiera.

Bombal González, Inés. 1991. "El diálogo político: La transición que no fue." Documento CEDES/61. Buenos Aires: CEDES.

Boylan, Delia. 1999. "Bureaucratic Reform in Developing Countries: A Comparison of Presidential and Parliamentary Rule." Paper prepared for the annual meeting of the American Political Science Association, Georgia, September 2–5.

Boylan, Delia. 2001. *Defusing Democracy: Central Bank Autonomy and the Transition from Authoritarian Rule*. Ann Arbor: University of Michigan Press.

Brinks, Daniel. 2003. "Democracy and the Rule of Law in Argentina, Brazil, and Uruguay: The Courts and Democratic Citizenship in the 1990s." Paper prepared for the XXIV International Congress of the Latin American Studies Association, Dallas, Texas, March 27–9.

Brysk, Alison. 1994. *The Politics of Human Rights in Argentina: Protest, Change, and Democratization*. Stanford, Calif.: Stanford University Press.

Bueno de Mesquita, Bruce, and David Lalman. 1992. *War and Reason*. New Haven: Yale University Press.

Burbank, Stephen, and Barry Friedman. 2002. *Judicial Independence at the Crossroads: An Interdisciplinary Approach*. Beverly Hills, Calif.: Sage.

Buscaglia, Edgardo, Maria Dakolias, and William Ratcliff. 1995. *Judicial Reform in Latin America*. Stanford, Calif.: Stanford University Press.

Caldeira, Gregory A. 1987. "Public Opinion and the U.S. Supreme Court: FDR's Court Packing Plan." *American Political Science Review* 81: 1139–53.

References

Cameron, C., A. Cover, and J. Segal. 1990. "Senate Voting on Supreme Court Nominees: A Neoinstitutional Model." *American Political Science Review* 84: 525–34.

Canes-Wrone, Brandice. 2003. "Bureaucratic Decisions and the Composition of Lower Courts." *American Journal of Political Science* 47(2): 205–14.

Carp, R. A., and Stidham, R. 2001. *Judicial Process in American*, 5th ed. Washington, D.C.: Congressional Quarterly Press.

Carrió, Alejandro. 1996. *La Corte Suprema y su independencia*. Buenos Aires: Abeledo-Perrot.

Carrió, Alejandro, and Alberto F. Garay. 1991. *La jurisdiccion "per saltum" de la Corte Suprema: Su estudio a partir del caso Aerolineas Argentinas*. Buenos Aires: Abeldo Perrot.

Carruba, Clifford J. 2002. "On the Evolution of Adjudication and Monitoring Mechanisms." Paper presented at the annual meeting of the Southern Political Science Association, Atlanta, Georgia.

Casper, Jonathan D. 1976. "The Supreme Court and National Policymaking." *American Political Science Review* 70 (March): 50–63.

Catterberg, Edgardo R. 1991. *Argentina Confronts Politics*. Boulder, Colo.: Lynne Rienner.

Cavallo, Domingo F. 2002. "What Will Happen If the Supreme Court Pronounces in Favor of the Savers?" Http://www.cavallo.com.ar/Weeklyopinion/court.html, accessed March 2003.

Cavarozzi, Marcello. 1986. "Political Cycles in Argentina since 1955." In Guillermo O'Donnell, Philippe C. Schmitter, and Laurence Whitehead, eds., *Transitions from Authoritarian Rule: Latin America*. Baltimore, Md.: Johns Hopkins University Press.

Chavez, Bill, John A. Ferejohn, and Barry Weingast. 2003. "A Theory of an Independent Judiciary." Paper presented at the Annual Political Science Association Meeting, Philadelphia, September 2003.

Clinton, Robert Lowry. 1994. "Game Theory, Legal History, and the Origins of Judicial Review: A Revisionist Analysis of *Marbury v. Madison*." *American Journal of Political Science* 38: 285–302.

Collier, David, and Ruth Berins Collier. 1991. *Shaping the Political Arena*. Princeton, N.J.: Princeton University Press.

CONADEP (Comisión Nacional sobre la Desaparición de Personas). 1997. *Nunca Más*, 3rd ed. Buenos Aires: Editorial Universitaria de Buenos Aires.

Conant, Lisa. 2002. *Justice Contained: Law and Politics in the European Union*. Ithaca, N.Y.: Cornell University Press.

Cooter, Robert, and Ginsburg, Thomas. 1996. "Comparative Judicial Discretion: An Empirical Test of Economic Models." *International Review of Law and Economics* 16: 245–313.

Coppedge, Michael. 1994. *Strong Parties and Lame Ducks: Presidential Partyarchy and Factionalism in Venezuela*. Stanford, Calif.: Stanford University Press.

Coppedge, Michael. 2003. "Popular Sovereignty versus Liberal Democracy in Venezuela." In Jorge I. Domínguez and Michael Shifter, eds., *Constructing Democratic Governance*, 2nd ed. Baltimore, Md.: Johns Hopkins University Press.

Corte Suprema de Justicia de la Nación Secretaria Letrada de Estadisticas. 1998. *Expedientes ingresados en la Corte Suprema de Justicia de la nacion por año.* Buenos Aires.

Correa Sutil, Jorge. 1993. "The Judiciary and the Political System in Chile: The Dilemmas of Judicial Independence during the Transition to Democracy." In Irwin P. Stotzky, ed., *Transition to Democracy in Latin America: The Role of the Judiciary.* Boulder, Colo.: Westview.

Crisp, Brian F., Erika Moreno, and Matthew Soberg Shugart. 2003. "The Accountability Deficit in Latin America." In Scott Mainwaring and Christopher Welna, eds., *Democratic Accountability in Latin America.* New York: Oxford University Press.

Dahl, Robert. 1957. "Decision-Making in a Democracy: The Supreme Court as a National Policymaker." *Journal of Public Law* 6: 279–95.

Dakolias, Maria. 1996. "A Strategy for Judicial Reform: The Experience in Latin America." *Virginia Journal of International Law* 36 (l): 168–231.

Demaris, Alfred. 1992. *Logit Modeling Practical Applications.* London: Sage.

Diez, Francisco, et al. 1994. *La Justicia La Argentina Informe.* Buenos Aires.

Domingo, Pilar. 1999. "Judicial Independence and Judicial Reform in Latin America." In Andreas Schedler, Larry Diamond, and Marc F. Plattner, eds., *The Self-Restraining State: Power and Accountability in New Democracies.* Boulder, Colo.: Lynne Rienner.

Echegaray, Fabian, and Carlos Elordi. 2001. "Public Opinion, Presidential Popularity, and Economic Reform in Argentina, 1989–1996." In Susan Stokes, ed., *Public Support for Market Reforms in New Democracies.* New York: Cambridge University Press.

Eckstein, Harry. 1975. "Case Study and Theory in Political Science." In Fred J. Greenstein and Nelson Polsby, eds., *Handbook of Political Science,* vol. 1: *Political Science: Scope and Theory.* Reading, Mass.: Addison-Wesley.

Epp, Charles. 1998. *The Rights Revolution: Lawyers, Activists, and the Supreme Court in Comparative Perspective.* Chicago: University of Chicago Press.

Epstein, Lee, and Jack Knight. 1996. "On the Struggle for Judicial Supremacy." *Law and Society Review* 30(1): 87–120.

Epstein, Lee, and Jack Knight. 1998. *The Choices Justices Make.* Washington, D.C.: Congressional Quarterly Press.

Epstein, Lee, and Jack Knight. 2000. "Toward a Strategic Revolution in Judicial Politics: A Look Back, a Look Ahead." *Political Research Quarterly* 53, no. 3 (Sept.): 625–61.

Epstein, Lee, Jeffrey A. Segal, Harold J. Spaeth, and Thomas G. Walker. 1994. *The Supreme Court Compendium: Data, Decisions, and Developments.* Washington, D.C.: Congressional Quarterly Press.

Eskridge, William N., Jr. 1991. "Reneging on History? Playing the Court/Congress/President Civil Rights Game." *California Law Review* 79.

Fallos de la Corte Suprema de Justicia de la Nación. Buenos Aires. Various years.

Ferejohn, John A. 1999. "Independent Judges, Dependent Judiciary: Explaining Judiciary Independence," *Southern California Law Review* 72.

References

Ferejohn, John, and Charles Shipan. 1990. "Congressional Influence on Bureaucracy." *Journal of Law, Economics, and Organization* 6 (Special Issue): 1–20.

Ferejohn, John A., and Barry Weingast. 1992. "A Positive Theory of Statutory Interpretation." *International Review of Law and Economics* 12.

Ferreira Rubio, Delia, and Matteo Goretti. 1998. "When the President Governs Alone: The *Decretazo* in Argentina, 1989–93." In John M. Carey and Matthew Soberg Shugart, eds., *Executive Decree Authority*. Cambridge: Cambridge University Press.

Finkel, Jodi. 1998. "Judicial Reform in Latin America: Market Economies, Self-Interested Politicians, and Judicial Independence." Paper presented at the Latin American Studies Association conference, Chicago, September 24–7.

Fiss, Owen. 1993. "The Limits of Judicial Independence," *25 University of Miami Inter-American Law Review* 58.

Fix-Fierro, H. 1998. "Judicial Reform and the Supreme Court of Mexico: The Trajectory of Three Years," *United States–Mexico Law Journal* 6 (spring).

Florángel Gómez. 2003. "Esperemos colocar un puñado de buenos jueces en el sistema judicial," *El Universal Digital*, http://politica.eud.com/informespecial/corrupcion. Cited in Michael Coppedge, "Popular Sovereignty versus Liberal Democracy in Venezuela." In Jorge I. Domínguez and Michael Shifter, eds., *Constructing Democratic Governance*, 2nd ed. Baltimore, Md.: Johns Hopkins University Press.

FORES (Foro de Estudios sobre la Administración de Justicia). 1988. *Diagnostico de la Justicia Argentina*.

Funston, Richard. 1975. "The Supreme Court and Critical Elections." *American Political Science Review* 69 (September): 795–811.

Gabrielli, Adolpho R. 1986. *La Corte Suprema de Justicia y la opinion pública, 1976–1983*. Buenos Aires: Abeledo Perrot.

Garay, Alberto F. 1997. "El precedente judicial en la Corte Suprema." In *Revista Jurídica de la Universidad de Palermo. Año 2, números 1 y 2* (April).

Gargarella, Roberto. 1996. *La Justicia frente al gobierno: Sobre el carácter contramayoritario del poder judicial*. Barcelona: Editorial Ariel, S.A.

Gargarella, Roberto. 1997a. "Después del diluvio: El perfeccionismo conservador en la nueva jurisprudencia de la Corte Suprema (1990–1997)." Mimeograph, Di Tella University, Buenos Aires.

Gargarella, Roberto. 1997b. "Recent Institutional Reforms in Latin America." Working paper 1997 (1), Centre for Development and the Environment, University of Oslo.

Garrido, Carlos Manuel. 1993. "Informe sobre Argentina." In Jorgé Correa Sutil, ed., *Situación y Políticas in América Latina*. Chile: Escuela del Derecho Universidad Diego Portales.

Garro, Alejandro M. 1983. "The Role of the Argentine Judiciary in Controlling Governmental Action under a State of Siege." *Human Rights Law Journal* 4 (3): 311–37.

Garro, Alejandro M., and Henry Dahl. 1987. "Legal Accountability for Human Rights Violations in Argentina: One Step Forward and Two Steps Backward." *Human Rights Law Journal* 8 (2–4): 283–344.

Gibbons, Robert. 1992. *Game Theory for Applied Economists*. Princeton, N.J.: Princeton University Press.

González Casanova, Pablo. 1970. *Democracy in Mexico*. Trans. Danielle Salti. New York: Oxford University Press.

Groisman, Enrique I. 1983. *Poder y Derecho en el "Proceso de Reorganización Nacional."* Buenos Aires: Centro de Investigaciones Sociales sobre el Estado y la Administración (CISEA).

Gunther, Richard, P. Nikiforos Diamandouros, and Hans-Jürgen Puhle, eds. 1995. *The Politics of Democratic Consolidation: Southern Europe in Comparative Perspective*. Baltimore, Md.: Johns Hopkins University Press.

Hamilton, Alexander. 1961 [1787]. *The Federalist Papers*. Ed. C. Rossiter. New York: Penguin.

Hammergren, Linn Ann. 1998. *The Politics of Justice and Justice Reform in Latin America: The Peruvian Case in Comparative Perspective*. Boulder, Colo.: Westview.

Helmke, Gretchen. 2002. "The Logic of Strategic Defection: Court-Executive Relations in Argentina under Dictatorship and Democracy." *American Political Science Review* 96: 2 (June).

Helmke, Gretchen. 2003. "Checks and Balances by Other Means: The Argentine Judiciary in the 1990s." *Comparative Politics* 35: 2 (January).

Helmke, Gretchen, and Mitch Sanders. 2003. "Modeling Motivations: A Game Theoretic Approach to Court-Executive Relations in Argentina." Paper presented at the annual meeting of the Political Science Association, Philadelphia, September 2003.

Henisz, Wittold. 2000. "The Institutional Environment for Economic Growth." *Economics and Politics* 12 (1): 1–31.

Hilbink, Lisa. 1999. "Exploring the Links between Institutional Characteristics of the Judiciary and the Substance of Judicial Decision-Making." Paper presented at the Conference on the Scientific Study of Judicial Politics, Texas A&M University, College Station, October 21–3.

Holmes, Stephen. 1995. *Passions and Constraints: On the Theory of Liberal Democracy*. Chicago: University of Chicago Press.

Iaryczower, Matías, Pablo Spiller, and Mariano Tomassi. 2002. "Judicial Decision-Making in Unstable Environments: Argentina 1935–1998." *American Journal of Political Science* 46.

Instituto de Gallup de la Argentina. 1994. *Estudio de Opinión Acerca de la Justicia en Argentina* 3. Cited in Maria Dakolias, "A Strategy for Judicial Reform: The Experience in Latin America," *Virginia Journal of International Law* 36 (1): 168 n. 5.

International Commission of Jurists. 1990. "Argentina: Controversy Surrounding the Judiciary." In *Review of the International Commission of Jurists*, no. 45.

International Commission of Jurists. 1999. *Attacks on Justice*, vol. 9. Annual report of the Centre for the Independence of Judges and Lawyers. Geneva, Switzerland. Http://www.icj.org/attacks/attacks.htm, retrieved July 15, 2000.

Jones, Mark P. 1997. "Evaluating Argentina's Presidential Democracy: 1983–1995." In Scott Mainwaring and Matthew Soberg Shugart, eds., *Presidentialism and Democracy in Latin America*. Cambridge: Cambridge University Press.

References

King, Gary, Robert Keohane, and Sidney Verba. 1994. *Designing Social Inquiry*. Princeton, N.J.: Princeton University Press.

Kreps, David M. 1990. *Game Theory and Economic Modeling*. Oxford: Clarendon.

Kritz, Neil. J. 1995. *Transitional Justice: How Emerging Democracies Reckon with Former Regimes*. Washington, D.C.: United States Institute of Peace Press.

Landes, William M., and Richard Posner A. 1975. "The Independent Judiciary in an Interest-Group Perspective," *Journal of Law and Economics* 18 (3).

Larkins, Christopher M. 1996. "Judicial Independence and Democratization: A Theoretical and Conceptual Analysis." *American Journal of Comparative Law* 44 (4): 605–26.

Larkins, Christopher M. 1998. "The Judiciary and Delegative Democracy in Argentina." *Comparative Politics* 30: 423–43.

Levitsky, Steven Robert. 1999. "From Laborism to Liberalism: Institutionalization and Labor-Based Party Adaptation in Argentina, 1983–1997." Ph.D. diss., University of California at Berkeley.

Levitsky, Steven Robert. 2000. "The 'Normalization' of Argentine Politics." *Journal of Democracy* 11 (2): 56–69.

Levitsky, Steven. 2003. *Transforming Labor-Based Parties in Latin America: Argentine Peronism in Comparative Perspective*. New York: Cambridge University Press.

Linz, Juan J. 1990. "The Perils of Presidentialism." *Journal of Democracy* 1 (1): 51–69.

Magaloni, Beatriz, and Arianna Sánchez. 2001. "Empowering Courts as Constitutional Veto Players: Presidential Delegation and the New Mexican Supreme Court." Paper presented at the annual meeting of the American Political Science Association, San Francisco, September 2001.

Mainwaring, Scott. 1990. "Presidentialism in Latin America." *Latin American Research Review* 25: 157–79.

Mainwaring, Scott, and Matthew Soberg Shugart, eds. 1997. *Presidentialism and Democracy in Latin America*. Cambridge: Cambridge University Press.

Mainwaring, Scott, Guillermo O'Donnell, and J. Samuel Valenzuela, eds. 1992. *Issues in Democratic Consolidation: The New South American Democracies in Comparative Perspective*. Notre Dame, Ind.: University of Notre Dame Press.

Malamud-Goti, Jaime. 1996. *Game without End: State Terror and the Politics of Justice*. Tulsa: University of Oklahoma Press.

Maltzman, Forrest, James F. Spriggs II, and Paul J. Wahlbeck. 2000. *Crafting Law on the Supreme Court: The Collegial Game*. New York: Cambridge University Press.

Manin, Bernard. 1994. "Checks, Balances and Boundaries: The Separation of Powers in the Constitutional Debate of 1787." In Biancamaria Fontana, ed., *The Invention of the Modern Republic*. Cambridge: Cambridge University Press.

Marks, Brian A. 1989. "A Model of Judicial Influence on Congressional Policymaking: *Grove City College* v. *Bell*." Ph.D. diss., Washington University in St. Louis.

McCann, Michael W. 1994. *Rights at Work: Pay Equity Reform and the Politics of Legal Mobilization*. Chicago: University of Chicago Press.

McCloskey, Robert G. [1960] 1994. *The American Supreme Court*, 2nd ed., revised by Sanford Levinson. Chicago: University of Chicago Press.

McCubbins, Matthew, and Thomas Schwartz. 1984. "Congressional Oversight Overlooked: Police Patrols versus Fire Alarms." *American Journal of Political Science* 28 (1): 165–79.

McGuire, James A. 1997. *Peronism without Peron: Unions, Parties, and Democracy in Argentina*. Stanford, Calif.: Stanford University Press.

Mejia-Acosta, Andres. 2000. "Weak Coalitions and Policy Making in the Ecuadorian Congress (1979–1996)." Paper presented at the Latin American Studies Association meeting, Miami.

Mendez, Juan E., Guillermo O'Donnell, and Paulo Sergio Pinheiro, eds. 1999. *The (Un)Rule of Law and the Underprivileged in Latin America*. Notre Dame, Ind.: University of Notre Dame Press.

Merryman, John Henry. 1985. *The Civil Law Tradition: An Introduction to the Legal Systems of Western Europe and Latin America*, 2nd ed. Stanford, Calif.: Stanford University Press.

Miller, Jonathan. 1989. "Control de constitucionalidad: El poder político del poder judicial y sus limites en una democracia." *El Derecho* 120: 919–29.

Miller, Jonathan. 1997. "Judicial Review and Constitutional Stability: A Sociology of the U.S. Model and Its Collapse in Argentina." Paper presented at Di Tella University, Buenos Aires.

Miller, Jonathan, María Angélica Gelli, and Susana Cayuso. 1995. *Constitución y poder político jurisprudencia de la Corte Suprema y técnicas para su interpretación*. Buenos Aires: Astrea.

Mishler, William, and Reginald S. Sheehan. 1993. "The Supreme Court as a Countermajoritarian Institution? The Impact of Public Opinion on Supreme Court Decisions." *American Political Science Review* 87: 87–101.

Moe, Terry M., and Michael Caldwell. 1994. "The Institutional Foundations of Democratic Government: A Comparison of Presidential and Parliamentary Systems." *Journal of Institutional and Theoretical Economics* 150: 171–95.

Molinelli, N. Guillermo. 1999. "La Corte Suprema de Justicia de la nación frente a los poderes políticos, a través del control de constitucionalidad, 1983–98." Presentado al IV Congreso Nacional de Ciencia Político (SAAO), Buenos Aires.

Molinelli, N. Guillermo, M. Valeria Palanza, and Gisela Sin. 1999. *Congreso, presidencia, y justicia en Argentina*. Buenos Aires: CEDI.

Moraski, B., and Shipan, C. 1992. "The Politics of Supreme Court Nominations: A Theory of Institutional Constraints and Choices," *American Journal of Political Science* 43: 1069–95.

Morgenstern, S., and Nacif, B. 2002. *Legislative Politics in Latin America*. New York: Cambridge University Press.

Morrow, James D. 1994. *Game Theory for Political Scientists*. Princeton, N.J.: Princeton University Press.

Munck, Gerardo L. 1998. *Authoritarianism and Democratization: Soldiers and Workers in Argentina, 1976–1983*. University Park: Pennsylvania State University Press.

Munger, Michael C. 2003. "The Stream That Rises above Its Source: Judicial Review and the Law." Paper presented at the annual meeting of the American Political Science Association, Philadelphia.

References

Murphy, Walter F. 1964. *The Elements of Judicial Strategy*. Chicago: University of Chicago Press.

Nino, Carlos Santiago. 1991. "The Duty to Punish Past Abuses of Human Rights Put into Context: The Case of Argentina." *Yale Law Journal*.

Nino, Carlos Santiago. 1992. *Fundamentos de Derecho Constitucional*. Buenos Aires: Astrea.

Nino, Carlos Santiago. 1993. "On the Exercise of Judicial Review in Argentina." In Irwin P. Stotzky, ed., *Transition to Democracy in Latin America: The Role of the Judiciary*. Boulder, Colo.: Westview.

Nino, Carlos Santiago. 1996. *Radical Evil on Trial*. New Haven, Conn.: Yale University Press.

Norden, Deborah. 1996. *Military Rebellion in Argentina: Between Coups and Consolidation*. Lincoln: University of Nebraska Press.

North, Douglass C., William Summerhill, and Barry Weingast. 2000. "Order, Disorder, and Economic Change: Latin America vs. North America." In Bruce Bueno de Mesquita and Hilton Root, eds., *Governing for Prosperity*. New Haven, Conn.: Yale University Press.

Octavio de Jesus, Marcelo, and Alejandra Ruscelli. 1998. "The Lasting Transition in the Judiciaries in South America: A Country Study." Paper presented at the XXI International Congress of the Latin American Studies Association, Chicago.

O'Donnell, Guillermo. 1979. *Modernization and Bureaucratic-Authoritarianism*. Berkeley: Institute of International Studies, University of California.

O'Donnell, Guillermo. 1992. "Delegative Democracy." Working paper no. 172, the Helen Kellogg Institute for International Studies, University of Notre Dame, Notre Dame, Ind.

O'Donnell, Guillermo. 1998. Horizontal Accountability and New Polyarchies. Working paper no. 253, the Helen Kellogg Institute for International Studies, University of Notre Dame, Notre Dame, Ind.

O'Donnell, Guillermo. 1999. *Counterpoints: Selected Essays on Authoritarianism and Democratization*. Notre Dame, Ind.: University of Notre Dame Press.

O'Donnell, Guillermo, and Philippe C. Schmitter. 1986. *Transitions from Authoritarian Rule: Tentative Conclusions about Uncertain Democracies*. Baltimore, Md.: Johns Hopkins University Press.

Organization of American States. 1980. *Annual Report of the Inter-American Commission on Human Rights*. Washington, D.C.

Osiel, Mark. 1986. "The Making of Human Rights Policy in Argentina: The Impact of Ideas and Interests on a Legal Conflict." *Journal of Latin American Studies* 18 (1): 135–80.

Palermo, Vicente, and Marcos Novaro. 1996. *Política y poder en el gobierno de Menem*. Buenos Aires: Grupo Editorial Norma.

Perry, H. W. 1991. *Deciding to Decide: Agenda-Setting in the U.S. Supreme Court*. Cambridge: Harvard University Press.

Poder Cuidadano. 1997. *Quien es quien en el poder judicial*. Buenos Aires: Perfil Libros.

Poder Judicial. 1996. *Poder Judicial de la Nacion Corte Suprema de Justicia Estadtisticas.* Argentina.

Prillaman, William C. 2000. *The Judiciary and Democratic Decay in Latin America: Declining Confidence in the Rule of Law.* New York: Praeger Press.

Przeworski, Adam. 1991. *Democracy and the Market.* Cambridge: Cambridge University Press.

Ramseyer, J. Mark, and Eric B. Rasmusen. 1996. "Judicial Independence in Civil Law Regimes: Econometrics from Japan." Working paper no. 37, Law and Economics (2nd series), University of Chicago Law School, Chicago.

Rios-Figueroa, Julio. 2003. "The Emergence of an Effective Judiciary: Fragmentation of Power and Judicial Decision-Making Evidence from the Mexican Supreme Court, 1994–2002." Unpublished manuscript.

Rock, David. 1985. *Argentina, 1516–1982: From Spanish Colonization to the Falklands War.* Berkeley: University of California Press.

Rogers, James. 2001. "Information and Judicial Review: A Signaling Game of Judicial Legislative Interaction." *American Journal of Political Science* 45: 84–99.

Rogers, James, and Georg Vanberg. 2003. "Affirming Lochner's Major Premise: The Superiority of Political Judges over Deferential Judges." Paper presented at the annual meeting of the American Political Science Association, Philadelphia.

Rogers, William D., and Paolo Wright-Carozza. 1995. *La Corte Suprema de Justicia y la seguridad jurídica.* Buenos Aires: Editorial Ábaco de Rodolfo Depalma.

Rohter, Larry. 1999. "Venezuelan Congress Moves to Defy Its Suspension by Rival Body." *New York Times.* Http://www.nytimes.com/library/world/americas/082799venezuela-politics.html. Accessed May 20, 2004.

Roniger, Luis, and Mario Sznajder. 1999. *The Legacy of Human-Rights Violations in the Southern Cone: Argentina, Chile, and Uruguay.* Oxford: Oxford University Press.

Rosberg, James. H. 1995. "Roads to the Rule of Law: The Emergence of an Independent Judiciary in Contemporary Egypt." Ph.D. diss., Massachusetts Institute of Technology.

Rosenberg, Gerald N. 1991. *The Hollow Hope: Can Courts Bring about Social Change?* Chicago: University of Chicago Press.

Rosenberg, Gerald N. 1992. "Judicial Independence and the Reality of Political Power." *Review of Politics* 54 (3): 369–88.

Rosenn, Keith. 1987. "Judicial Independence." *Inter-American Law Review* 19 (1): 3–35.

Schedler, Andreas, Larry Diamond, and Marc F. Plattner. 1999. *The Self-Restraining State: Power and Accountability in New Democracies.* Boulder, Colo.: Lynne Rienner.

Schultz, David A., ed. 1998. *Leveraging the Law: Using the Courts to Achieve Social Change.* New York: Peter Lang.

Schwarz, Carl. 1977. "Rights and Remedies in the Federal District Courts of Mexico and the United States." *Hastings Constitutional Law Quarterly* 4.

Scott, Robert. 1964. *Mexican Government in Transition.* Urbana: University of Illinois Press.

References

Scribner, Druscilla. 2003. "Judicial Compliance and Defiance: Supreme Court Decision-Making on Challenges to Exceptional Authority in Chile and Argentina," Paper presented at the annual meeting of the American Political Science Association, Philadelphia, September 2003.

Segal, Jeffrey A. 1997. "Separation-of-Powers Games in the Positive Theory of Congress and Courts." *American Political Science Review* 91: 28–44.

Segal, Jeffrey A., and Harold J. Spaeth. 1993. *The Supreme Court and the Attitudinal Model*. Cambridge: Cambridge University Press.

Segal, Jeffrey A., and Harold J. Spaeth. 2002. *The Supreme Court and the Attitudinal Model Revisited*. Cambridge: Cambridge University Press.

Shklar, Judith N. 1986. *Legalism: Law, Morals, and Political Trials*. Cambridge: Harvard University Press.

Shugart, Matthew Soberg, and John Carey. 1994. *Presidents and Assemblies*. New York: Cambridge University Press.

Siavelis, Peter, M. 2000. *The President and Congress in Postauthoritarian Chile: Institutional Constraints to Democratic Consolidation*. University Park: Pennsylvania State University Press.

Signorino, Curtis S. 1999. "Strategic Interaction and the Statistical Analysis of International Conflict," *American Political Science Review* 93 (2): 279–97.

Smith, William. 1991. "State, Market, and Neoliberalism in Post-Transition Argentina." *Journal of Interamerican Studies and World Affairs* 33 (4): 45–82.

Smulovitz, Catalina. 1995. "Constitucíon y poder judicial en la nueva democracia Argentina: Las experiencia de las instituciones." In Carlos Acuña et al., eds., *La nueva matriz politica Argentina*. Buenos Aires: Ediciones Nueva Visión.

Snow, Peter G. 1975. "Judges and Generals: The Role of the Argentine Supreme Court during Periods of Military Government." Jährbuch des Öffentlichen Rechts der Gegenwart. Tübingen: J. C. B. Mohr.

Snyder, Frederick E. 1984. "State of Siege and Rule of Law in Argentina." *Law of the Americas* 15: 503–18.

Spiller, Pablo T., and Rafael Gely. 1990. "A Rational Choice Theory of Supreme Court Statutory Decisions with Applications to the *State Farm* and *Grove City* Cases." *Journal of Law, Economics, and Organization* 6 (2): 263–300.

Spiller, Pablo T., and Rafael Gely. 1992. "Congressional Control or Judicial Independence: The Determinants of U.S. Supreme Court Labor-Relations Decisions, 1949–1988." *RAND Journal of Economics* 23 (4): 463–92.

Staton, Jeffrey K. 2002. "Judicial Activism and Public Authority Compliance: The Role of Public Support in the Mexican Separation of Powers System." Ph.D. diss., Washington University in St. Louis.

Staton, Jeffrey K. 2003. "It Can Happen in a Hurry: Rational Learning about Judicial Legitimacy." Paper presented at the annual meeting of the American Political Science Association, Philadelphia.

Stephenson, Matthew C. 2002. "Court of Public Opinion: Government Accountability and Judicial Independence." Paper presented at the annual meeting of the American Political Science Association, Boston, September 2002.

Stokes, Susan C. 1999. "What Do Policy Switches Tell Us about Democracy?" In Adam Przeworski, Susan C. Stokes, and Bernard Manin, eds., *Democracy, Accountability, and Representation*. Cambridge: Cambridge University Press.

Stokes, Susan C. 2001. *Mandates and Democracy: Neoliberalism by Surprise*. Cambridge: Cambridge University Press.

Stotzky, Irwin P., ed. 1993. *Transition to Democracy in Latin America: The Role of the Judiciary*. Boulder, Colo.: Westview.

Sunstein, Cass R. 1996a. "Constitutional Myth-Making: Lessons from the *Dred Scott* Case." Occasional paper from the University of Chicago Law School no. 37, Chicago.

Sunstein, Cass R. 1996b. "The Supreme Court, 1995 Term Forward: Leaving Things Unsaid." *Harvard Law Review* 110 (1): 4–101.

Tate, Neal C., Stacia L. Haynie, Reginald Sheehan, and Donald R. Songer. 2002. "Regime Support and Appellate Courts: A Comparative Analysis of Litigation Outcomes." Paper presented at the annual meeting of the American Political Science Association, Boston.

Timerman, Jacobo. 1981. *Preso sin nombre, celda sin número*, 2nd ed. Barcelona: El Cid.

Toharia, José. 1975. "Judicial Independence in an Authoritarian Regime: The Case of Contemporary Spain." *Law and Society Review* 9 (spring): 475–96.

Tsebelis, George. 1997. "Decision-Making in Political Systems: Veto Players in Presidentialism, Parliamentarism, Multicameralism, and Multipartism." *British Journal of Political Science* 25: 289–325.

Tsebelis, George. 2002. *Veto Players: How Political Institutions Work*. New York: Russell Sage Foundation.

Vanberg, Georg. 1999. "The Politics of Constitutional Review: Constitutional Court and Parliament in Germany." Ph.D. diss., University of Rochester, N.Y.

Vanberg, Georg. 2000. "Establishing Judicial Independence in Germany: The Impact of Opinion Leadership and the Separation of Powers." *Comparative Politics* 10: 299–326.

Vanberg, Georg. 2001. "Legislative-Judicial Relations: A Game Theoretic Approach." *American Journal of Political Science* 45: 346–61.

Verbitsky, Horacio. 1993. *Hacer la corte: La creación de un poder sin control ni justicia*. Buenos Aires: Planeta Espejo de Argentina.

Verner, Joel G. 1984. "The Independence of Supreme Courts in Latin America: A Review of the Literature." *Journal of Latin American Studies* 16: 463–506.

Von Lazar, Arpad. 1971. *Latin American Politics*. Boston: Allyn and Bacon. Cited in Joel G. Verner, "The Independence of Supreme Courts in Latin America: A Review of the Literature," *Journal of Latin American Studies* 16 (1989): 467.

WOLA (Washington Office on Latin America). 2000. *Deconstructing Democracy: Peru under Alberto Fujimori (Executive Summary)*, February. Http://www.wola.org/perudeconstructingdemo.html, retrieved July 27, 2000. *Journal of International Law* 36 (1): 168 n. 5.

References

Yamin, Alicia Eli, and Ma. Pilar Noriega. 1999. "The Absence of the Rule of Law in Mexico: Diagnosis and Implications for a Mexican Transition to Democracy." *Loyola of Los Angeles International and Comparative Law Journal* 21, no. 3 (July).

Yates, Jeff. 2002. *Popular Justice: Presidential Prestige and Executive Success in the Supreme Court.* Albany: State University of New York Press.

Index

abstention, 109–111, 117
Acción por la República (liberal party), 90
Acevedo, Sergio, 148
Acordada 44 (Argentine Supreme Court), 85–86
activism, judicial, 5–6, 31, 172
Adams, John, 21
Aerolineas Argentinas (Fontenla) case (Argentine Supreme Court), 22–24, 157
Agosti, Orlando Ramón, 68
Alfonsín, Raúl, 18; human/civil rights and, 131–135, 141; judges under, 14, 23, 74, 75–84, 93, 95, 96, 100–101, 102–103, 104, 106, 107–108, 110, 111, 112, 114, 115, 119, 121, 131–135, 142, 143–144; on Menem's third term bid, 137; military and, 76–80, 81–82; Pacto de Olivos signed by, 88, 89, 119, 138; Peronists' opposition to, 80, 132–134; quid pro quo agreement of, 88, 135; Radical Party collapse and, 79–84, 93, 94, 131–133
Allende government (Chile), 162–163
Alliance for Jobs, Justice, and Education, 90–92, 93–94, 136–137, 139, 140–141
Alvarez, Carlos ("Chacho"), 91–92
Alywin, Patricio, 164

amnesty, granting of, 134
Amnesty International, 72
amparo cases. *See* appeals
Anzorreguy, Hugo, 87
appeals: acceptance, 111–113; court (Argentine), 143, 175; impeachment and, 126; procedures (Argentine Supreme Court), 176–177; *recurso de amparo*, 22, 105, 138, 178–179; *recurso extraordinario*, 4, 133, 176, 177; *recurso ordinario*, 176, 177; *recurso de queja*, 177; variable of, 105, 106, 108, 120
appointments, judicial. *See* selection, judicial
Aramayo case (Argentine Supreme Court), 132
Argentina, 14, 39, 73; collapse of, 145–152; constitutions of, 38, 61, 69, 72, 88, 135, 136–138, 140, 157, 175, 176, 181; de facto v. de jure governments of, 63; democracy in, 11, 17–18, 66, 142; Dirty War in, 74, 76, 115, 130; economic policy in, 73, 79, 80–81, 84–85, 88, 145–146, 151–152, 157; hyper-presidentialist system in, 36, 38; Malvinas fiasco in, 74; presidency in, 1, 3, 10–11, 36, 43, 63–65; privatization in, 22; protest in, 73, 145–146, 148, 150, 152, 162; sequential voting in, 39; social

Index